2004 √

ROI *selling*

INCREASING REVENUE, PROFIT, & CUSTOMER LOYALTY THROUGH THE 360° SALES CYCLE

MICHAEL J. NICK & KURT M. KOENIG

KAPLAN PUBLISHING

President, Kaplan Publishing: Roy Lipner
Vice President and Publisher: Cynthia A. Zigmund
Acquisitions Editor: Michael Cunningham
Senior Managing Editor: Jack Kiburz
Interior Design: Lucy Jenkins
Cover Design: Jody Billert, Billert Communications
Typesetting: the dotted i

Published by Kaplan Publishing,
a division of Kaplan, Inc.

Printed in the United States of America

06   07   10 9 8 7 6 5 4 3

Library of Congress Cataloging-in-Publication Data

Nick, Michael J.
    ROI selling : increasing revenue, profit + customer loyalty through the
    360 degree sales cycle / By Michael J. Nick & Kurt M. Koenig.
        p.   cm.
    Includes bibliographical references and index.
    ISBN 0-7931-8799-0 (hbk.)
    1. Selling.   I. Koenig, Kurt M.   II. Title.
HF5438.25.N526 2004
658.8′1—dc22

                                                                    2004009128

Dedication

To the loves of my life, Jonathan and Jessica. I will forever be grateful for the time you gave me and for the maturity, patience, and understanding you showed while I wrote this book. Also to my mother, Nicki, who taught me to love the written word and to believe this project could happen.

—Michael Nick

To my family, especially Bill, Joan, and Karl, who made it all possible; and Mel, Isabelle, and Andrew, who make it all worthwhile.

—Kurt Koenig

C o n t e n t s

PART THREE
INTEGRATING ROI INTO YOUR SALES AND MARKETING PROCESSES

If you are a sales professional, having a friendly relationship with a client is a wonderful thing. It certainly makes doing business a lot more pleasant and usually more productive too. That's why all good salespeople invest time and effort in developing rapport with customers, especially customers they intend to do business with for a long time.

But imagine that your close contact in your most important customer organization resigns, retires, or is fired. What would you say if that customer's CEO then came to you and asked you to describe the value you had delivered to the CEO's firm? What would you do? Could you explain the value that you provided in language that the executive would understand?

Unfortunately, most salespeople would be challenged to express the value they provide to customers. Our firm, Sales Performance International, has consulted with more than 500,000 sales professionals worldwide, and we've seen an appalling inability of the majority of salespeople to accurately describe the value they provide to their customers in a complete and compelling way.

Too often, I see salespeople abandon the calculation of value from a potential purchase, delegating this important step entirely to the customer. Many salespeople fail to calculate the potential return on investment for what they are trying to sell because they don't know how to do it—or, even worse, they are afraid they can't justify the investment! But these salespeople run a terrible risk. Without an understanding of the potential value they will receive, customers will demand a lower price, choose an alternative solution, or decide not to buy at all.

In my book *The New Solution Selling*, I described the importance of value justification in winning sales opportunities. Top-performing sales professionals recognize that they must constantly establish and demonstrate value in every part of each evolving relationship with a customer.

The best of sales relationships are based (and sustained) on customers' understanding of the value that you deliver to them.

In this groundbreaking book, Michael Nick and Kurt Koenig describe a repeatable process for establishing and demonstrating the potential value that sales professionals can deliver to customers. The principles described in *ROI Selling* fill a glaring void in most sales professionals' repertoire of essential sales skills and abilities.

For years, I have recommended that every company provide its sales-people with models to assist them with value justification. In this book, Michael and Kurt provide a logical, straightforward process for develop-ing expressions of value that customers will understand fully—thus rais-ing the level of professionalism of salespeople that embrace and apply this critical approach.

ROI Selling provides a practical road map that can help all sales-people—novice or expert—to navigate the once arcane world of value analysis and justification. Sales professionals who master the art of value justification enjoy significant advantages, including faster closing of sales, initiation of new sales opportunities, minimized discounting, and avoidance of no decisions. In short, these salespeople enjoy greater pro-fessional and personal success—and you can too.

Good luck and good selling!

Keith M. Eades, CEO, Sales Performance International, and author
of *The New Solution Selling*

WHY BUY THIS BOOK?

This book is for every sales professional facing the challenge of differentiating and selling products and services in a competitive market. Whether you are a sales manager responsible for team results or an individual "road warrior," *ROI Selling* helps you develop and deploy tools you can integrate with your existing sales and marketing methodologies, programs, and systems to dramatically increase revenues from new sales as well as from your existing customers.

Until now, the benefits of ROI Selling have been available only to businesses possessing the wherewithal to hire consultants and dedicate personnel to designing and implementing a program. The authors have helped giant corporations, including Oracle, Microsoft Great Plains, Hewlett-Packard, and Rockwell International along with many others, develop and implement winning ROI Selling programs. With publication of this book, the powerful selling tools and techniques that had been that exclusive preserve of leading corporations are revealed to smaller companies and individual salespeople.

Thank you for taking the time to read *ROI Selling*. We hope that you find this book useful and enlightening. We believe the materials we've included will enable you to make a smooth transition from selling features and functions to selling value.

Please join us in discussions regarding ROI in the sales process, marketing programs, and Sales Force Automation implementations, or just contact us at info@roi4sales.com or visit our Web site at http://www.roiselling.net.

"The secret of business is knowing something that nobody else knows."

ARISTOTLE ONASSIS

We want to acknowledge the following ROI4Sales customers: Oracle, Hewlett-Packard, Microsoft Great Plains, Rockwell Automation, GEAC, InfraActive, Pentawave, Excelergy, Solution Technologies Inc., MindGent, Sales Performance International (Solution Selling®), Piuma, FirstScoop, Penta Technologies, Netliant, VerticalNet Solutions, ToolWatch, LRS, Entek, Alpine Systems, and CrossAccess, all of whom helped us develop these concepts and ideas into this wonderful guide to building and using value justification in the sales process.

A very special thank you to Melissa Reiser for her encouragement, research, and assistance in developing our value matrix models and examples throughout the book.

Special thanks to all the people at Rockwell Automation, especially Jennifer Clement and Ted Matwijec, without whose support I sincerely believe we would never have completed this book.

I would like to thank Jim Kanir for his input over the years as it relates to sales process, Bob Makowski, Bob Populorum "Poppy," Karl Koenig, Harvey Shovers, Bob Kantin, Rob Schaefer, Kai Evenson, Brian Sommer, Lynn Wallace, Zev Laderman, Don Kafka, Andy Vabules at IBIS, Rick McCarthy, Steve Smidler, Jim Herkert, and Scott Sherman; all of whom over the years have helped us develop many pieces of the ROI selling model.

To Dan Bizub, our CPA and financial consultant, thank you so much for your help on the ROI Financial Dashboard. We could never have done it without you.

A very special thank-you to Keith Eades, Tim Sullivan, and especially Jimmy Touchstone from Sales Performance International for their help and assistance throughout this project.

We also want to thank John Willig, our agent, for believing in this project and finding the fine folks at Dearborn Trade Publishing. Also, thank you Michael Cunningham and all the staff at Dearborn. They are amazing people to work with. Thank you!

Last, and certainly the key to the success of this book, is Lorna Gentry, who spent endless hours reading, editing, and researching the principles of ROI Selling. Lorna, thank you so much.

Solution Selling® is a registered trademark of Sales Performance International (SPI).

*R*OI *Selling* is about building and using compelling return on investment (ROI) models to help generate more new sales of your products and services and to improve relationships and revenue opportunities with your existing customers. The ability to present solid ROI data to back up your value proposition in the sales process is becoming "table stakes" in business-to-business selling—you need ROI sales tools to be in the game. The ROI Insider on CIOSearch.com recently noted that "more than 80 percent of IT buyers now rely on vendors to help them quantify the value proposition of solutions. In fact, many CIOs now elevate the ability of a vendor to proactively justify their solutions to one of the top five most important selection criteria."

Like many other disciplines, the key to successful ROI Selling lies in doing a better job than your competition. This book walks you through building a superior ROI toolkit that does the following:

- Fits into your existing sales programs and methodologies and your Sales Force Automation tools.
- Provides a two-way feedback loop to maximize synergy with, and effectiveness of, your marketing programs.
- Helps your sales team be more effective at every stage of the sales process.
- Produces a result that your prospects and customers will find believable and compelling.
- Cements customer satisfaction after a sale by documenting the results produced by your products and services.

How This Book Can Help You

ROI Selling teaches you techniques for demonstrating the *true* return on investment offered by your products or services to your customers. Return on investment occurs when a company realizes *an increase in revenue, a reduction of cost,* or *an avoidance of cost,* as a result of investing in a product or service. These three types of returns are what we (you and I in this book) are going to build our ROI model around. We will associate specific features of your product or service with one of these three types of returns. We will identify, define, and quantify each return type. The quantification process helps us to create the data analysis document and mathematical algorithms in the final ROI model.

There are many reasons companies use return on investment in their sales process. For example, our customers have told us they needed sales training, a competitive edge, or a new angle on an old method. This book contains many techniques that will help you increase your revenue, reduce your cost of sale, and potentially avoid very expensive marketing programs that simply won't work.

Important Tools before, during, and after the Sale

The techniques you learn in *ROI Selling* provide great value to your company both during and after the sales process. During the sale, the techniques presented in *ROI Selling:*

- Give you and other salespeople within your organization specific questions to ask at each stage of the process and a framework for recording a prospect's responses.
- Extend your existing sales methodology by providing a structured approach to analyzing the prospect's answers.
- Emphasize the pain or cost that customers will experience if they don't buy or defer buying your products or services.
- Provide tangible and compelling justification and differentiation for your products and services.

ROI Selling also shows you a simple yet elegant solution for gaining valuable knowledge *after* the sale to help you improve future sales and marketing processes. The recognition that sales and customer relationship management are more like an ongoing cycle than a one-time process is another product of the existing competitive climate. Sales activity no longer ends when you close the deal. Maximizing (and communicating) the value you produce for your customers is a critical success factor in retaining their loyalty and driving future revenues from follow-on sales and referrals. Realizing that objective demands a new, highly proactive approach to managing customer relationships.

The innovation that truly excites companies that have participated in our workshops is called *360 Degree ROI*. The 360 Degree ROI provides you with a methodology for conducting what we call value assessments with your customers, using ROI tools after the sale to prove the value that customers actually receive from your products and services. The 360 Degree ROI Value Assessment process involves benchmarking your customers' actual results against the projected ROI data you developed during the sales process, using the same criteria and measurements. Even if many of your competitors offer ROI analysis during the sale, your ability to back it up with postsale analysis will add to your credibility and help you stand apart from the pack.

Organization-Wide Benefits of ROI Selling Techniques

ROI Selling does more than tell you how to develop an ROI sales and postsale value assessment toolkit. The book also provides you with specific guidance in integrating ROI tools and techniques into:

- Your existing sales program or methodology
- Your Sales Force Automation program, turning it from just a tracking system into a proactive management and forecasting tool
- Your marketing activities, creating powerful synergies between your sales and marketing messages

The challenges of differentiating and selling products and services under extremely competitive market conditions have spawned a number of sales training and management programs. One of the most powerful aspects of ROI Selling is the fact that it is not another sales program. ROI Selling is a set of value justification tools that you can use to enhance any sales methodology. We developed the ROI Selling program to complement the leading sales training programs by arming your sales team with hard, tangible information about the returns your customers will gain from purchasing and using your products and services. In fact, in this book we provide specific guidance for integrating ROI Selling with your existing sales program to make it more powerful and effective.

ROI Selling Overview— How This Book Is Organized

ROI Selling is organized in three major parts designed to present the ROI process in a logical, linear order. The following sections briefly describe each of these parts in detail.

Part One: Laying the Foundation: Collecting and Organizing ROI Data

Your customers and prospects must find your ROI proposition to be completely credible and believable. The credibility of your ROI tools depends greatly on the quality and relevance of the information on which the calculations in your model are based. Therefore, the initial information-gathering phase is a critical determining factor in the success of your ROI Selling program.

In Part One we describe a proven process to gather the data you need to build your ROI Selling tools and provide a framework that helps you organize that information to support development of your ROI model. The following is a quick overview of the information you will gather and document in this phase:

- Chapter 1, "Understanding the ROI Development Process," introduces you to the basic concepts of ROI Selling by providing a broad overview of the entire ROI process and introducing you to the templates and forms you'll use in your own ROI Selling practices.
- In Chapter 2, "Creating Why Buy Statements," we show you how to identify and record reasons why companies and individuals buy

products like yours and how to use this information as a valuable component of your ROI Selling toolkit.

- In Chapter 3, "Defining Business Issues," you learn to create well-written business issue statements and to use them in partnership with why buy statements as the foundation for the remaining stages of creating the ROI model.

- In Chapter 4, "Identifying the Stakeholders," we show you how to identify the decision makers within your prospect's organization who are most affected by the problem, issue, or goal outlined in your business issue statement.

- Chapter 5, "Describing Desired Outcomes," explains how to craft statements that express the resolution or outcome the stakeholders want or expect as a result of buying and using your products and services.

- In Chapter 6, "Identifying Features and Solutions," we help you identify the features of your product or service that your prospect can use to achieve the desired outcome.

- In Chapter 7, "Assigning ROI Categories and Value Metrics," you explore the heart of the ROI model. ROI categories describe the form of ROI (cost reduction, cost avoidance, revenue increase) your prospect will realize as a result of purchasing your product or service. Value metrics are the units of measure—such as reduced man-hours or expenditures—used to quantify those returns.

Part Two: Building the Perfect ROI Model

The second part of the book presents the process for synthesizing the information you have gathered into a set of tools you can use during and after the sales process to calculate and demonstrate the value that your products and services are capable of producing for your prospects and customers. Here's what you'll find in Part Two of *ROI Selling:*

- In Chapter 8, "Creating Value Statements," you learn to craft value statements that can help you understand the specific value that your products or services are capable of delivering to your prospects. Value statements synthesize the data you gathered in

Part One into a single statement for each linked why buy statement, business issue, and desired outcome.

- In Chapter 9, "Analyzing the Value Matrix," you learn to analyze the data you've gathered in your ROI Value Matrix and organize that data to make a concise and compelling ROI model.

- In Chapter 10, "Developing Key Pain Indicators," we show you how to write key pain indicators, also known as KPIs. KPIs are the questions describing key pains, issues, or goals your customers and prospects experience. Asking the right questions and obtaining the right information from your customers is a key success factor in building a sound ROI model. When you develop key pain indicators, you turn each value statement into a question that resonates with your customers and prospects and helps them articulate the specific, measurable impacts of their business issues.

- Chapter 11, "Creating Needs Analysis Questions," shows you how to create the questions you'll use to solicit specific information from a prospect that will drive the ROI calculation for the prospect's unique set of business issues. A well-designed Needs Analysis Questionnaire provides added value to your sales activities by providing a "script" for dialogue with prospects, thereby helping sales personnel (especially new or less experienced reps) express knowledge of, and empathy for, a prospect's business issues.

- Chapter 12, "Building the ROI Calculations," describes the process of creating the calculations you use within your ROI model. The ROI model contains mathematical logic that uses the ROI categories and value metrics for each business issue to translate your prospects' responses to the Needs Analysis Questionnaire into calculations of the projected ROI they can realize from use of your products and services.

- Chapter 13, "Designing the ROI Needs Analysis Questionnaire Interface," describes how to put together the actual mechanism you use for recording the information you've gathered and calculating the resulting ROI. Our customers generally use an electronic spreadsheet application such as Microsoft Excel or Lotus 1-2-3 to create the ROI model. These applications have become ubiquitous in the business world. If you are not familiar with them, we recommend that you recruit a friend or associate to help you with this stage of the process.

- In Chapter 14, "The ROI Financial Dashboard," you learn techniques for creating this important presentation tool. The ROI Financial Dashboard features tables, charts, and graphics to deliver a compelling and easy to understand summary of the projected ROI your prospect can expect as a result of using your products and services. Your ROI dashboard is a killer sales tool that will supercharge the effectiveness of your sales presentations and proposals.
- Chapter 15, "360 Degree ROI Selling," shows you how to build after-the-sales performance tracking into your sales methodology. By returning to your customer's business at a predetermined time after your product or service has been implemented, you're able to document the ROI actually produced and compare it with the projections you created during the sales process. During the sales process, offering the 360 Degree ROI Value Assessment shows the prospect your commitment to delivering on your promises. After the sale, it reinforces your relationship with the customer, presents an opportunity to proactively identify and address any issues that may have come up as the customer starts using your products, and provides real-world data for you to incorporate into future ROI models and presentations.

Part Three: Integrating ROI into Your Sales and Marketing Processes

This is where the rubber meets the road. One of the most powerful aspects of ROI Selling is its ability to fit into and strengthen your existing sales processes, Sales Force Automation tools, and marketing programs, no matter what sales methodology and software you use. In Part Three we provide specific guidance on how to integrate the ROI Selling toolkit you developed in Parts One and Two with your existing programs. Here's what you'll find in Part Three:

- Chapter 16, "ROI in the Sales Process," provides solid advice for putting ROI Selling to work for you. Every sales process consists of a series of steps or phases designed to move your prospect toward the "close." In this chapter we break down the sales cycle into its component phases and describe how you can use your ROI Selling tools to be more effective and produce better results in each step of the process, no matter what sales methodology you use.

- Chapter 17, "Integrating ROI Selling and Sales Force Automation," shows you how to use your ROI sales tools with an existing automated sales system. Many companies and sales professionals use Sales Force Automation (SFA) software packages to help manage and track the progress of the sales cycle. This chapter tells you how to leverage the power of ROI Selling and your SFA software by linking and using them in a seamlessly integrated fashion.

- In Chapter 18, "ROI Marketing," you learn how to incorporate the power of ROI into your marketing campaigns and communications. ROI Selling has become much more than just a sales process tool for many of our customers. As you learn in this chapter, ROI Selling, through deployment of 360 Degree Value Assessments, can become part of the overall value proposition you present to the marketplace.

Reference Material

As we have seen, Parts One, Two, and Three of this book tell you how to develop and deploy your ROI selling tools. The Appendixes and Glossary offer you a number of resources you will find helpful throughout those processes:

- Appendix A, "Examples and Templates," contains examples and template forms that you can use as a guideline in developing your ROI Selling toolkit. Parts One and Two contain many examples to illustrate the concepts we are discussing, but the contents of this Appendix provide additional examples for your reference.

- Appendix B, "Conducting an ROI Workshop," tells you how to set up and conduct an ROI workshop for the information-gathering activities described in Part One of the book. Earlier, in the Introduction, we described how ROI Selling started as a program to be implemented by companies or departments and deployed to a sales force. This book serves the dual purpose of documenting the ROI Selling program for corporate deployment and bringing the power of ROI Selling to individual salespeople for the first time. If you are reading this book to learn how to develop and deploy ROI Selling tools for your company or department, Appendix B gives you the information you need to present the information you've learned in this book to your sales force and deploy ROI techniques throughout your sales department.

- The Glossary of terms is a consolidated quick reference guide to the terminology used throughout *ROI Selling*. In writing this book, we've used terminology that is common in marketing and sales force management and automation; and we introduce a number of terms that are specific to the ROI Selling program. As a rule, we define each term the first time we use it and offer reminders about terms' meanings at key points in the book. The Glossary collects these terms into one easy-to-use listing.

How to Use This Book

ROI Selling is intended as a guide to developing and deploying ROI sales tools according to a specific, proven methodology that has been developed over the course of the authors' combined four decades of sales experience and their many consulting engagements helping companies design and implement ROI Selling programs. As you've just read, the book's information is organized to lead you through the process of creating and deploying a superior ROI toolkit for the products and services that you sell. Therefore, our recommendation is to read the book through in sequence. Even if you will be an end user of the ROI Selling tools in your company and may not participate in their development, understanding the thoughts and concepts that went into the design will help you be a more effective user.

Other readers, such as marketing personnel who may be focused on integrating ROI Selling into their company's marketing programs and campaigns, will also benefit from a brief acquaintance with the underlying concepts of *ROI Selling*. These individuals should read the Introduction and Chapter One carefully, skim the remaining chapters in Parts One and Two, and then focus their attention on Part Three.

Because the concepts involved in creating the model build upon each other in a carefully designed sequence, we strongly suggest that all readers review the chapters in order.

Please keep in mind the primary purpose of this book is to guide you through developing an ROI model. It will not sell your product for you. It is only a sales tool to be used by your sales force, marketing staff, and, in some cases, investors. The value matrix you build will help create and refine your messaging to the market. It can help investors understand the value proposition you offer to your customers and prospects. Your sales force will use the matrix in their sales process, forecasting, and as a prequalification questionnaire.

LAYING THE FOUNDATION
*Collecting and Organizing
ROI Data*

"It is not the employer who pays the wages; he only handles the money. It is the product that pays the wages."

HENRY FORD (1863–1947),
American automobile engineer and manufacturer

1

UNDERSTANDING THE ROI DEVELOPMENT PROCESS

ROI Selling is a guide to developing powerful ROI sales tools and integrating them into your sales and marketing processes, programs, and systems. The first two parts of the book walk you through the process of creating a set of ROI Selling tools for your products and services. This chapter is an overview of that process intended to provide context as you work through the individual steps.

If we think of those processes as making up a sort of journey or expedition for you and your associates, it may be helpful to take a look at the destination. Figure 1.1 is an example of one of the key products you will produce through the ROI Selling process, the ROI Financial Dashboard. The dashboard summarizes the tangible returns on investment your prospect will receive from using your products and services.

The ROI Financial Dashboard is a very powerful selling tool. Companies we have worked with to develop and implement ROI Selling programs incorporate their ROI dashboards into presentations and proposals to illustrate the potential returns they are offering their prospects and—a key point—the cost of not buying. One recent innovation presents this in the form of cost per day of not buying. You will learn more about the ROI Financial Dashboard itself in Chapter 14 and more about integrating all aspects of ROI Selling, including the dashboard, into your sales and marketing programs in Chapters 16 through 18.

FIGURE 1.1 THE ROI FINANCIAL DASHBOARD

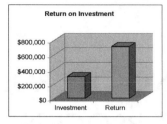

Return on Investment

Financial Dashboard Summary	
ROI Selling Investment:	$300,000
Savings from Cost Reductions:	$200,000
Savings from Cost Avoidances:	$300,000
Savings from Revenue Increases:	$212,159
Estimated Savings:	$712,159
Financial Dashboard Summary Metrics	
Return on Investment Percentage	237%
Payback Period: (Months)	8.1
Factor: 8% Net Present Value:	$332,784
Internal Rate of Return	137%
Start-up 90 After payback period,	$51,168
Factor: Days Monthly cost to wait:	
Key PAIN Indicators	
Reduction in cost of sale	$85,000
New account rep time:	$75,000
Cost per lead:	$89,000
Revenue per lead:	$120,159
Account debrief:	$65,000
Increase service sales:	$63,000
Customer life cycle:	$90,000
Channel partners:	$125,000
Total value estimation from KPIs:	**$712,159**

Return by Category

Increases 30%   Reductions 28%

Avoidances 42%

Key PAIN Indicators

Gathering Information

The information-gathering phase of ROI development helps you and your sales associates reorient your thinking toward the customer's perspective. The features that your products and services offer play an important part in the ROI calculation, but you will identify the most important features and solutions as a result of analyzing a customer's needs and issues instead of leading with product.

Automobile options offer a simple example of this principle. Drivers who spend a lot of time in their cars in hot weather want to be comfortable and to arrive at their destinations looking reasonably fresh. Air-conditioning delivers this result, but customers aren't really buying air-conditioning; they're buying the comfort it delivers. The savvy salesperson focuses on the good feeling that air-conditioning produces for a customer rather than specifications and features. Therefore, the information-gathering process starts with the customer and moves to product features.

The companies we have worked with to build ROI Selling programs generally work through the information-gathering process in a workshop setting, where a brainstorming atmosphere provides the additional benefit of team building and knowledge transfer. Because one of our primary objectives in writing this book was to bring the benefit of ROI Selling to individual salespeople, we show you how to work through the information-gathering exercise on your own. In designing information-gathering ROI tools, you will:

- Reconfirm your understanding of the issues and needs that drive customers' purchase decisions.
- Pinpoint the decision makers who are most likely to be affected by each issue.
- Link the features offered by your products and services to specific outcomes that your customers are seeking as a result of their implementation.
- Identify and document the specific paybacks (ROI) your customers will receive in terms of reducing costs, avoiding costs, or increasing revenue as a result of using each feature.

You will build up these concepts by working through the following steps, which correspond to the remaining chapters in Part One:

- **Creating why buy statements.** Why buy statements articulate reasons people and companies buy products and services like those you sell—not your specific product or service but the category. For example, why do people buy cars? At this stage we are looking at the general decision to purchase an automobile, not why people ultimately decide to buy Fords or Lexuses. "We need to reduce our sales cycle" is an example of a why buy statement.

- **Defining business issues.** Business issues are the specific needs or problems a customer seeks to solve as a result of buying and using your products and services. For example, "When the sales cycle drags on too long, we lose the sale: the customer decides not to buy at all or buys from the competition."

- **Identifying stakeholders.** People buy from people. Face time with prospective customers is a precious commodity. You want to be sure that you are talking to the right people about the right issues. As you learn later in this book, all stakeholders share two key qualifications—one, they are directly affected by business issues and, two, they are in a position to influence the purchase decision. In the examples cited above, the president, CEO, CFO, and VP of Sales might be the logical stakeholders for this particular business issue.

- **Describing desired outcomes.** What specific result does the stakeholder expect? This outcome is not a feature of a product or service—the stakeholders in our example don't expect or desire a specific sales tool; they want results. Their desired outcome could be stated thus: "Reduce the amount of time from meeting with prospect to closing the sale."

- **Attaching features and solutions.** Aha! We are finally ready to talk about product. One result of this approach is that a product feature will only make it into the ROI model if it addresses a specific business issue by producing the desired outcome, keeping you focused on your customer's needs. In our example, such a feature would be "ROI dashboard shows prospect the cost of not purchasing from us by day, week, month, year, and so on." Again the product feature will only make it into your model if it produces a tangible return on investment.

- **Assigning ROI categories and value metrics.** The ROI category defines whether the outcome will deliver ROI as a result of one of the following three categories: *cost reduction, cost avoidance,* and *revenue increase.* The value metric provides a unit of measure for the ROI; for example, "Reduced cost of sale." By quantifying the length of the existing sales cycle and presenting research to support the projected reduction in the sales cycle to be expected from purchasing your product or feature, you can demonstrate the means by which the proposed product or feature helps the stakeholders attain their desired outcome.

- **Creating value statements.** Value statements synthesize all of the above information into a single "back of the business card" summary statement. The value statement for our example might read: "Reduce your cost of sale by reducing the sales cycle." Chapter 8 describes value statements in more detail and explains how to create the most effective statements for your ROI model.

As you research, create, and gather this information, remember to do so by *putting yourself in your customers' shoes.* It is crucial to understand the importance of providing this information and devising solutions from your customers' perspective. Your customers and prospects determine the need for your product or service. The business issues and desired outcomes used to build your ROI model must be relevant and meaningful to your customers from their point of view for the model to be compelling and credible.

Recording the Information: The ROI Value Matrix

You will record all of the information you gather in the process listed above in a ROI Value Matrix. The value matrix is a table that lists ROI selling data in a tabular format with one row for each item, including:

- Business issue
- Desired outcome
- Stakeholders
- Feature/Solution
- Category
- Value metric (unit of measurement)
- The value matrix takes the form of a table or spreadsheet that lists, in individual rows, one set of the above data for each individual issue or problem. Figure 1.2 shows the preceding elements organized in a value matrix for ROI Selling. It should give you an idea of what to expect going forward and what your own matrix will look like.

Be sure to take your time in the ROI Value Matrix development process. You don't have to build your value matrix in a day; in fact, some

FIGURE 1.2 A TYPICAL ROI VALUE MATRIX

ROI Selling Value Matrix

No.	Why Buy?	Business Issue	Desired Outcome	Stakeholder	Feature	Category	Value Metric	Value Statement
1	We are discounting too much and need to reduce or eliminate discounting . . .	because constant discounting is costing us a great deal of revenue.	We want to reduce or eliminate discounting.	President, VP Sales, CFO	ROI Financial Dashboard shows current cost of status quo, NPV, IRR, ROI % and payback period.	Increase revenue.	Recapture discounted dollars	Reduce or eliminate discounting by proving your value exceeds the cost.
2	We need to reduce our sales cycle . . .	because when a sale lingers too long, our cost of sale continues to rise.	We want to reduce the length of our sales cycle.	VP Sales, CFO	ROI Financial Dashboard displays "cost of waiting," "cost of status quo," and "cost of delay" calculations.	Reduce cost.	Cost of sale	Reduce your cost of sale by shortening the sales cycle.
3	We need a competitive edge . . .	because our win ratios are declining from previous years of growth.	We want to increase our win ratio.	VP Sales, VP Marketing	ROI Needs Analysis Questionnaire changes the paradigm from selling features to selling value.	Increase revenue.	Additional sales	Increase revenue from closing more opportunities.

ROI projects take months to complete. The more complex your product, the more time it will take to dissect the value proposition. Your ultimate goal should be building a tool that will convince your prospects that if they don't buy from you now, they stand to lose more money than they would have invested in your products and services in the first place. Remember, your products must reduce their costs, increase their revenue, and/or help them avoid potential costs.

Throughout this book, we explain each column (section) of the value matrix in detail and provide examples to promote new ideas and conversation. Also, we provide a list of key concepts at the end of each section to stimulate thought processes and help keep you on track. As you complete each step in developing your ROI Value Matrix, you will be amazed at how much information you have gathered and, best of all, what a tremendous sales tool you have developed.

Building the Perfect ROI Model

The information in this book is based on the premise that you start by defining the answers about your customers, products, and services, and then formulate the questions that will drive the development of your ROI model. But formulating the right questions is only a part of the entire ROI process. You also need to offer your prospects proof of the value to their business of your products or services. The mathematics behind the questions are what will set you apart from your competitors. You will not only prove your value with the ROI model and its calculations, you will show your prospects there is a cost associated with not buying your company's products or services. Remember, status quo is your number one competitor.

With a solid ROI model, you can help your prospects better understand their primary needs and assist them in uncovering other needs that may have been less obvious when they started the process. Remember, this concept of tangible ROI modeling is about creating the questions that lead back to reasons to buy from you and, at the same time, associating features in your products that resolve your prospect's business issues. That is what understanding your value proposition is about.

Remaining Steps for Completing the ROI Model

After you have gathered the initial information and recorded it in the ROI Value Matrix, other steps for you in the process of building an ROI model include the following:

- Defining value statements for each line in the matrix.
- Analyzing the value matrix to eliminate duplication of benefits and sources of ROI and group-related items. Remember—credibility is essential to customer acceptance of your ROI model, so you want to avoid any appearance of double-counting ROI.
- Developing the Needs Analysis Questionnaire, which will become the primary vehicle for data collection and analysis during the sales process (see Appendix A, Examples and Templates, for an example of a Needs Analysis Questionnaire). This is an exercise in turning the value statements into questions, called key pain indicators (KPIs). These questions are transferred from the Needs Analysis Questionnaire to the "questions" column of the completed ROI Value Matrix.
- Creating an ROI dashboard that presents a one-page graphical summary of the project results for any given prospect (Appendix A contains three examples of ROI Financial Dashboards). As we stated at the beginning of this chapter, the dashboard will be your primary vehicle for communicating the ROI message during the sales process. Therefore, time and attention to detail in terms of both content and presentation are especially important when you create your dashboard.
- Creating a 360 Degree ROI Value Analysis template for use in postsale reviews of the value you have actually delivered to your customers. See Appendix A for an example of a 360 Degree ROI Value Analysis template.

Using Software to Build the ROI Model

We use Microsoft Excel and Microsoft Visual Basic as development tools when we build ROI models for our customers—Excel to record information and perform calculations, and Visual Basic to spice up the presentation. We strongly suggest that you use some type of software, especially for the calculations, which can be any spreadsheet program available on the market. The algorithms can get very complex, and you may find yourself tweaking and tuning models for individual customers. Therefore this model is an ideal application for a spreadsheet program. You will use your spreadsheet to do the following:

- Capture information.
- Deliver a final ROI questionnaire.
- Complete the mathematical algorithms.
- Create the ROI dashboard presentation document.
- Collect results to measure your postsale success.

Stimulating Thought Processes

To repeat a key point, formulating and asking the right questions of your prospects is the key to creating a credible and compelling ROI model. As you embark on the journey of developing your model, whether working alone or in a group, consider the following exercise that we use to kick off our ROI workshop sessions. The purpose of the exercise is to get everyone who's involved in building the ROI model thinking about how important it is to develop the right questions and how having and using these questions appropriately can help salespeople drive to get the answers they need in the information-gathering phases of the sales cycle.

Jennifer Clement is with Rockwell Automation and is a participant in our ROI Value Matrix workshop. I chose Jennifer for no particular reason other than she was in the back row. She was looking apprehensive and appeared to be wondering why she needed to participate in this exercise.

I took a blank piece of paper and wrote the following words in large capital letters on it: NINE OF HEARTS. Next, I turned the paper face down on the podium without showing it to anyone in the room.

I pointed out there are four suits in a deck of playing cards: ". . . diamonds, spades, clubs, and hearts. Jennifer, please choose two of them."

Jennifer replied, "Clubs and hearts."

I then asked her to narrow her selection to one of them, "Clubs or hearts?"

She selected clubs.

I then asked, "What does that leave?"

Jennifer confidently stated, "Hearts."

My next suggestion: "There are three levels to choose from in the hearts line of playing cards: high hearts, low hearts, and middle hearts . . . please choose two."

Jennifer's response: "High and low."

Next I asked, "What does that leave?"

"Middle hearts," said Jennifer.

"Now focusing on middle hearts, you may choose the six, seven, eight, or nine. Please choose two of them."

"Six and seven."

Once again, I asked her, "What does that leave?"

"The eight and nine of hearts."

"Jennifer, we are almost through here, but can you just select one more card. Of the eight and nine of hearts, please choose one of the two and say it out loud."

Jennifer shouted out loud, "Nine of hearts!"

I then confidently turned over the piece of paper on the podium showing the words in big letters: NINE OF HEARTS. As with many audiences, the group reacted as though I was David Copperfield and had just made an elephant appear on the podium. The point here, as I knew from the beginning, is that Jennifer *would* choose the nine of hearts. There was no slight of hand and certainly no magic.

"How did you do that?" is very often the next question from the participants. The answer, which you may already have figured out, is that *I knew the answer* before I started asking the questions. By knowing the answer, I hold all the information I need to create a series of questions that drive Jennifer toward the logical answer I want. ROI selling is not about manipulating the prospect's answers. It is about knowing the answers (your product, market, and reasons to buy) and offering choices that guide your prospect to a logical conclusion. That conclusion is the purchase of your product or service.

Once again, follow the steps as outlined in this book, don't skip forward, and, most important, try to enjoy the process. Many of our customers have found the process as rewarding as the final deliverable ROI model. Your sales force and product marketing staff are the best candidates to participate in these exercises, but you may want management to be involved too. Product developers and software programmers are usually too emotionally attached to products to offer much help, but feel free to experiment. Remember, the more people involved early in the process, the greater the likelihood of a successful outcome.

2

CREATING WHY BUY STATEMENTS

No matter what product or service you sell, a well-constructed ROI model based on an ROI Value Matrix built solidly from your customer's perspective is a tremendous tool for training your sales team, understanding your market, and qualifying the value you deliver to your customers. Creating why buy statements is the first step in building an ROI Value Matrix.

Why buy statements are phrases used to describe the emotional reasons people or companies buy products and services like yours. The why buy statement is a personalized expression that you craft strictly from your customer's or client's perspective. Your objective in writing these statements is to capture every reason someone would buy a product or service like yours and then gather these reasons into a coherent list. These statements fill the first column of the ROI Value Matrix and are the foundation on which the matrix data is built.

When we conduct ROI workshops, many participants discover that this phase of the process helps them pull together information on their product and assess its potential values in ways they never had before. And creating effective why buy statements has value beyond building the value matrix itself. By carefully crafting why buy statements for the value matrix, you will:

- Define the real reasons people buy products like yours.
- Better understand the emotion behind purchasing products or services.
- Appreciate and evaluate customers' success stories.
- Gain confidence in the value your products are capable of delivering.
- Understand buyer and industry trends.

For example, we worked with Oracle's Application group for Web site commerce development. This group sells software, consulting, and other tools to companies that are trying to add commerce to their Web sites. We asked this question: "Why do people buy Web site commerce automation tools?" The Oracle team told us their customers would respond with answers like the following:

- "We are losing business; we can't get a transaction-based Web site live quickly enough."
- "There are too many errors in product configuration when trying to order on our Web site."
- "We want to be able to sell 24/7."

Each of these answers became the basis for the why buy statements Oracle used in its ROI Value Matrix.

In this chapter, you learn how to create effective why buy statements that will capture all of the emotional reasons a prospective client might have for purchasing your products or services. You also learn how to use these statements as the foundation for the remainder of your ROI Value Matrix and as important tools for understanding your market and the many ways your products and services can meet the demands of that marketplace.

Key Concepts and Guidelines

Why buy statements are a critical component of the ROI Value Matrix and an important tool in understanding your company's products, services, and customer base. Keep these key concepts and guidelines in mind as you craft your own why buy statements:

- **Put yourself in your prospects' shoes.** As you create and capture your why buy statements, it is important to phrase them from your customers' or prospects' point of view. Understanding why people buy products or services like yours will help uncover the issues your company and product need to address in your solution. It is critical for the success of your ROI model that you define each reason people buy products or services like yours from *their* (the buyers') viewpoint.
- **Personalize your statements.** Use prompter words, such as these:
  - I want to . . .
  - I need to . . .
  - We need to reduce . . .
  - It is necessary for us to have . . .
  - We need to streamline . . .
  - I must eliminate . . .
  - We must organize . . .
  - We need to better . . .
  - We want to improve . . .

  You are trying to capture an emotional response to this question: "Why would I buy your product or service?"
- **Focus on a product or service category.** Focus on the category of product you sell, not the product itself. For example, imagine that you work for a company that sells laptop computers. Why buy statements for this company should express why people buy laptop computers in general rather than why people specifically choose Dell, IBM, or Sony laptop computers. By focusing on a category, you eliminate your product biases, which ultimately helps you create a more credible ROI model.
- **Talk directly to the decision makers.** When creating and defining your why buy statements, target them squarely at decision makers within your customers' companies or businesses. It serves no purpose to define a reason to buy that is meaningless to the person who will buy from you. (You learn more about how to identify these decision makers in Chapter 4, "Identifying the Stakeholders.")
- **Don't worry about measuring value here.** At this stage of the value matrix building process, it isn't necessary to consider whether the impact of a why buy statement is measurable. As you build your

value matrix, other stages in the process require you to associate quantifiable and measurable results with your why buy statements.

- **Cast a broad net.** Keep in mind this is a classic brainstorming exercise, so at this point there is no such thing as a "bad" why buy statement. The objective for this first step is to try and document any and all reasons people buy products or services like yours.

- **Keep it simple.** Each why buy statement must stand on its own as a single reason. Participants in our workshops often mix their thoughts by combining what are really multiple why buy statements or issues into one statement. By including only one reason in each why buy statement, you're better able to address the specific business issue, desired outcome, stakeholder, solution, and so on for that specific reason for purchasing your product or service.

You learn more about each of these basic concepts and guidelines in later sections of this chapter.

Digging Deep to Understand Buyer Motivations

On weekends I sometimes attend swap meets. If you have never attended a swap meet, I encourage you to visit one in the near future. I am constantly amazed at the things people buy and sell. I see items like parts of toys, tattered furniture, dented pots and pans, auto parts that I couldn't identify if I had to, old torn clothes, pieces of mismatched jewelry, and fruit cake that looks 20 years old. And, all of it is lying on the ground or on a blanket, in boxes, or atop milk crates and plywood. Most of it seems like stuff you and I would consider useless.

Sometimes I say out loud, "Why would anyone buy this stuff?" The vendors tell me, "You would be surprised at what people are looking to buy." My children remind me that one person's junk is another person's treasure. I so desperately want to understand the reason for this, but the bottom line is simple: People buy for all sorts of reasons, regardless of the product or merchandise, and some people buy goods and services others might believe to be bad choices. The point here is that people will buy almost anything if they have a reason and perceive value.

Your mission in this exercise is to state, as simply and concisely as possible, all of the reasons someone would buy products or services like the ones you sell.

Understanding How to Create Powerful Why Buy Statements

It is important to understand the people and companies that make up the market in which you're selling. When listing all the reasons your customers buy products or services like yours, be sure to capture the issues your buyers face every day—whether you have a solution for them or not. Always try to use easy-to-understand language when entering data into the Why Buy? column of the ROI Value Matrix table. For example, in Figure 2.1 you see sample data from a Why Buy workshop on a sales training program similar to Solution Selling®. Let's take a look at how each of these why buy statements was created and how well it fits with the fundamental concepts of and guidelines for creating these statements.

Including Measurable Goals

The first why buy statement in Figure 2.1, *"I want to reduce our cost of sale,"* is more than just an emotional reason for buying a product or service; the desired outcome is actually defined in the statement. "Cost of sale" is both measurable and quantifiable. Assuming reasonably good recordkeeping, you can evaluate the cost of sale for your fiscal or other reporting periods (e.g., this year versus last year). The difference between the two points in time provides hard data you can measure and evaluate for success.

FIGURE 2.1 WHY BUY VALUE MATRIX TABLE—SALES TRAINING PROGRAMS—INCORRECT

Product	Why Buy?
Why buy a sales training program?	I want to reduce our cost of sale.
	I want to increase revenue per closed lead and reduce our cost of generating leads.
	Reduction in the amount of time spent doing account debriefs.

The first why buy statement in Figure 2.1 is well written because it is direct and simple and contains a measurable outcome, but it is not necessarily typical of all why buy statements. Not all why buy statements you gather at the first stages of this process are going to include measurable and quantifiable goals, but that's OK. As we noted earlier, at this point in the process you are concentrating on why people buy the type of products and services you sell, so don't worry whether the statement includes a measurable outcome. Say it, capture the statement, and move on! As the process unfolds, each statement becomes measurable or will be removed from the matrix.

Limiting Each Statement to a Single Goal or Idea

The next sample why buy statement in Figure 2.1, *"I want to increase revenue per closed lead and reduce our cost of generating leads,"* breaks one of our rules for building why buy statements by incorporating two reasons or goals (increase revenue and reduce cost) into a single statement. To craft the most effective why buy statements, you must break down your thought so that each statement contains just one, single reason or concept. Although the two goals in this example are related (and might be used together later in a Needs Analysis Questionnaire), it is important at this stage to deal with just one thought at a time. If you combine or mix goals or ideas within a single why buy statement, it becomes difficult later on to calculate specific costs and gains associated with a particular statement.

Writing Clear, Concise, and Personalized Statements

The last why buy sample statement in Figure 2.1, *"Reduction in amount of time spent doing account debriefs,"* is stated incorrectly. It is missing a strong personalization and defined audience for the goal. It might be better stated as, "I want to reduce the amount of time spent conducting account debriefs with my sales team," which presents the statement much more directly from the stakeholder's personal point of view.

To be successful at building high-quality and objective ROI models, it is necessary for you to be the customer. You need to feel your customers' pain and live their everyday experiences and frustrations. When you are using phrases like "I want . . ." and "I need . . .," you are forcing the creation of objective and credible why buy statements that can be felt as an issue, problem, or goal by your prospect's stakeholders.

With the changes we made to the statements shown in Figure 2.1, our value matrix table now looks like the one shown in Figure 2.2.

FIGURE 2.2 WHY BUY VALUE MATRIX TABLE—CORRECTED

Product	Why Buy?
Sales training program	I want to reduce our cost of sale.
	I want to increase revenue per closed lead.
	I want to decrease our cost of generating sales leads.
	I want to reduce the amount of time spent conducting account debriefs with my sales team.

Improving Sample Why Buy Statements

Let's look at another example of a why buy value matrix table, this time for talent acquisition and/or recruiting software. Try to correct the way the why buy statements are phrased in the examples shown in Figure 2.3.

FIGURE 2.3 WHY BUY VALUE MATRIX TABLE—HR/RECRUITING SOFTWARE AND SERVICES

Product	Why Buy?
HR/recruiting software and services	We want to improve the talent acquisition process for selecting candidates so it costs less to hire them.
	Eliminate managing multiple job boards.
	Web site is not current.
	We want access to more candidates.

The first why buy statement in Figure 2.3, *"We want to improve the talent acquisition process for selecting candidates so it costs less to hire them,"* is wordy and runs right into the perceived value or outcome the customer is seeking. There is no need, when creating why buy statements, to extend the phrase to include what the prospect expects as a return. Better stated, this example would read, "We want to reduce the cost of selecting and hiring candidates."

The second example in Figure 2.3, *"Eliminate the need to manage multiple job boards,"* is an easy-to-measure why buy statement that only needs to be personalized. Simply add the phrase "We want to . . ." at the beginning of the sentence, making it "We want to eliminate the need to manage multiple job boards."

The third example in Figure 2.3, *"Web site is not current,"* is stated in a way that is not personalized, doesn't express a goal, and is too general because it does not refer to a particular section of the prospect's Web site. Because this particular example is intended to refer to the career section of the prospect's Web site, the why buy statement should make this intent clear. It is important that you understand a prospect's issue, pain, or goal when creating why buy statements. By changing this statement to read "We need to keep the employment opportunity data on our Web site current," you are stating a clear goal for the organization. In addition to referencing a goal, this why buy statement now expresses an implicit requirement for definition and measurement of what the word *current* actually means. The time frame expressed by the word *current* must be defined to be measurable.

As you build your value matrix and define the other elements of the ROI equation, many of the outcomes arising from your why buy statements are driven by time saving. It will become critical to define the time period for the assessment to prove its value. For example, if a job opening is filled but the career section of your Web site is not updated, the person managing the résumés will waste time (human capital cost) sorting through them to weed out those sent to apply for the filled position. The old adage, "Time is money," is true when it comes to dealing with value estimation.

Finally, the last why buy statement in Figure 2.3, *"We want access to more candidates,"* needs to be a little more specific—clarity is critical when creating why buy statements. By making this statement more specific, it will be easier to define the goal's starting and ending points for measurement. Also, this why buy statement as phrased could be hiding multiple needs. If we added a phrase to the statement—for example, ". . . [more candidates] from our help-wanted advertising program," or ". . . [more candidates] from our college recruiting talent acquisition pool"—we are then able to help the prospect measure the results from each program. Crafting the statement with this level of detail should help you better understand your prospect's needs in each area of recruiting. Therefore, we suggested that our client create a separate line item in the value matrix for each of these why buy statements.

Figure 2.4 displays the corrected why buy statements from Figure 2.3.

FIGURE 2.4 CORRECTED VERSION OF THE WHY BUY VALUE MATRIX TABLE FOR HR/RECRUITING SOFWARE AND SERVICES

Product	Why Buy? Original	Why Buy? Corrected
HR/recruiting software and services	We want to improve the talent acquisition process for selecting candidates so it costs less to hire them.	We want to reduce the cost of selecting and hiring candidates.
	Eliminate managing multiple job boards.	We want to eliminate the need to manage multiple job boards.
	Web site is not current.	We need to keep the employment opportunity data on our Web site current.
	We want access to more candidates.	We want our college recruiting program to add more candidates to our talent acquisition pool.

Figures 2.5 and 2.6 illustrate additional why buy statement samples from other industries. You may want to reference these examples as you begin building your own why buy statements. Figure 2.5 includes why buy statements designed for advertising programs.

FIGURE 2.5 WHY BUY VALUE MATRIX TABLE, ADVERTISING
PROGRAMS

Product	Why Buy?
Advertising programs	We need to improve our image.
	We have a new product we want to promote.
	We need to increase our revenue quickly.
	We want to reduce our inventory of certain products.

Figure 2.6 is from one of our many Rockwell Automation workshops; in this example, Rockwell's sales force was creating why buy statements for the sale of extended warranties and ongoing maintenance contracts to their manufacturing customers.

FIGURE 2.6 WHY BUY VALUE MATRIX TABLE, MAINTENANCE
AGREEMENTS—ROCKWELL AUTOMATION

Product	Why Buy?
Maintenance agreements	We need to reduce the amount of time our staff spends trying to figure out maintenance issues.
	We need to use automatic updates to keep our system current.
	We want to know about issues before we experience a problem.
	We want after-hours technical support.

Summary

Why buy statements are the foundation for building a comprehensive value matrix. Keep the following summary points in mind when you develop your why buy statements to make sure you are creating a solid foundation for your ROI model:

- Write why buy statements to capture every emotional reason a prospective client might want to buy your product or service.
- When crafting why buy statements, remember to understand your market, to focus on a product or service category (rather than a specific product or service itself), to speak directly with decision makers, and to put yourself in your customers' shoes.
- Start your why buy statements with one of the statement prompter words: *I want, I need, We want, We need,* and so on.
- Confine your why buy statements to one goal or idea per statement.
- Be sure each why buy statement is phrased as a pain, an issue, or a goal of the organization or individual.
- Keep your statements simple.

3

DEFINING
BUSINESS ISSUES

The first step in developing an effective ROI Selling approach is determining why your prospects need to purchase your products or services by creating the why buy statements described in Chapter 2. In that chapter, you developed statements that capture the problems, issues, or goals that motivate stakeholders to purchase products or services like yours, as expressed from the stakeholders' personal perspective.

You document the situations and circumstances that inspire the feelings expressed in your why buy statements by creating business issue statements, the second step in building the ROI Value Matrix and the ROI model. In the ROI Selling methodology, a *business issue* is the quantifiable logical explanation for the pain, issue, or goal expressed within each why buy statement. A well-written business issue statement sets the stage for calculating the costs of losses experienced as a result of these issues and therefore the savings to be gained by buying your company's products or services.

In this chapter, you learn to create well-written business issue statements and use them in partnership with why buy statements as the foundation for the remaining stages of creating the ROI model.

Five Rules for Creating Effective Business Issue Statements

There are five rules in developing business issue statements that you can use to define and measure the results and the ROI your products and services deliver. The foundation of your ROI model is built on the objectivity you bring to developing these statements. Because each of the following rules is critical to the creation of an objective and credible ROI model, be sure to follow them in creating your own business issue statements.

Rule 1: Put yourself in your customer's shoes and state the business issue from the customer's standpoint. This is a fundamental principle that we reiterate throughout the book and is perhaps the simplest rule for building sound business issue statements. This rule is such an important part of the process of creating effective business issue statements and your entire ROI model that we emphasize it both here and in this chapter's key concepts. Your business issue statements must resonate with your target audience. Writing statements that speak from your customers' perspective is critical to gaining their buy-in to the results your products or services deliver.

Rule 2: Focus on decision makers. This is another fundamental principle. The issues and outcomes in your ROI model help you close sales only if they are meaningful to the stakeholders who can make or influence the purchase decision.

Rule 3: Use the word *because*. In your business issue statements, always use the word *because* to prompt a response. For example: Read the reason to buy—that is, the why buy statement—out loud, and at the end of the statement add the phrase ". . . because <blank>" and fill in the blank. Here are some examples of phrases that might follow the word *because* in your business issue statements:

- . . . it is too costly to . . .
- . . . there is not enough . . .
- . . . of the time issue with . . .
- . . . there's a chance of missing . . .
- . . . it takes too much time . . .

- . . . of potential errors with . . .
- . . . it is not up-to-date . . .
- . . . it is difficult to . . .

Rule 4: Phrase the business issue statement from the standpoint of a loss, and tie it specifically to a cost. You can follow this rule in most cases simply by turning your why buy statements into statements of loss. For example, if your why buy statement is "I want to improve my company's recruitment results," your business issue statement might be ". . . because my company spends too much money finding and locating new hires." Always remember that pain is the best motivator for your prospects to buy from you, and *pain comes from loss!*

Rule 5: The loss stated in your business issue statement should be measurable and quantifiable. Although measurable and quantifiable may seem like the same thing, they are not. Measurable refers to the ability to "measure a result." Quantifiable refers to a numeric response. Especially in the early stages of the sales cycle, salespeople are asking questions and gathering information. In the process, we often ask questions that don't require a numeric response. When building an ROI model, it is absolutely necessary for you to obtain information that can be used in a mathematical equation. And when applying this rule, make sure you reference the specific pain, issue, or goal you included in your why buy statement. Ambiguity will compel you to redefine your business issue statements later. The more specific your definition, the easier for you to create a credible and objective ROI model later.

E *v e r y o n e* **F** *e e l s   t h e* **P** *a i n   o f* **L** *o s s*

After the Green Bay Packers lost to the Minnesota Vikings a few years ago, Dan Marino came to Green Bay to interview Brett Favre. After Marino offered the usual greeting, Favre responded, "Considering we just lost to Minnesota at home, I've had better days." Then Marino said, "You know, in the latter part of my career, that was the most difficult thing to deal with, the losing. The wins you expect; I expect to win every week. When you do, it's no big deal, but I don't expect to lose."

Key Concepts and Guidelines

Business issue statements present unemotional business-related facts that logically justify the emotional responses expressed by the why buy statements you learned to create in Chapter 2. As you craft business issue statements, your customers' real issues, pains, and goals become clearer and better defined. In the process of writing these statements, keep these points in mind:

- **Take out the emotion.** Although it was important to understand a prospect's reasons to buy from an emotional perspective in the why buy statements, business issues look behind each of those emotional statements to find the actual, practical purpose of, or cause for, the pains, issues, or goals referred to.

- **State business issues from standpoint of loss.** Your prospect will be better able to feel the pains, issues, and goals put forward in your why buy and business issue statements if they can be internalized. As humans, we tend to feel the pain of loss twice as much as we feel the pleasure from an equivalent amount of gain. Reactions to the swings in the stock market over the past couple of years are a good example. When the markets were booming, most people watched their portfolios grow dramatically. Those who may have seen their portfolio grow 10 percent during a hot week often had a response that was positive but not ecstatic—for example, "It's no big deal." However, if the same investor *lost* 10 percent in a week, the reaction, the feeling of pain, would almost certainly be much more intense than the pleasure derived from the equivalent gain.

- **Tie the loss to a cost.** When you write your business issue statements, be sure that you tie each loss that you identify directly to an associated cost to the customer's business.

- **Where possible, focus on tangible costs and savings.** As you create business issue statements, pay attention to whether the cost you are associating with the issue, pain, or goal is tangible or intangible. If the issue has both tangible and intangible costs associated with it, focus on the tangible result. For example, an intangible savings might be improved employee satisfaction, whereas lower employee turnover is a tangible savings that could result from the intangible improvement in satisfaction. You can help your customers measure their employee turnover and quantify the cost of replacing employees. It is much more difficult to place a value on and quantify employee satisfaction—especially in a way that is sufficiently compelling to drive prospects toward a purchase decision.

- **Put yourself in your customers' shoes.** Now and throughout the process of building your ROI model, it is very important to look at the issues, pains, and goals expressed in your business issue statements through your customers' eyes. The credibility of your ROI model depends completely on the ability of your customers and prospects to relate to the pains and issues on which the ROI calculations are based.

Creating Business Issue Statements

Let's take a look now at some sample business issue statements created for a sales training program. In Figure 3.1, you see a value matrix table in which we have completed the business issue statements that are associated with why buy statements we wrote and discussed in Chapter 2. In this section, we examine each of these business issue statements in detail to determine how well they follow the five rules for creating business issue statements that you learned earlier in this chapter.

FIGURE 3.1 WHY BUY/BUSINESS ISSUE VALUE MATRIX TABLE

Product	Why Buy?	Business Issue
Sales training program	I want to reduce our cost of sale . . .	because the sales cycle is too long and our costs continue to rise as the deals linger.
	I want to increase our revenue per closed lead . . .	because the cost of our marketing programs continues to rise without an increase in our close ratio.
	I need to reduce the amount of time spent conducting account debriefs with my sales team . . .	because debriefs aren't a productive use of our reps' and managers' time.

Being Specific

The first example, *"I want to reduce our cost of sale because the sales cycle is too long and our costs continue to rise as the deals linger,"* follows our five rules:

Rule	Example	Conforms?
State from customer's point of view	"the sales cycle . . . our costs"	Yes
Important to decision maker/influencer	Rising cost of sale	Yes
Start with "because"	"because the sales cycle . . ."	Yes
Tie loss to a cost	"sales cycle too long" (the loss) tied to "the rising cost of sale" (the cost)	Yes
Use quantifiable and measurable costs	Cost of sale	Yes

It is important for your why buy and business issue statements to complete the "pain" thought: "I would buy from you because I have this pain. The reason for my pain is . . ." Associating a specific reason with the pain provides the basis for measuring and quantifying the loss, which ultimately feeds the ROI calculation.

Testing Statements with Examples

Sometimes you may need to study business issue statements closely and test them using examples from actual customer experiences to determine if they carefully follow the five rules for effective business issue statements. The second why buy statement in Figure 3.1, for example, states, *"I want to increase our revenue per closed lead because the cost of our marketing programs continues to rise without an increase in our close ratio."* The issue in this example is really not the rising cost of marketing programs. It is the fact that close ratios have not increased proportionately with the increase in the marketing department's spending on lead generation programs. The author of this statement made these assumptions:

- Marketing is spending more on lead generation to increase the quality of leads produced. For example, our marketing department is upgrading booth position at trade shows, investing in technology for product display, presenting additional targeted advertising, and tightening its message to more specifically targeted, qualified buyers.
- Because these lead generation programs are more focused, they should produce better-qualified leads.
- Close ratios should increase based on the increased number of better qualified, better targeted leads being generated.

N *o t e*

It is also important to make sure terms are defined. *Close ratio* could mean the ratio of closed sales to either raw leads or qualified leads. In this example, we are referring to the total number of leads generated from specific marketing programs.

When you are creating business issue statements and feel the data is valid but you aren't able to convey the cost savings or revenue increases described by the statement, try using an example such as a case study, customer success story, or outside research to validate your theory. You will find that the use of real-life examples often helps clarify and validate a cost saving or revenue increase your product or service has produced in the past.

Does ". . . because the cost of our marketing programs continues to rise without an increase in close ratio" meet our five rules for creating a business issue statement? Let's check the statement against each rule:

Rule	Example	Conforms?
State from customer's point of view	"our marketing programs . . ."	Yes
Important to decision maker/influencer	Rising cost of marketing programs	Yes
Start with "because"	"because the cost of . . ."	Yes
Tie loss to a cost	Close ratio (the loss) is tied to the rising cost of marketing (the cost)	Yes
Use quantifiable and measurable costs	Margin	Yes

Building Business Issue Statements in a Workshop

If you are building your value matrix in a workshop environment, stories are excellent ways of transferring valuable product knowledge. When the business issue statement *I want to increase our revenue per closed lead because the cost of our marketing programs continues to rise without an increase in our close ratio* was proposed in a workshop, we challenged the workshop participant on his assumptions. He gave us these examples showing why the business issue statement is valid:

If you spend $10,000 on a marketing program that generates 100 leads, your average cost per lead generated is $100. ($10,000 / 100 = $100)

If you close two of the leads, your close ratio is 2 percent. If your gross margin generated from your average sale is $5,000, then the gross margin revenue generated from this program is $10,000. For the sake of this simple example (no other factors considered), you broke even on the program.

If your next program cost $20,000 and you generated the same number of leads (100), your average cost per lead would double to $200. If your sales team again closes two deals at $5,000 in gross margin per deal, you are still generating $10,000 in total gross margin. Using the same logic as above, you have lost money on this program by spending $20,000 and generating only $10,000 in gross margin.

A sales training program could help the customer address this situation in two ways: either improve the close ratio by giving the sales team tools and techniques to close more of the leads that marketing generates, or give them tools (like ROI selling!) to increase the amount of gross margin generated by each deal. The ideal outcome would be a higher close ratio and more margins per deal!

We ultimately agreed; these examples satisfied us that the business issue statement was logical.

By using examples to illustrate the issues addressed in the statement and by checking the statement against the five rules, we were able to determine that tracking close ratios as they relate to specific marketing programs is a valid way to measure the programs' success or failure. As a result, the business issue statement in the second example in Figure 3.1 is a valid expression of pain and loss.

Considering the Costs of Lost Opportunities

The last example in Figure 3.1, *"I need to reduce the amount of time spent conducting account debriefs with my sales team because debriefs aren't a productive use of our reps' and managers' time,"* suggests an "opportunity cost" loss. In this example, the opportunity costs result from the fact that although debrief is essential for a smooth sales operation, it doesn't directly generate income. Further, the time your sales representatives spend tied up in debrief is time they can't spend doing things that *do* generate new income, such as prospecting for new business and closing deals. Therefore, the pain addressed in this business issue statement is one of lost opportunities to generate income. In general, it is more difficult to calculate the true costs of lost opportunities than it is to calculate the costs of other, more tangible loss types. Nonetheless, losses associated with opportunity cost can be significant. As we move through the process of building your ROI model, you will be able to see how we use the value estimation tool to calculate the losses addressed in these examples. For now, let's consider whether this example meets our five rules for business issue statements.

Rule	Example	Conforms?
State from customer's point of view	"our reps and managers . . ."	Yes
Important to decision maker/influencer	Too much time for reps and managers	Yes
Start with "because"	"because debriefs aren't a productive use. . . ."	Yes
Tie loss to a cost	Loss of time causes a cost in productivity	Yes
Use quantifiable and measurable costs	Time	Yes

We particularly like the use of *"our"* in the last example. It internalizes the loss of time. We can all feel the pressure of time in everyday life. The business issue statement does meet our five rules.

Evaluating the Effectiveness of Business Issue Statements

To make sure we have fully communicated how important it is that your business issue statements are stated correctly, let's take a look at a few more examples. Try to select the most effectively worded business issue statements from the three examples shown in Figure 3.2.

FIGURE 3.2 ASSESSING WHICH BUSINESS ISSUE STATEMENT IN THIS VALUE MATRIX FOR A SALES TRAINING PROGRAM IS THE BEST

Product	Why Buy?	Business Issue
Sales training program	We want to increase our existing customers' life cycle . . .	because the cost of obtaining new customers is much higher than the cost of keeping our existing customers.
	We are losing customers too fast . . .	because existing customers are complaining too much, and we want customer satisfaction to increase.

The first business issue statement in this figure, *"Because the cost of obtaining new customers is much higher than the cost of keeping our existing customers,"* definitely meets each of the five rules for effective business issue statements:

Rule	Example	Conforms?
State from customer's point of view	"our existing customers . . ."	Yes
Important to decision maker/influencer	"Keeping customers" and "cost of obtaining new customers"	Yes
Start with "because"	"because the cost of . . ."	Yes
Tie loss to a cost	Loss of customers and cost of obtaining new customers	Yes
Use quantifiable and measurable costs	Difference between the cost of obtaining new customers and retaining existing customers	Yes

Now let's consider the second example in Figure 3.2, *"We are losing customers too fast."*

Rule	Example	Conforms?
State from customer's point of view	"We are losing . . ."	Yes
Important to decision maker/influencer	"losing customers . . ."	Yes
Start with "because"	"We are losing . . ."	NO
Tie loss to a cost	*What is the cost of losing customers? Obviously, it is a bad thing, and the answer may be obvious. It needs to be stated clearly.*	NO
Use quantifiable and measurable costs	*We need a clear statement of the cost to determine whether it is measurable and quantifiable.*	NO

The general lesson from the last two points in this table is to not leave anything to conjecture. There is no harm in too much data when building an ROI Value Matrix.

Let's see how the last example in Figure 3.2, *"Because existing customers are complaining too much, and we want customer satisfaction to increase,"* lines up with the rules for business issue statements."

Rule	Example	Conforms?
State from customer's point of view	"we want customer satisfaction . . ."	Yes
Important to decision maker/influencer	"customers are complaining too much"	Yes
Start with "because"	"because existing customers . . ."	Yes
Tie loss to a cost	*Again we need more information to understand what the loss and cost really are.*	NO
Use quantifiable and measurable costs	*Without clearly defined loss and cost, we don't have data to measure and quantify.*	NO

The relationship between the loss, the pain, and the cost is vital to developing well-written business issue statements that can drive compelling results in your ROI model. This business issue needs to be improved by adding a quantifiable measure, such as the impact of poor customer references on new sales.

The analysis of the sample statements against the five rules stated earlier in this chapter demonstrates that the first example, "Because the cost of obtaining new customers is much higher than the cost of keeping our existing customers," is the best business issue statement in this group and can serve as a model for the business issue statements you develop for your products and services.

Quantifying Tangible and Intangible Costs and Savings

Just as the business issue statement must be directly tied to a specific loss, effective why buy statements should be directly linked to the business issue statement. Chapter 1 has described how the process of working through why buy statements, business issues, stakeholders, outcomes, and feature/solutions supplies the information you need to calculate the ROI your products and services can produce for your prospects and customers. The potential savings offered by your products and services are clearly a key element of that process. Being aware of the difference between tangible and intangible savings is important as you phrase your why buy and business issue statements.

Because why buy statements are the emotional expression of a pain, loss, or goal, these statements often reference what we call an intangible, or *soft dollar,* savings. A soft dollar return measures savings achieved by reducing or eliminating the costs of one activity, with the assumption that the savings will be shifted to a more attractive activity. In other words, instead of reducing costs, avoiding costs, or increasing revenue, a soft dollar savings shifts the delivered value to another activity. Our experience has shown that including intangible, or soft dollar, savings diminishes the credibility of your ROI model. Keep this important point in mind when crafting business issue statements based on such why buy statements.

To better understand the difference between tangible and intangible savings, the following examples illustrate the process of calculating intangible costs and soft dollar returns.

In the first example, let's look at a value estimation calculation for an executive's time-saving activity. Here are the three steps we took in this calculation:

1. To illustrate the point, we developed a model for one of our clients that shows a one-hour-per-week reduction in the amount of time an executive must spend running reports.
2. We calculated the value of one hour of an executive's time.
3. Next, we showed the total amount of time and dollars saved annually.

This example is a classic representation of a soft dollar return. The time the executive saves is likely to be used for many other activities. Though it may seem to constitute real dollar savings at first glance, the savings are difficult to quantify and therefore open to being disputed or dismissed. Many people might respond to this example by reminding us that the executive is still going to be at work doing something else. Because of the variety of executive responsibilities, it is not possible to say, "The executive will have 50 additional hours per year to do X, which is worth this much money." The response is likely to be, "It is merely shifting time, not really saving time." This example illustrates a type of savings that is highly unlikely to resonate with a customer or prospect. You must be very sensitive to this type of issue because, once a prospect discovers any hole or gap in the reasoning behind your ROI model, the credibility (and therefore value) of the entire model is thrown into question.

Though calculating the soft dollar savings associated with an executive's time can be difficult, time savings can be quantified in a more tangible fashion for other types of personnel. Consider the example of a business that produces software for call centers. One of its clients has a call center that supports 40 call takers, each of whom receives about 20 calls a day. The software company

N *o t e*

You should quickly realize as you work through the exercises in this book that you will have at least a 20 to 1 ratio of tangible versus intangible lines in your value matrix. We highly recommend you eliminate the intangibles. Your goal is to recognize the intangibles as early as possible in the ROI Value Matrix building process and eliminate them from your value matrix.

proposes a solution to the call center that can save each call taker 5 minutes per call, or 80 minutes per day. The consistent and repetitive nature of the call takers' duties (in contrast with the duties of an executive) allow us to present this as a tangible savings because it enables each call taker to take more calls per day. The additional time provided by the software company's product increases the call center's output on the primary measurement of employee productivity. This increase in output leads to (at least) a cost avoidance; the call center avoids having to hire additional personnel because the customer is getting more productivity from existing personnel.

In these two examples, you see that we can measure the impact of an additional five minutes per call taker, but we cannot measure the impact of the extra hour we supplied the executive. There is some irony here in that virtually everyone will agree the executive's time is vastly more valuable to the customer's business than is the call taker's. The difference lies in being able to present an ironclad calculation of the savings for the call takers.

The issue of tangible versus intangible savings should work itself out as you build the value matrix. As you move forward in this book and in the process of building your value matrix, each column into which you enter data requires you to include a quantifiable and measurable element—for example, "I want to reduce *consultant turnover* because it is too costly to replace our subject matter experts." Avoid such nonquantifiable statements as, "I want to increase our consultants' satisfaction because they are leaving the company to go elsewhere." When you get to the point of assigning ROI categories and value metrics, the lack of quantifiable and measurable elements in a why buy and business issue statement will prompt you to eliminate the item from the matrix.

Summary

In this chapter, you have learned how to craft well-written business issue statements. Here are the important points you learned in this chapter:

- Business issue statements quantify the pain, issue, or goal in the why buy statement that can be addressed by your company's products and services.

- When writing business issue statements, remember the five rules:
    1. State the business issue from the customer's perspective.
    2. Focus on decision makers.
    3. Use the word *because.*
    4. Phrase the business issue statement from the standpoint of a loss and tie it specifically to a cost.
    5. Make the loss stated in the business issue fully quantifiable.
- Ask questions and use examples to refine your business issues.
- Test your business issue statements against the rules you've learned in this chapter.
- Be sensitive to tangible versus intangible costs and savings.

4

IDENTIFYING THE STAKEHOLDERS

Identifying stakeholders is the third step in the ROI information-gathering process. It involves correctly identifying the decision makers within your prospect's organization who are most affected by the pain, issue, or goal outlined in your business issue statement. Stakeholders are the individuals who have the most to gain by purchasing your products or services—and the most to lose if they don't make the purchase.

Stakeholders play a significant role in ROI Selling. As a salesperson, your ability to identify stakeholders directly relates to your ability to identify allies within a customer's organization; in the process, you can also find potential problem areas. People buy from people. Finding the right people to work with in your sales efforts—both in terms of the pain they are feeling and in their ability to influence the purchase decision—is one of the most essential skills for every sales professional. That is why most, if not all, selling methodologies teach this technique in great detail.

The process of identifying stakeholders is critical to understanding your market and your prospects' goals for purchasing your products. Here are some of the key benefits of this phase of the ROI analysis:

- **You learn more about your customers and your products when you assign pain to the position.** You are identifying the stakeholders who most directly associate with the pain, issue, or goal you expressed in your business issue statement. Understanding which people in your prospects' or customers' organizations are affected by each business issue statement will help you later as you define the specific desired outcomes your customers expect from the purchase of your products or services.

- **You learn how to sell "broad and deep."** Sometimes we get "happy ears" and hear only what we want to hear from that one person in a customer's or prospect's organization with whom we have developed a relationship. This mistake can be fatal to the sale and ultimately to the salesperson's career. Completing the ROI Value Matrix helps you realize that many people within these organizations can influence the decision to buy or not to buy from you. By identifying the stakeholders who "own" your business issue statements, you increase your ability to broaden your contact base within your customers' or prospects' organizations—and you're targeting those individuals most capable of making or influencing the buying decision.

- **You hone your competitive edge.** In most sales situations, no single person will know, or have access to, all the information required to complete an ROI model. During the data-gathering process, you have a unique opportunity to bond with the decision makers and influencers throughout your customers' and prospects' organizations. Your understanding of their issues, pains, and goals will set you apart from your competition.

Identifying stakeholders has benefits for your entire sales and marketing efforts. It is always important for your marketing and sales personnel to "stay on the same page" by promoting the same message to the same stakeholders. As a result of thinking through which issues, pains, or goals are associated with a particular stakeholder and which features or solution your product or service provides to address those issues, you will be able to supply the necessary data for a compelling ROI analysis and presentation.

Key Concepts and Guidelines

In the first two columns of your value matrix, you captured the emotional and logical reasons people buy products or services like yours.

The following key concepts and guidelines help you understand how to identify, associate, and document all of the decision makers and decision influencers who experience the issues, pains, and goals you documented in your why buy and business issue statements:

- **Focus on decision makers and influencers.** When you identify the people (by position in a customer's organization) who will be most affected by the business issues you've outlined, focus on positions that make or influence purchase decisions.
- **Do not include staff who cannot make purchasing decisions.** This is a logical corollary to the previous point. We recognize the importance of talking with many people within a prospect's or customer's organization. Even though it is often possible to collect valuable background information from individuals who are not in a position to "pull the trigger" and buy your products, you want the line items in your value matrix and ROI dashboard to resonate with decision makers. Therefore, do not include the titles of individuals who cannot make or influence the buying decision as stakeholders in your value matrix.
- **Consider the impact.** How will the purchase of (or the failure to purchase) your products or services affect these stakeholders? Who has the most to lose as a result of the business issue? Who is feeling the pain, living with the issue, or most likely to bring up the reason to buy as a goal? Next, consider who has the most to gain from the resolution of this issue (in effect, the purchase of your products or services). Your stakeholders come from both sets of individuals: those with the most to gain and those with the most to lose.
- **Record the position title in your value matrix.** Record in the "Stakeholder" column of the value matrix the position titles of the individuals most affected by the pain or issue outlined in your business issue statement.

Mastering Stakeholder Identification

In Chapters 2 and 3, we discussed a number of sample why buy and business issue statements to start building the ROI Value Matrix. Here,

One of our customers, Constructware, sells online collaboration tools to the construction industry. Constructware's products clearly affect the productivity and effectiveness of administrative staff. Administrators use Constructware's tools to expedite documents like change orders, blueprints, and payment draws. In the construction industry, these documents often make the difference between being paid and not being paid. Therefore, the administrative staff position is very important to the business process. However, administrators do not make the decision to purchase collaboration tools. In fact, it is rare that administrators even influence the decision to purchase or not to purchase. Therefore, Constructware decided it would serve no purpose to include administrators in their value matrix worksheet.

we'll continue to build on those examples by identifying the stakeholders for each of those why buy/business issue statements.

Our first example uses the why buy and business issue statements we developed for sales training programs. This example shows how you can identify either a single stakeholder or multiple stakeholders for a single why buy/business issue statement.

Identifying Multiple Stakeholders for an Issue

The first row of the value matrix shown in Figure 4.1 states, *"I want to reduce our cost of sale because the sales cycle is too long and our costs continue to rise as the deals linger."* The issue included in this statement is likely to affect several people within a selling organization. The first of these individuals is, of course, the VP of Sales. "Lingering deals" is an issue just about

T *i p*

If you have difficulty identifying who the stakeholders are, we suggest that you ask yourself or your team, "Who did we sell to in the past?" By looking deep into your existing customer base, you can learn who the stakeholders will be on future deals by recalling which individuals and job positions drove the decision-making process in your previous sales.

FIGURE 4.1 VALUE MATRIX—SALES TRAINING PROGRAM—STAKEHOLDER

Product	Why Buy?	Business Issue	Stakeholder
Sales training program	I want to reduce our cost of sale . . .	because the sales cycle is too long and our costs continue to rise as the deals linger.	VP Sales CFO
	I want to increase our revenue per closed lead . . .	because the cost of our marketing programs continues to rise with no increase in close ratio.	VP Marketing VP Sales
	I need to reduce the amount of time spent conducting account debriefs with my sales team . . .	because debriefs aren't a productive use of the reps' and managers' time.	VP Sales

S*eeing* S*takeholders* M*ore* C*learly*

Another of our clients, Excelergy Corporation, learned a lot about the stakeholders it sells to when participants from that company built a value matrix in one of our workshops. Excelergy develops and sells software to companies who trade energy. In all the years they have been in business, Excelergy's primary sales target has been the CIO or VP of Technology. Excelergy told us repeatedly that their sale is a "technical" sale. During the value matrix workshop, however, participants from Excelergy found themselves consistently listing CFO and CEO in the stakeholder column of the matrix. The Excelergy workshop participants arrived at this conclusion based on their analysis of the business issues they identified for their customers. They realized that many of the issues addressed by their products actually cause more pain at the CEO/CFO level than at the CIO and VP of Technology level. This revelation is changing the way Excelergy plans to sell in the future, as the company promotes the value it is capable of delivering to its customers' CFOs and CEOs.

every VP of Sales would like to resolve. In fact, we all experience the lingering deal syndrome; as sales professionals, time is our enemy. (In Chapter 15, "ROI in the Sales Process," we discuss the effect of a lingering deal as it applies to integrating ROI into your existing sales process.)

Take a look within the prospect's organization and determine which other individuals would be adversely affected by this business issue. We believe the CFO is also a candidate for feeling the pain of a lingering deal. Lack of cash flow will quickly rise to the top of the CFO's list of issues when sales opportunities don't close as projected. Therefore, at least two people—the VP of Sales and the CFO—could be listed in the "Stakeholder" column for this why buy/business issue statement.

Who Stands to Lose? Who Stands to Gain?

The next example in Figure 4.1, *"I want to increase our revenue per closed lead because the cost of our marketing programs continues to rise with no increase in close ratio,"* also affects multiple people within the organization. The VP of Marketing and the VP of Sales are likely candidates to feel the most pain as a result of this issue. After reviewing who has the most to lose by an issue, take a moment to identify who has the most to gain by resolving the issue. Put yourself in your customers' or prospects' shoes once again and ask yourself the following questions:

- "If we do reduce the cost of marketing programs, who within the organization will benefit most?"
- "If we increase close ratio, which individuals will benefit the most?"

In both instances the VP of Sales and the VP of Marketing are probably the greatest beneficiaries of a successful campaign.

T *i p*

It is not uncommon for a business issue statement to affect more than one position positively or negatively within an organization. However, it is unusual for the same issue to affect one position positively and another negatively. If you encounter such an issue, you may want to rephrase the business issue to eliminate the ambiguity, or leave it off your value matrix altogether, as the offsetting positive and negative impact is not likely to improve your ROI model.

When Is a Single Stakeholder the Right Choice?

The final example in Figure 4.1, *"I need to reduce the amount of time spent conducting account debriefs with my sales team because debriefs aren't a productive use of the reps' and managers' time,"* is really an issue only for the VP of Sales. Look at this phrase closely and decide who "I" really is. As stated early in this chapter, the key to success in identifying the stakeholders in your ROI Selling process (and correctly filling in the "Stakeholder" column in the ROI Value Matrix) is correctly identifying the person or persons making the why buy statement. As a salesperson, your effectiveness in this task will also affect your ability to identify allies—and potential roadblocks—within your customer's organization.

There is a debate among sales methodology experts whether a business issue can affect multiple people within an organization. Is there a connection, chain, or link between stakeholders? Some believe that if an organization appoints an executive to manage people, projects, and programs, you need only to list the person this business issue statement or pain affects most—in other words, the executive who is responsible for that area of the company. The key word here is *most*. Based on experience in our own selling careers and on the experiences of our customers, we firmly believe that you should list every decision maker and influencer affected by the situation outlined in your business issue statement. With that list in mind, you'll be able to articulate the right message to the right people within an organization as you work your way from stakeholder to stakeholder. People within an organization are linked—they share pain regardless of whom it affects most.

If you employ a sales methodology such as Solution Selling®, TAS, Miller Heiman, and the like, we encourage you to check with your sales methodology vendors on their thoughts and suggestions regarding stakeholders and to update your value matrix to reflect the methodology your company has adopted with respect to single versus multiple stakeholders.

Identifying Stakeholders Who Have Different Stakes within the Same Statement

The value matrix in Figure 4.2 displays the results of an ROI Value Matrix workshop conducted for an advertising agency.

FIGURE 4.2 VALUE MATRIX INCLUDING STAKEHOLDERS FOR
AN ADVERTISING PROGRAM

Product	Why Buy?	Business Issue	Stakeholder
Advertising	We have a public relations (image problem) issue from a tampered-product incident and need a positive exposure . . .	because the public refuses to purchase our products for fear of fatal results— (reduced sales).	VP Sales
	We have a new product we want to promote . . .	because without public awareness of the value this new product delivers, we will not meet our sales projections.	VP Sales
	We want to reduce our inventory of certain overstocked merchandise . . .	because the storage, carrying, and inventory management costs continue to rise.	VP Sales CFO VP Logistics

---

Figure 4.2 illustrates three reasons to buy advertising programs. Notice how in the first two rows of the value matrix (Figure 4.2), the only stakeholder is the VP of Sales. The last statement, however, lists three stakeholders: VP of Sales, CFO, and VP of Logistics. Each stakeholder has something different to lose and something different to gain:

- The issue for the VP of Logistics could be an overstock on a particular product, pointing to the fact it may have been overpurchased or overproduced.
- Overstock can mean lower margins, excessive carrying costs, and potentially poorly managed inventory control policies—all issues the CFO must take into account.
- On the other hand, the VP of Sales may benefit from an overstock situation and have an opportunity to increase sales with a special advertising program and perhaps a lower price on the overstocked products.

Adding Stakeholders to Your Value Matrix

Continue down the "Stakeholder" column in your value matrix and assess each line to determine which decision makers or influencers have the most to gain and the most to lose by purchasing or not purchasing your products or services. If you are not able to identify a stakeholder for each business issue statement, either commit to finding out who the stakeholders are or eliminate the issue from the value matrix. If, after all of your research, you are unable to identify a stakeholder for your why buy and business issue statements, it means no one will feel that pain. Therefore, the issue is not likely to help you build a credible or objective ROI model or to close the sale.

As we complete the value matrix, some items will drop off because we cannot justify including them. Don't worry about this unless you find yourself dropping a very large number of items. Based on our customers' experiences, you should expect about 20 percent of the items from the initial why buy statements to be eliminated or combined for various reasons. It is all part of the exercise and will help your sales team focus on the most important issues.

Having associated stakeholders with the why buy statements and the business issue statements, we are ready to define the desired outcomes that the stakeholders are seeking.

Summary

Identifying stakeholders is a way of looking inside the mind of your prospect and personalizing the pain expressed in your why buy and business issue statements by linking them to specific individuals. Stakeholder identification is a critical part of building a credible and objective ROI. Your ability to associate pains, issues, and goals with decision makers and influencers increases your ability to understand and communicate the value you are capable of delivering. In the next chapter, you use this knowledge to identify how the stakeholders want to resolve their issues, pains, and goals. In the meantime, the following summary provides some additional information to think about as you begin the process of adding stakeholders to your ROI Value Matrix:

- Identifying the stakeholder for a why buy/business issue statement involves determining which decision maker(s) within your prospect's organization made the why buy statement and is most affected by the problem or goal expressed in the business issue statement.
- When identifying stakeholders, be sure to consider who has the most to gain and who has the most to lose from the pain, issue, or goal referenced in the why buy statement.
- From the group of stakeholder candidates, add to your list of stakeholders only those individuals who can make or influence a buy decision.
- Remember that it is OK to list multiple positions for each business issue statement.
- Different stakeholders can have different goals, gains, pains, or losses associated with a single business issue.

5

DESCRIBING DESIRED OUTCOMES

The information-gathering phase of building your ROI model follows a logical sequence. In previous chapters, you've learned how to craft compelling why buy and business issue statements as preliminary steps in the ROI Selling process. You also learned how to identify stakeholders—the decision makers within your prospect's organization who are most affected by each business issue and therefore have the most to gain or lose as a result of a purchase decision. The desired outcomes you list in your ROI Value Matrix are the results your stakeholders seek to achieve from their why buy and business issue statements. Determining desired outcomes is the fourth step in creating your ROI Value Matrix.

Though every desired outcome is unique, all perform the same functions. A well-written desired outcome does the following:

- **Relates the issue, pain, or goal to the outcome.** Desired outcomes must specifically relate to the issue, pain, or goal in the why buy statement. Depending on your products or services, we recommend documenting the answer by saying "Therefore, . . .
  - I need to reduce . . .
  - We want a way to . . .
  - It must . . .

- **Resolves the business issue statement.** A desired outcome must resolve the business issue statement with which it is associated. In other words, when you expressed the reason to buy in the why buy statement, you referred to a pain, issue, or goal. In the business issue statement, you explained the pain, issue, or goal your customer is hoping to resolve or achieve. In this step, you must resolve the business issue and give your customer or prospect a reason to buy from you . . . now.

- **Focuses on the business issue rather than specific products or services.** When you're writing desired outcomes, keep your focus strictly on the business issue at hand. Don't think about specific product features or service functions your company can offer, because at this point they don't mean much to your prospect. Concentrate on the business issue and the outcomes your customers are likely to want and need to resolve that issue.

- **Contains specific details for measuring success.** It is critical to be as specific as possible when creating desired outcomes. Clearly state the issue your customers want resolved and the measurement you'll use to assess your success. An example of a vague desired outcome would be, "We want our consultants to work harder." This example fails to express any real measurement criteria on which to base an assessment of success or failure. Better stated, the example might read, "We need to increase our consulting group's billed hours by X percent this year to reach our revenue goals." Stated this way, we can stop time, measure the current situation, and then come back later and measure success after we have delivered a solution to increase our customer's billing hours.

Learning how to craft effective desired outcomes offers a number of benefits to you as a salesperson and to your sales organization. In addition to helping you to better understand exactly what business issues your products are capable of resolving, creating desired outcomes helps you understand if there are holes in the products, services, or solution you are delivering. If you identify a significant why buy, business issue, and desired outcome that customers cannot address with your products and services, you may have discovered an opportunity to improve your competitive position through product development.

The desired outcome plays a major role in the development of your ROI model. In Chapter 8, "Creating Value Statements," you learn how to create and articulate statements of the value your products or services offer, which will be based on the desired outcomes you are defining now. When you get to the point of designing the look and feel of your ROI model, we recommend you use the desired outcome in the Needs Analysis Questionnaire that you also learn about in Chapter 8.

Key Concepts and Guidelines

As with all other tasks in the process of exploring and creating the data you use in your ROI Value Matrix, determining your customers' desired outcomes requires some thoughtful practice in the techniques we describe. In other words, practice makes perfect. Your proficiency will grow as you become more comfortable with the individual components of the ROI model and how they fit together. These fundamental concepts should guide you in the process and help build your ROI modeling skills:

- **Understand your prospects' expectations.** If you don't know what a prospect's expectation is regarding the outcome or result of using your products or services, how can you possibly meet or exceed it? For example, if your prospect has stated that he wants to increase revenues, do you understand by what metric the prospect will be judging that increase? Is the prospect hoping for an increased number of sales, or will he look for an increased average sale amount?
- **Point out the cost of doing nothing.** When needs are known to exist, there is always a cost to doing nothing. Calculating and presenting a credible statement of the cost of not purchasing your products or services is a key to your sales success. Like most selling methodologies, we subscribe to the principle that the status quo is the biggest competitor all salespeople have to deal with. More deals are lost from a customer's or prospect's doing nothing than to all of the competitive products in the market.
- **Understand the difference between a desired outcome and a why buy statement.** Desired outcomes often sound a lot like why buy statements. They are not! You must understand the "real" expectation from the issue, pain, or goal referenced in the why buy statement. Remember, your why buy statement is an emotional

C *l o s e - u p   o n*   **C** *u s t o m e r s*

Don Kafka is the president of ToolWatch, one of our customers. Don had us add an additional calculation to his ROI model. He wanted to be able to show his prospects the monthly cost of doing nothing. Don asked us to insert a calculation of a customer's total current cost before using Don's solution and then compare that to the total projected cost if ToolWatch delivered all the value it estimated. The difference between the current and projected cost is the savings delivered by ToolWatch. We then divided the total savings figure by 12 months. The result is the monthly savings the prospect could realize from implementing ToolWatch. It is also the monthly cost of deferring the purchase decision. In the example shown in Figure 5.1, the potential savings is $5,000 per month. Obviously, every month the customer delays buying and implementing the solution, the savings would not be realized, and the $5,000 cost/loss continues to accumulate.

response to the question, "Why buy this product?" Given the data you now have (why buy, business issue, and stakeholder), the desired outcome statement should be able to answer the question, "What quantifiable and measurable result will resolve your problem?" What is your desire for resolving your issue? Put yourself back in your stakeholders' shoes and try to think in terms of a measurable deliverable that your prospects would want to resolve their business issue.

- **You must be able to produce the desired outcome.** Remember, you can promise the moon, but can you deliver? It is important that your desired outcomes are realistic and attainable through existing features in your products or services.

FIGURE 5.1 COST OF STATUS QUO TABLE—TOOLWATCH

Activity	Result
Current annual cost of managing tools:	$300,000
Annual cost if ToolWatch is implemented:	$240,000
Annual savings:	$60,000
Monthly savings ($60,000/12 months):	$5,000

Creating Desired Outcomes

The next examples illustrate many different ways of creating desired outcomes, and all are based on the data we've added to the ROI Value Matrix in previous chapters. Figure 5.2 contains the examples we'll reference in this section of the chapter.

Using Measurable Terms

In Figure 5.2, *"I want to reduce our cost of sale because the sales cycle is too long and our costs continue to rise as the deals linger"* describes a VP of Sales's primary issue, pain, or goal. The VP's desire to resolve the pain comes in the form of the desired outcome: "I want to reduce the time to revenue and shorten the sales cycle." This very specific statement describes the medicine the VP of Sales needs to resolve her pain, issue, or goal. The desired outcome contains quantifiable and measurable words that

---

FIGURE 5.2 VALUE MATRIX—DESIRED OUTCOME—SALES TRAINING PROGRAM

Why Buy?	Business Issue	Stakeholder	Desired Outcome
I want to reduce our cost of sale . . .	because the sales cycle is too long and our costs continue to rise as the deals linger.	VP Sales CFO	I want to shorten the sales cycle.
I want to increase our revenue per closed lead . . .	because the cost of our marketing programs continues to rise with no increase in close ratios.	VP Marketing VP Sales	I want to increase our close ratios.
I need to reduce the amount of time spent conducting account debriefs with my sales team . . .	because debriefs aren't a productive use of the reps' and managers' time.	VP Sales	I want to reduce the time reps and managers spend conducting account debriefs.

tie the why buy statement and business issue statement together. The result is a statement that you can use to deliver a solution and to measure the results after the solution has been implemented (see Chapter 15, "360 Degree ROI Selling," for more information on measuring the actual ROI achieved after the sale).

Connecting the Why Buy and Business Issue Statements

The second line of Figure 5.2 reads, *"I want to increase our revenue per closed lead because the cost of our marketing programs continues to rise with no increase in close ratios; therefore I want to increase our close ratios."* This example illustrates the concept that the desired outcome should closely connect the why buy statement or business issue statement. There is no harm in similarities between the desired outcome and the why buy statement so long as the desired outcome contains a quantity you can measure once you deliver the solution. In this example, we restate and amplify the why buy statement and business issue statement by adding the specific, measurable objective of "increasing the close ratios." In other words, if customers can close more of the sales they attempt by using our products and services, we have provided them with a credible reason to buy from us. Using ROI Selling, we can cement our case by documenting the results with the customer's own data.

E x t e n d i n g   t h e   R O I

One of our clients offers a "try and buy" on its products and services. This client gives prospective customers its products to use for four to six weeks and measures successes along the way. Our client will even refund a customer's money if it doesn't hit certain defined levels of success. If the customer decides to keep the product after the first four to six weeks, our client commits to an additional follow up in 9 to 12 months to measure how much success the customer has had since purchasing our client's product. Our client has defined, documented, and verified the value it is capable of delivering by using postsale analysis to identify what its customer base considers a successful implementation. As a result, this client has made ROI a program, not an event.

The next example also illustrates the use of quantifiable terms in the desired outcome statements. The last line in Figure 5.2 reads, *"I need to reduce the amount of time spent conducting account debriefs with my sales team because debriefs aren't a productive use of the reps' and managers' time; therefore, I want to reduce the time reps and managers spend conducting account debriefs."* This is another situation in which we have included a metric—in this case, "time"—our customers can use to measure our success on delivery. We can easily measure the account debrief time by phone records or logs from managers.

Thinking Outside the Box

In the next example, shown in Figure 5.3, we see the why buy and business issue statements added to an ROI Value Matrix for an advertising program.

The why buy and business issue statements in this example are unique and perhaps don't apply to many companies. However, a public relations problem is very real and most common in today's business-to-business market. The desired outcome— *"A positive advertising campaign that will improve our image and result in an increase in sales over the next X quarters"*— aligns directly with the goal of improving the company's image, as expressed in the why buy statement. This desired outcome also aligns with the business issue statement of recovering from "reduced sales." The VP of Sales

FIGURE 5.3 VALUE MATRIX—DESIRED OUTCOME—ADVERTISING PROGRAM

Why Buy?	Business Issue	Stakeholder	Desired Outcome
We need to improve our image in the wake of a tampered-product incident that became a public relations problem . . .	because the public refuses to purchase our products for fear of fatal results (reduced sales).	VP Sales	A positive advertising campaign that will boost our image and result in an increase in sales over the next X quarters

in this example wants to turn the image problem around and sell more product by convincing the public the safety issues have been addressed.

When you state a desired outcome, be sure to phrase it carefully so that it contains a measurable, numeric outcome. In the desired outcome shown in this example, "increasing sales over X quarters" can be measured to see if the desired outcome has been met or exceeded.

Testing and Improving Desired Outcomes

Try to identify the missing link between the why buy statement and business issue statement in Figure 5.4. Following the figure, we discuss each of the desired outcomes and illustrate the correct way to phrase each.

FIGURE 5.4 VALUE MATRIX—DESIRED OUTCOMES

Why Buy?	Business Issue	Stakeholder	Desired Outcome
We need a competitive edge . . .	because we are losing business to our competitors, who use ROI modeling in every sale over $100,000.	VP Sales VP Marketing	To beat the competition
I need to help our prospects justify the cost of this purchase to management . . .	because their executive management is now requiring an ROI on all capital purchases. Without it, our contacts cannot get budgeted for the funding on our project.	VP Sales	Want to train our sales team how to read financial statements so they can talk intelligently about net present value (NPV) and internal rate of return (IRR).
We need to reduce or eliminate sales force discounting . . .	because excess discounting is costing us a great deal of revenue on every deal.	VP Sales CFO	We need to reduce or eliminate discounting.

The first example in Figure 5.4, *"To beat the competition,"* is not a good desired outcome statement because it is missing several of the needed components for measuring potential success:

- There is no term or phrase within the statement that offers a measurable basis for success.
- The desired outcome doesn't directly link the why buy statement to the business issue statement. Our why buy statement points out the need for a competitive edge and the business issue statement points out that competitors are using ROI modeling. The outcome alludes to competition but doesn't suggest a solution that directly competes with the use of ROI modeling.

A better way to state the desired outcome would be: "We need to implement sales tools to increase our close ratios." Moving from "We need to beat the competition" to "We need a set of sales tools to increase our close ratios" may seem like a big leap. However, when our client brought this desired outcome up in a workshop, our challenge was simple: "How do you beat the competition?" He confidently stated, "By increasing our close ratio!" Increasing your close ratio is definitely a measurable desired outcome.

The second example in Figure 5.4, *"Want to train our sales team how to read financial statements so they can talk intelligently about net present value (NPV) and internal rate of return (IRR),"* misses the point of the why buy and business issue statement. First, this desired outcome statement needs to be rephrased to more accurately reflect the customer's point of view. Ability on the part of the sales team to understand a financial statement is not what your customer is looking for. As stated in the why buy and business issue statement, an ROI model is what your customer is looking for. A better way to phrase this desired outcome: "We want an ROI tool our customers can use to justify the cost of purchasing our solution."

The last example in Figure 5.4, *"We need to reduce or eliminate discounting,"* is specific and measurable. You can document your total discounts as a percentage of sales today, implement a policy or solution to reduce discounting, and measure the percentage again in a year. What is missing from this statement is the desired solution. In other words, the CFO wants sales to stop discounting but offers no resolution that helps the team say, "We can or cannot do that." When you enter a desired outcome statement, it must offer a specific resolution to the issue at hand. A better way to phrase this desired outcome statement might be: "We need a set of sales tools to reduce or eliminate discounting by proving we are delivering more value than our products cost." Although you might expect the CFO to state her desired outcome here as simply, "We need to quit discounting," that statement is too general to break down and measure. Besides, your objective in creating the entire ROI model is to help your customers think through what they really want and how they can realistically use your products or services to get there.

Summary

Writing effective desired outcomes requires that you fully understand the expectations your prospects have for the resolution of the issue, pain, or goal presented in each line of the ROI Value Matrix. Remember, if you don't understand your prospect's expectation, it is likely to be impossible to meet or exceed it. On the other hand, if you incorrectly guess what the prospect is expecting, it could be disastrous for the sale. Therefore, creating these elements of the ROI Value Matrix requires a great deal of thought and careful practice. Here is a summary of the important points you learned in this chapter about writing effective desired outcomes for your ROI Value Matrix:

T *i p*

When you're writing your own desired outcomes, remember that it is important to capture as much specific data as possible. Be sure you look at the answers from your prospect's viewpoint. Focus on measurable deliverables. Your statement cannot be "blue sky." Test your desired outcome statements with the following sentence: "If we can help you to [insert desired outcome statement], will you purchase from us?" This is one of the bases for building a credible and objective ROI model.

- Desired outcomes provide a resolution for the business issue with which they are associated.
- Desired outcome statements should always tie your why buy statements to your business issue statements.
- Desired outcome statements can be similar to why buy statements with the addition of a tangible, quantifiable result that can be measured.

- Always relate the desired outcome statement to a single need (e.g., a single why buy statement and business issue statement). Split the statement if the desired outcome is too complex.
- Be as specific as possible.
- State your desired outcome from your customer's or prospect's point of view.
- Be sure your desired outcome contains specific quantifiable and measurable details for measuring success.
- Stick to deliverables that you are able to produce with your existing product or service. Avoid stating your desired outcome as a "blue sky" wish.

6

IDENTIFYING FEATURES AND SOLUTIONS

Through this point in the ROI information-gathering process, we have stressed the importance of putting yourself in your customer's or prospect's shoes. The chain of reasoning from why buy to business issue to desired outcome must speak loudly and clearly to the stakeholders for your ROI model to be compelling and credible, both of which are essential to the desired result: a sale.

Having set the context of customer expectations and desires, we are ready to start matching them up with the products or services you offer. Identifying the features and solutions that your products or services can provide is the fifth step in developing your ROI Value Matrix. A feature/solution is a specific function of your products or services. The feature/solution you associate with a specific line on your value matrix must resolve the prospect's or customer's business issue, meet (or exceed) the stakeholder's expectation for the desired outcome, and (of course) give the prospect a reason to buy from you. Examples might include:

- A module within your software application that delivers specific value (e.g., a depreciation module that calculates depreciation of fixed assets so that customers don't have to do it manually).

- An outsourced service your company provides, such as managing hazardous waste documentation, which is not among your customers' core competencies.
- A particular feature of your product or a particular piece of equipment.

In this chapter, you learn how to identify and apply at least one feature/solution to every issue, pain, or goal you defined in the value matrix. Once you establish this link, you have the magic to succeed with ROI Selling.

Key Concepts and Guidelines

Each column of your value matrix builds on the next. At this stage of the process, you need to state the solution that will resolve the why buy and business issues of your stakeholders by achieving their desired outcomes. Here are some key concepts and guidelines to help you complete this exercise:

S *pecific* S *olutions* B *oost* C *redibility*

Rockwell Automation contracted with us to build an ROI model for its maintenance group. We spent a day identifying the reasons people buy maintenance or service agreements, what business issues these customers face, and their desired outcomes. When it came to entering the features/solutions of the Rockwell maintenance program, we cited solutions like 24/7 phone support and online diagnostic services. It would have been easy for Rockwell's staff to simply say, "We can modify our service to resolve any issue or handle any problem . . . after all, Rockwell invented the program." If you take the approach that you can go back and rework a product or solution to "do anything" and stray from a focus on features and solutions you can deliver today, your model will lack objectivity and, as a result, will not be credible to your prospects. Rockwell identified several service offerings currently available in its arsenal and applied each one to the issues, pains, and goals we listed in its ROI model.

- **Never enter "wishware."** To keep your ROI model credible, it is critical to be honest with yourself and enter only features and functions your product currently offers. Regardless of their products or services, salespeople are always eager to talk about the next version or revision or update or upgrade. Avoid this temptation. You need to be honest and enter only solutions you can provide *now*.

- **Sometimes there are holes.** Sometimes there are reasons to buy, business issues, and desired outcomes that your product or service can't address. That's OK—it's a rare market in which one or more vendors have developed the "100 percent solution."

- **Always be specific.** In the introduction to this chapter, we listed several examples of features/solutions. Each of these examples contains specific functions that resolve a specific issue, pain, or goal. If your products or services offer multiple features that may play a role in the solution, list as many as should make sense to a reader unfamiliar with your products. We strongly encourage you to avoid simply listing a product's name as the solution.

T *i p*

Remember what you learned in Chapter 5, "Describing Desired Outcomes"; if you have defined a significant why buy, business issue, and desired outcome that customers can't address with your products or services, you may have discovered a product development opportunity. Though you can't list future products as solutions for existing issues in your value matrix, this information can be a great benefit to the ongoing success of your company.

Finding the Knowledge within Your Organization

Now it's time to gather information from the product experts in your company. Identifying the best solutions and features offered by your company's line of products or services requires an in-depth understanding of your products' features and functions and how your customers use them. When you seek out product experts, we recommend you avoid product architects or designers because of the emotional tie they often have with their products. A better choice is knowledgeable sales staff, support staff, product marketing people, and perhaps management with a good understanding of a product's capabilities. The knowledge base you want to tap into are people who have a strong knowledge of how customers use your product or service to solve real life issues.

Assessing the Value Matrix and Identifying Features/Solutions

With the information you gain from your product experts in mind, read each line of the value matrix one at a time and match the statements in those lines to specific products or features offered by your business. As you read each line, connect the columns with the words *because* (after the why buy statement) and *therefore* (after the business issue statement in the form: [Why Buy? <because> Business Issue <therefore> Desired Outcome].

For example, Figure 6.1 shows one line of the value matrix table for Solution Selling®.

Using the above formula, this example would be read aloud as: *"I want to reduce our cost of sale* because *the sales cycle is too long and our costs continue to rise;* therefore, *I want to reduce the time to revenue and shorten the sales cycle."* It is not unusual for this reading of the statements to sound somewhat redundant. That is perfectly acceptable and indicates logical consistency across the chain.

During workshops we read each line item on the value matrix out loud for the group to consider and comment on. If you build your own value matrix as an individual, we still recommend that you read each line out loud. Hearing the entire chain of reasoning out loud is a good

---

FIGURE 6.1 VALUE MATRIX TABLE

Why Buy?	Business Issue	Stakeholder	Desired Outcome
I want to reduce our cost of sale.	The sales cycle is too long and our costs continue to rise.	VP Sales	I want to reduce the time to revenue and shorten the sales cycle.

double-check for the question, "Would anyone really say this?" Hearing, in addition to reading, also reinforces the message and stimulates different processing areas in your brain, adding perspective to your understanding of the issue. As you read the value matrix, analyze whether the reason to buy and the business issue are:

- **Logical.** We encourage an open, brainstorming approach to developing why buy statements because, at that stage of the process, it is important to capture every possible reason—regardless of whether your products can fulfill all of the reasons or whether all of the reasons support a credible and compelling ROI model. Because we allow any answer to the reasons people buy products like yours, sometimes you'll find that the data you have entered into the matrix doesn't make sense as it relates to your product offering. For example, if you sell advertising for a living and one of the why buy statements you recorded is "Improve the graphics in presentations," you may conclude, on considering this statement, that it doesn't make sense to spend money on an entire advertising campaign just to acquire new graphics.
- **Relevant.** Ensuring that your value matrix line items are relevant to your products or services is as important as validating the logic. For example, if you sell outsourced training programs, and the why buy statement is "Ensure a cost-effective implementation," your offering may not be relevant for this issue. Outsourced training may not always contribute to a cost-effective implementation and may in fact increase the cost of implementation.
- **Attainable.** It is critical to your success in this exercise to recognize your ability as a company to attain the expected results. You must be able to meet or exceed the stakeholder's expectations for the desired outcome. Review each item and decide if you are capable of delivering a product or service that will resolve your prospect's issues and give the prospect a reason to buy from you.
- **Measurable.** Finally, you must ensure that the desired outcome produced by your solution is measurable. Ask yourself, "Can I stop the clock and measure my prospect's current situation and then assess my delivery by measuring again at a later date? I must be able to prove the value I delivered."

Once you have read a line from the value matrix out loud, decide what feature of your product can meet or exceed the desired outcome, resolve the stakeholder's business issue, and give your prospect a tangible reason to buy from you. Enter the feature or solution into your value matrix and move on to the next line item.

Remember, you may not be able to find solutions within your existing products or services for every business issue. When that's the case, you must be willing to recognize the "hole" in your company's offerings. But also be ready to eliminate some of the business issues as being outside your company's mission. If some of your customers' reasons to buy, business issues, and desired outcomes seem farfetched and you're missing features to support them, consider how important those issues, outcomes, and features are to your overall product and market strategy before spending any amount of time and energy on them in the ROI process or product development activity. If listed issues and outcomes are remote or insignificant, drop them from your value matrix.

Matching Specific Features/Functions to Issues and Outcomes

When identifying features or functions that best address the business issues and desired outcomes in your ROI model, remember that simple is always better. For example, try to think in basic terms, along the lines of "Why does a child buy candy?" Use straightforward phrases for the most impact. You want the information in your ROI model to come through loud and clear to your prospects. If the reasoning is too complex and needs a lot of explanation, it will lose impact.

In the example shown in Figure 6.2, we have returned to our sales training example.

Note that for each of the examples in Figure 6.2, Sales Performance International's (SPI) Solution Selling program provides product features that will meet the desired outcome for the VP of Sales, the CFO, and the VP of Marketing and resolve their business issue. In all three instances, the answers are specific Solution Selling tools or features. They directly address the issues and are products that exist today in the Solution Selling portfolio. This example is interesting because SPI is a services company that provides sales training programs, including tools such as *pain*

FIGURE 6.2 VALUE MATRIX—FEATURE/SOLUTION—SALES TRAINING PROGRAMS

Why Buy?	Business Issue	Stakeholder	Desired Outcome	Feature/Solution
I want to reduce our cost of sale . . .	because the sales cycle is too long and our costs continue to rise as the deals linger.	VP Sales CFO	I want to shorten the sales cycle.	Solution Selling Sales Process and Job Aids
I want to increase our revenue per closed lead . . .	because the cost of our marketing programs continues to rise with no increase in close ratios.	VP Sales VP Marketing	I want to increase our close ratios and improve revenue per lead produced by marketing.	Solution Selling Sales Process and Pain Sheets
I need to reduce the amount of time spent conducting account debriefs with my sales team . . .	because debriefs aren't a productive use of the reps' and managers' time.	VP Sales	I want to reduce the time managers spend conducting account debriefs.	Solution Selling Sales Management and GRAF

sheets. Although SPI's services may at first glance seem less tangible than a product like a Sales Force Automation software application that might help address some of the same issues, we documented the fact that SPI's services provide a wide array of tangible, measurable returns on investment for SPI's customers.

Combining Features, Functions, and Services as Solutions

Figure 6.3 presents four examples of adding a product or solution to the value matrix. Each line contains data that is different in nature. The ROI Selling client with whom we created this ROI Value Matrix specializes in developing software that assists HR managers with their recruiting practice (for our purposes here, we'll call this company Ranking Systems, Inc.). The solutions proposed in this example are based on a combination of product features, functions, and services.

The first line of this example, *"The Rank-and-Match application will narrow the list of candidates based on education, experience, and capability test scores,"* identifies a feature of the software offered as a solution. The Rank-and-Match engine filters out unqualified candidates and leaves the HR manager with a list of candidates who are qualified, thus improving the quality of the candidate pool. Because the process is automated, this solution meets the prospect's desired outcome perfectly.

Line two in Figure 6.3, *"Ranking Systems, Inc., will leverage its close partnerships with and manage all job board relationships like Monster.com, Headhunter.net, and ten other candidate pools . . ."* is a different sort of entry. It is not a product or a service. Rather, it is a statement of the vendor's capabilities in the form of a partnership. Line two in Figure 6.3, *"Rank-and-Match software narrows the list of candidates. In addition, we provide a custom candidate screening by our specialists that is specific to our customers' needs, wants, and desires,"* adds an element of service that bolsters the Rank-and-Match engine product to achieve the desired outcome of a "narrowed list of qualified candidates." The why buy statement requests a "better way to qualify candidates." By automating the filtering process and then following up with a targeted interview, the vendor ensures that the client gets only the most-qualified candidates available in the market.

Line three in Figure 6.3, *"Ranking Systems, Inc., handles all advertising, candidate screening, Web site maintenance, and interaction with hiring man-*

FIGURE 6.3 VALUE MATRIX—FEATURE/SOLUTION—HUMAN RESOURCES SOFTWARE

Why Buy?	Business Issue	Stakeholder	Desired Outcome	Feature/Solution
We want to improve our talent acquisition pool . . .	because it is too time consuming for us to review all of these unqualified résumés.	VP Human Resources	Automation to narrow the list of candidates to a size we can handle—eliminate the unqualified candidates in the talent pool	The Rank-and-Match application will narrow the list of candidates based on education, experience, and capability test scores.
We need access to a larger pool of qualified candidates . . .	because the existing pool does not contain enough qualified candidates, forcing us to hire outside headhunters.	VP Human Resources	Access to a larger qualified talent pool	Ranking Systems, Inc., will leverage its close partnerships with and manage all job board relationships like Monster.com, Headhunter.net, and ten other candidate pools to increase our volume of incoming applicants.
I need a better way to qualify candidates . . .	because Human Resources is getting too much invalid data on incoming candidates—it takes too long to narrow down the lists.	VP Human Resources	A narrowed list of qualified candidates	Rank-and-Match software narrows the list of candidates. In addition, we provide a custom candidate screening by our specialists that is specific to our customers' needs, wants, and desires.
We must eliminate redundancy of working with recruiter and posting open positions . . .	because the time it takes to do both is overwhelming.	VP Human Resources	A single point of contact with no duplication for recruiting talent	Ranking Systems, Inc., handles all advertising, candidate screening, Web site maintenance, and interaction with hiring managers and Human Resources. No chance for redundancy.

agers and Human Resources. No chance for redundancy"—uses a mixed approach. In this example, multiple elements of delivery, products, services, and other capabilities all stated together are used to describe how a vendor can meet or exceed the prospect's desired outcome, resolve the business issue, and give the prospect a reason to buy. The mixed approach is most effective when you must meet several major needs masked in one request.

Evaluating Other Examples

To further illustrate the feature/solution column, we have included four additional examples in Figure 6.4 covering various industries. Review the examples and determine how the features and solutions listed in this table could be improved.

The first line of Figure 6.4's feature/solution states, *"ABC Jets has more than 20 jets."* Although this is in effect a feature offered by the vendor, it doesn't exactly spell out how ABC Jets manages its inventory of jets and how it is going to resolve the issue of "on-demand charter services." A more appropriate response might be: *"ABC Jets has corporate jet service 24/7 guaranteed by the more than 20 jets in our inventory."* Notice the difference in the two statements. The original statement simply states a fact without describing the action to be taken. The second spells out how the vendor uses the more than 20 jets to have charters available 24/7.

In the second line of Figure 6.4, the feature/solution states, *"XYZ Software, Inc., has a committee that monitors FASB requirements and enables us to update for new regulations."* There are two primary issues with this example: (1) The statement never clearly states what this committee is going to do to resolve the issue, and (2) it doesn't directly address the desired outcome of "a system that enforces the FASB requirements." A more appropriate feature/solution might be, *"XYZ Software, Inc., has a committee that monitors the changes in FASB requirements and automatically alerts you of changes and possible compliance issues."*

The third example in Figure 6.4 states, *"Application service provider (ASP) collaboration software with custom workarounds for security."* This line item also fails to address the desired outcome. First and foremost, try to avoid the use of terms like *custom* and *workaround*. The credibility of your

FIGURE 6.4 SAMPLE VALUE MATRIX FOR FEATURE/SOLUTION

Product	Why Buy?	Business Issue	Desired Outcome	Feature/Solution
Charter aircraft	We need the ability to fly anywhere at anytime day or night	because our clients require face-to-face service, and we need the flexibility to fly to our clients on demand and cannot wait for commercial flights.	On-demand charter services available around the clock and at a moment's notice	ABC Jets has more than 20 jets.
Leasing software	We need to avoid costly audits and lawsuits by the government resulting from noncompliance with Financial Accounting Standards Board (FASB) regulations	because we could lose our business or end up paying thousands to millions of dollars in fines.	We want a system that enforces FASB requirements.	XYZ Software, Inc., has a committee that monitors FASB requirements and enables us to update for new regulations.
Online collaboration	We are afraid of losing all of our data from an insecure system	because we risk payment delays, security breaches, and potential nonpayments from inaccurate or illegally accessed data.	We want a safe and secure method of accessing and managing secured data.	Application service provider (ASP) collaboration software with custom workarounds for security
Advertising program	We need to promote a new product to a certain demographic	because if we don't reach the targeted demographic, the product launch will fail, and we will not reach our revenue targets or breakeven goals.	Need an advertising program targeted to our chosen demographic.	Acme Advertising Agency has experience with demographically targeted campaigns.

entire ROI model relies on limiting your feature/solution entries to hard-and-fast deliverables from currently available products and services. Although this line item is better than the previous examples, it is missing one element: the *how!* If the business issue is a fear of losing data, and the desired outcome references the need for a "safe and secure method of accessing and managing secure data," then your feature/solution must explain specifically how you intend to meet stakeholders' expectations and resolve the business issue. For this example our rewrite reads as follows: *"Application service provider (ASP) collaboration software is an Internet-based online collaboration tool with built-in security based on log-on and password."* This statement is broken into three pieces:

1. The application is Internet based.
2. It comes with built-in security.
3. The security is based on log-on and password.

The data is safe because it is off-site, and it is secure because of the security measures employed by the developer.

The last example in Figure 6.4, *"Acme Advertising Agency has experience with demographically targeted campaigns,"* is just a simple statement of fact that, like some of the previous examples, doesn't specifically address the desired outcome or business issue. The business issue references the prospect's need to promote a new product to a "certain" demographic; the desired outcome states that a need therefore exists for an advertising program targeted to a chosen demographic. Notice how the statements use the verbs *promote* and *advertise.*

In both cases, the feature/solution as described is likely to fall short of the stakeholder's expectations. We rewrote the feature/solution to read, *"Acme Advertising Agency's research department conducts demographic studies in major cities prior to making recommendations for an advertising campaign. In addition, our customer base is filled with examples of successful demographic-specific advertising campaigns."* We realize this feature/solution is lengthy. We always advise our customers, when defining features and solutions, not to be too concerned with word counts. It is far more important to get the right verbiage and express the message clearly when creating your feature/solution statements.

The new value matrix with a corrected feature/solution column is displayed in Figure 6.5.

FIGURE 6.5 SAMPLE VALUE MATRIX FOR FEATURE/SOLUTION—CORRECT VERSION

Product	Why Buy?	Business Issue	Desired Outcome	Feature/Solution
Charter aircraft	We need the ability to fly anywhere at anytime day or night . . .	because our clients require face-to-face service, and we need the flexibility to fly to our clients on demand and cannot wait for commercial flights.	On-demand charter services available around the clock and at a moment's notice	ABC Jet's corporate jet service, available 24/7, is guaranteed by the more than 20 jets in our inventory.
Leasing software	We need to avoid costly audits and lawsuits by the government resulting from noncompliance with Financial Accounting Standards Board (FASB) regulations . . .	because we could lose our business or end up paying thousands to millions of dollars in fines.	We want a system that enforces FASB requirements.	XYZ Software, Inc., has a committee that monitors the changes in FASB requirements and automatically alerts you of changes and possible compliance issues.
Online collaboration	We are afraid of losing all of our data from an insecure system . . .	because we risk payment delays, security breaches, and potential nonpayments from inaccurate or illegally accessed data.	We want a safe and secure method of accessing and managing secured data.	Our ASP (application service provider) software is an Internet-based online collaboration tool with built-in security based on log-on and password.

(continued)

FIGURE 6.5 continued

Product	Why Buy?	Business Issue	Desired Outcome	Feature/Solution
Advertising program	We need to promote a new product to a certain demographic. . . .	because if we don't reach the targeted demographic, the product launch will fail, and we will not reach our revenue targets or breakeven goals.	Need an advertising program targeted to our chosen demographic.	Acme Advertising Agency's research department conducts demographic studies in major cities prior to making recommendations for an advertising campaign. In addition, our customer base is filled with examples of successful demographic-specific advertising campaigns.

Summary

In this chapter, you've learned some of the basic guidelines and processes for matching your customers' business issues and desired outcomes with solutions based on your company's products and services. Remember these key pieces of information from this chapter:

- When completing the features/solution column of the ROI Value Matrix, enter only existing features of your product or service.
- Be as specific as possible.
- Don't be too concerned with word counts—long explanations are acceptable.
- It is OK to enter services, partnerships, or other currently available mixed approaches that resolve issues.
- Avoid the word *custom* when entering the solution or feature.
- Don't enter the term *workarounds*.
- Whenever possible, use specific features of your product or service rather than entering the name of an entire product line or set of services.

7

ASSIGNING ROI CATEGORIES AND VALUE METRICS

To make sure we are establishing an appropriate context for the important concept of assigning ROI categories and value metrics, let's review the chain of logic we have developed to arrive at this point, as expressed in the following series of questions:

- Why do people buy products like yours?
- What business issues, pains, or goals are prospects trying to resolve as they relate to the reason to buy?
- Who in a prospect's organization is affected most by these issues?
- What is the desired outcome or expectation of those individuals?
- What product or service feature or solution do you offer that delivers the desired outcome, meets or exceeds the prospect's expectation, and gives the prospect a reason to buy from you . . . now?

At this stage of the process, you must also ask:

- What type of ROI does your solution deliver (revenue increase, cost reduction, or cost avoidance)?

In this chapter, we talk about choosing and recording data in two closely related columns of the ROI Value Matrix: ROI category and value metric. This phase of developing your ROI model is closely linked with the features and solutions we discussed in Chapter 6, because the ROI category and value metric describe the ROI produced by the specific features and solutions you've identified and recorded in your value matrix. In this chapter, you learn to assign and enter into the ROI Value Matrix an ROI category and value metric—the sixth and seventh steps in building your ROI model. The information in this chapter teaches you the last steps in the information-gathering phase of building your ROI model! After this stage, your value matrix will include only the tangible hard dollar savings your product has to offer, and you will be ready to start the actual process of building the model as described in Part Two.

Understanding ROI Categories and Value Metrics

ROI category is the label used to describe the benefit of the features/solutions you expect to deliver to your customer or prospect. We use only three ROI categories in ROI selling:

1. **Cost reduction.** Features/solutions in this category lead to a reduction in cost, regardless of where the reduction comes from. Examples of features or solutions that fall into this category include overhead reductions, staff downsizing, lower raw material costs, automation that replaces a manual effort and thus reduces your cost of manufacturing, and so on.
2. **Cost avoidance.** Features/solutions that fall into this category enable your customer or prospect to avoid taking on expenditure. This category is often misunderstood, because the avoidance may actually become a cost reduction. Examples of features or solutions that fall into this category include avoiding fines for noncompliance and avoiding the need to hire additional personnel to perform tasks that could be automated using your feature/solution.
3. **Revenue increase.** Features/solutions in this category lead to an increase in top-line revenue. It is important to note that these revenue increases may or may not lead to increased profits and margin (we expand on this concept later in the chapter). Examples of revenue increases include increasing the average amount or revenue per sale or increasing the number of sales.

Our experience from developing models with many ROI Selling clients has shown that just about every value you can deliver falls into one of these three categories. We use revenue increase, cost reduction, and cost avoidance to ensure that the ROI you associate with your feature/ solution is tangible. In Chapter 11, we tell you how to apply mathematics to the Needs Analysis Questionnaire responses you obtain from your customers to calculate the ROI your products and services are capable of producing. You will find it difficult, if not impossible, to calculate ROI for intangible items. Even if you could figure out an ROI formula for intangible items, keep in mind the need for credibility when building ROI models. Intangibles in your ROI model provide opportunities for your prospects to raise questions about the validity of the entire model. Using the three ROI categories helps ensure that you end up with a credible finished product.

After you have assigned ROI categories, the next step in the process of building the ROI Value Matrix is assigning a value metric to each feature/solution. The value metric is the unit of measure used to describe the ROI category delivered by the feature/solution. The value metric must be quantifiable and measurable. For example, if the ROI category is cost reduction, then the value metric could be the cost of human capital. Or if the ROI category is revenue increase, then the value metric could be increased Web site transactions leading to additional sales. The value metric is simply a measurable explanation of your ROI category. This metric gives your prospect a clear and precise statement of how the benefit delivered by the proposed feature or solution will be measured.

In order for you to accurately identify the ROI category and value metric for your ROI Value Matrix statements, those statements must have sound and tangible desired outcomes (if you are not comfortable with this concept, review Chapter 5, "Describing Desired Outcomes"). We have encouraged you to avoid nontangible issues and outcomes such as improving customer satisfaction. Although improving customer satisfaction is important, it is difficult to quantify in an ROI model. It is critical to be sure that the outcomes remaining in your value matrix at this point can be quantified into a tangible unit of measure. If you find they cannot, either replace them with something that is quantifiable, manipulate them to include a measurable element, or eliminate them from the value matrix.

Key Concepts and Guidelines

These key concepts and guidelines for entering the ROI category and value metric help assure you that you are entering only tangible items into your value matrix:

- **This is where you understand and quantify the value you're offering.** Each piece of information you have accumulated thus far (why buy, business issue, desired outcome, stakeholders, and feature/solution) has led you toward an understanding of your prospect's pain, issue, or goal. In this stage of the process, you quantify precisely the value you are capable of delivering.

- **Not profit, not margin.** Occasionally, we're asked why we don't include "increase profit" as an ROI category, as many organizations want to increase their profits. We don't use this category for a simple reason: If you can manipulate the numbers, it doesn't count. Profit be manipulated, and therefore it can't be used as an ROI category.

Note

You can manipulate an existing nontangible savings by changing the measurement to get the result you are looking for. For example: There are widely accepted calculations in the marketplace that will determine the lifetime value of a customer. You can use this calculation to determine the cost of losing a customer as a result of dissatisfaction or other reasons. Further, you may want to simply change customer satisfaction to a metric you can measure, such as customer turnover. Ask yourself: What is our annual customer turnover?

The next potential category we are challenged with is margin increase. We believe we've covered this possibility within the existing categories. When you break down what an increase in margin really is, you typically find that it's a cost reduction. If your margins have increased, you have either reduced your cost or raised your price to achieve this outcome.

- **The value metric must be measurable.** If you are going to increase revenue, avoid costs, or reduce costs, then the value metric you assign to each of these categories must be measurable. You must provide a valid means for measuring your company's ability to deliver the solution as well as the success achieved by your prospect after putting your solution in action. For example, a measurable metric might be a reduction in the amount of time spent performing a task, whereas a nonmeasurable metric is a reduction in the amount of time it takes our customers to navigate our Web site and place orders.

Assigning Categories and Value Metrics

In the following examples, note that we have purposely limited categories to those listed above and that each of the categories is tangible and measurable. Figure 7.1 lists several examples of ROI categories and value metrics. In each example, we first categorize the proposed product or feature and then assign a specific value metric to the solution. As you read through each of these examples, evaluate the category and value metric data against the criteria for these elements given earlier in the chapter.

ROI Value Matrix Statements

Look at the reason to buy and the business issue in the first line item of Figure 7.1, *"I want to reduce our cost of sale because the sales cycle is too long and our costs continue to rise as the deals linger."* In the business-to-business (B2B) world, where salespeople must often make face-to-face calls on prospects to close an opportunity, sales expenses can compound when deals linger on without closing. The cost of sale can be made up of many factors, including travel expenses, material expenses, and the human capital costs of your sales team, presale engineers, proposal department and sales support staff, and so on. Therefore, the ROI category for this feature/solution is reduce a cost because we are talking about cutting the expenses related to prolonged sales processes.

To complete the value metric, we must ask ourselves, "What cost are we trying to reduce?" In this case the answer is in the why buy statement: ". . . reduce our cost of sale." How do we accomplish this? By using the Solution Selling® feature/solution to reduce the sales cycle as stated in the desired outcome.

FIGURE 7.1 VALUE MATRIX—SALES TRAINING PROGRAMS—CATEGORY/VALUE METRIC

Why Buy?	Business Issue	Stakeholder	Desired Outcome	Feature/Solution	Category	Value Metric
I want to reduce our cost of sale . . .	because the sales cycle is too long and our costs continue to rise as the deals linger.	VP Sales CFO	I want to reduce the time to revenue and shorten the sales cycle.	Solution Selling Sales Process and Job Aids	Reduce cost.	Reduce the cost per sale
I want to increase our revenue per closed lead . . .	because the cost of our marketing programs continues to rise with no increase in close ratio.	VP Marketing VP Sales	I want to increase our close ratio and improve our revenue per lead produced by marketing.	Solution Selling Sales Process and Pain Sheets	Increase revenue.	Increase close ratio
I need to reduce the amount of time spent conducting account debriefs with my sales team . . .	because debriefs aren't a productive use of the reps' and managers' time.	VP Sales	I want to reduce the time sales managers spend conducting account debriefs.	Solution Selling Sales Management, GRAF	Reduce cost.	Reduce account rep and manager time (human capital cost)

On the second line in Figure 7.1, the why buy business issue statement declares, *"I want to increase our revenue per closed lead because the cost of our marketing programs continues to rise with no increase in close ratio."* This tells us quite clearly that the ROI category is increase revenue. The revenue referred to is stated in the desired outcome: "I want to increase our close ratio and improve our revenue per lead produced by marketing." The vendor in this case, SPI, determined that the revenue increase would most likely be produced by an increase in the number of sales closed. Therefore, this statement is about improving the close ratio, which leads to an increase in the number of sales and thus an increase in revenue. Conceptually, if you close a higher proportion of your opportunities, your overall revenue should increase as well (provided you don't use discounts or other price reductions to improve the close ratios and thus give away the potential revenue increase).

Finally, the last example in Figure 7.1 reads, *"I need to reduce the amount of time spent conducting account debriefs with my sales team because debriefs aren't a productive use of the reps' and managers' time."* This statement refers to a loss of productive time for both the sales and management teams. When you are able to reduce the amount of time a salesperson or sales manager spends performing nonsales activities, you are reducing a major cost to the organization. Some would argue that this particular item could be expressed as an increase in revenue, because if the reps have more time to sell, they will generate more sales and thus increase revenue. This type of revenue increase can be difficult to quantify and measure. You might be able to capture the number of selling hours spent annually and divide the total by the revenue generated by each salesperson. However, logic tells us that if a salesperson has urgent sales activities to perform, that person would most likely skip the account debrief for the week. Also, most sales personnel don't adhere to a strict 40-hour work week. Successful reps spend the time necessary to "get the job done." Therefore, the ROI category that fits best in this instance is reduce a cost in the form of a reduction in time spent conducting debriefs.

N *o t e*

We did a simple survey with salespeople that indicated outside salespeople spend only about 30 to 50 percent of their time selling. The rest of their time is spent on debriefing, paperwork, and traveling.

Identifying Unstated Goals within the Desired Outcome

Figure 7.2 illustrates three additional examples of ROI categories and value metrics that are a bit more difficult to follow than the previous ones. In this section, we discuss the thought processes involved in assigning ROI categories and value metrics to each of these statements, so you can clearly see the logic behind our choices.

The first line in Figure 7.2 begins with the following why buy and business issue: *"We want to improve our talent acquisition pool because it is* too time consuming *for us to review all of these unqualified résumés."* The business issue points us toward a time-consuming task that needs to be expedited and leads us to the desire to reduce the cost of human capital required to perform this task. Illustrating our recommendation that you read through the entire line on the value matrix as you progress through these steps, we can confirm this by rereading the desired outcome: "Automation to narrow the list of candidates down to a size we can handle—eliminate the unqualified candidates in the talent pool." Although it is not stated directly in the desired outcome, the desire is to reduce the amount of time spent doing this task manually. Sometimes you must analyze a statement like this and select the real meaning of the customer's goal.

The second example in Figure 7.2 states, *"We need access to a larger pool of qualified candidates because the existing pool does not contain enough qualified candidates, forcing us to* hire outside headhunters." Once again, the desired outcome does not point out an obvious choice for an ROI category. The desired outcome reads, "Access to a larger qualified talent pool." This statement, along with the why buy statement and business issue, does suggest that without a larger qualified talent pool, there will be additional costs. We are fortunate that the business issue directs our attention specifically to the cost of outside headhunter fees. Take note that the annual amount spent on headhunter fees is measurable and quantifiable. Therefore, we want to reduce the cost of recruiting resources and, in particular, reduce or eliminate the cost of headhunter fees.

The last example in Figure 7.2 states, *"We must eliminate redundancy of working with recruiters and posting open positions because* the time it takes *to do both is overwhelming."* The desired outcome is a single point of contact with no duplication for recruiting talent. This is another statement

FIGURE 7.2 VALUE MATRIX—CATEGORY/VALUE METRIC—HUMAN RESOURCES SOFTWARE

Why Buy?	Business Issue	Stakeholder	Desired Outcome	Feature/Solution	Category	Value Metric
We want to improve our talent acquisition pool . . .	because it is too time consuming for us to review all of these unqualified résumés.	VP Human Resources	Automation to narrow the list of candidates down to a size we can handle—eliminate the unqualified candidates in the talent pool	The Rank-and-Match application narrows the list based on education, experience, and capability test scores.	Reduce cost.	Reduce the amount of time it takes to screen applicants.
We need access to a larger pool of qualified candidates . . .	because the existing pool does not contain enough qualified candidates, forcing us to hire outside headhunters.	VP, Human Resources	Access to a larger qualified talent pool	Ranking Systems, Inc., will leverage our close partnerships and manage all job board relationships, such as: Monster.com, Headhunter.net, and ten other candidate pools to increase our volume of incoming applicants.	Reduce cost.	Reduce the time and expense of building your talent pool.
We must eliminate redundancy of working with recruiters and posting open positions . . .	because the time it takes to do both is overwhelming.	VP Human Resources	A single point of contact with no duplication for recruiting talent	Rank-and-Match software narrows the list. In addition, we provide a custom candidate screening by our specialists that is specific to our customer's needs, wants, and desires.	Reduce cost.	Reduce the cost of paying both job boards and recruiters for same candidates; eliminate our Web site mgmt. costs.

that does not lead us to an obvious ROI category. To make it easier to understand, let's turn the statement around: "If we gave you a single point of contact with no duplication for recruiting talent . . . would you reduce your costs, increase revenue, or avoid costs?" The answer is that it would reduce the customer's cost of human capital by reducing the time it takes to track and fix redundancies. Keep this turnaround technique in mind as you build your own ROI categories and value metrics.

Assigning Multiple Categories to Multiple Features

As you complete the value matrix, you are likely to encounter situations where multiple features may work together to solve a single business issue. For example, to improve the talent acquisition pool, you may need tools to assess the quality of the pool as well as find ways to increase the number of candidates by attracting additional talent into the pool. To accomplish this, you need to look at more than one feature and more than one category.

When you find that a line item is addressed by multiple feature/solutions and ROI categories, we suggest that you add as many lines as needed to list each feature and category in your value matrix separately. For example, Constructware has a unique software application that helps construction companies reduce their litigation costs as described in Figures 7.3 and 7.4.

The one row in Figure 7.3 combines two ROI categories into a single value matrix line item; we don't recommend this approach. Our experience is that you must create separate lines of the ROI Value Matrix to accommodate multiple features, solutions, categories, and metrics, as shown in Figure 7.4. Addressing each feature and category separately is the only way you can properly

T *i p*

Because we are familiar with the human resources software product on which this example is based, it is easy for us to explain the issues and solutions. As you build your ROI model, you will quickly notice there is no substitute for product knowledge. Be sure to consult with the most knowledgeable personnel to whom you have access as you build your ROI Value Matrix. The bonus here (ROI for you) is the transfer of product knowledge in a "protected" real-world environment.

FIGURE 7.3 WHY BUY VALUE MATRIX—CONSTRUCTWARE ONLINE COLLABORATION TOOLS—SINGLE EXAMPLE

Why Buy?	Business Issue	Stakeholder	Desired Outcome	Feature/Solution	Category	Value Metric
We need to manage our risk . . .	because our cost of litigation continues to rise because of our inability to meet occupancy schedules.	Owner, general contractor, project managers	Reduce our litigation costs; capture our on-time delivery bonuses.	Our dashboard, cost management features, and budgeting module	Reduce cost/ increase revenue.	Litigation cost reductions, revenue increases from receiving bonus for on-time delivery

FIGURE 7.4 WHY BUY VALUE MATRIX—CONSTRUCTWARE ONLINE COLLABORATION TOOLS—ROI CATEGORY SPLIT INTO TWO LINES

Why Buy?	Business Issue	Stakeholder	Desired Outcome	Feature/Solution	Category	Value Metric
We need to manage our risk . . .	because our cost of litigation continues to rise because of our inability to meet occupancy schedules.	Owner, general contractor, project managers	Reduce our litigation costs.	Our dashboard, cost management features, and budgeting module	Reduce cost.	Litigation cost reductions.
We need to manage our risk . . .	because our cost of litigation continues to rise because of our inability to meet occupancy schedules.	Owner, general contractor, project managers	Capture our on-time delivery bonuses.	Our dashboard, cost management features, and budgeting module	Increase revenue.	Receive bonuses for on-time delivery.

lay out your ROI Needs Analysis Questionnaire and develop your ROI calculations
when we start working on Part Two.

Analyzing a Variety of Value Metrics

Sometimes, cost savings or revenue increases exist in addition to human capital or
increasing sales. In the examples shown in
Figure 7.5, we define different units of measure you may come across as
you assign value metrics to your ROI categories.

In Figure 7.5, the value metric in the first line is "Recapture the dollars we discounted." Most salespeople feel a perceived need to grant discounts to close business. Our value matrix indicates that we can increase
revenue by reducing discounting using the features listed in the feature/
solution column.

The second example references a reduction in the cost per closed
lead generated by marketing. Improved close ratios mean more sales
from each marketing program and a lower marketing cost for each closed
deal. In both of these examples, the value metric is based on the vendor's ability to stop and measure a cost or expense and return after implementation and measure again. The third example is similar to the other
examples; it proposes human capital as the value metric of the reduced
cost resulting from the use of a meeting planning company.

Summary

It is impossible to overstate the value of the data you have gathered
in your ROI Value Matrix. By successfully completing Part One of *ROI
Selling*, you have created a compilation of every reason someone buys
products like yours. You have listed the business issues, pains, and goals
they face, their desired outcomes or expectations, and, of course, the
positions of the decision makers who own these issues. In Chapter 6, you
associated a product feature or solution to each of the line items on your
value matrix that describe the issues, pains, or goals your prospects face.

FIGURE 7.5 VALUE MATRIX—ROI SELLING—ROI CATEGORY/VALUE METRIC

Why Buy?	Business Issue	Stakeholder	Desired Outcome	Feature/Solution	Category	Value Metric
We are discounting too much . . .	because the competition is trying to increase market share.	VP Sales	Reduce or eliminate discounts	Cost of waiting calculations and estimated value delivered on the ROI Financial Dashboard	Increase revenue.	Recapture the dollars we discounted.
Our cost per lead continues to rise.	because close ratios are not increasing on leads generated by marketing.	VP Sales, VP Marketing	Need to increase close ratios	Needs Analysis Questionnaire and Executive Summary	Reduce cost.	Marketing cost per closed lead generated
The cost of planning and executing our meetings continues to rise . . .	because meeting planning is not our core competency.	VP Marketing	We need to reduce our ongoing cost of meetings.	Meeting planning company that focuses on event planning	Reduce cost.	Human capital for planning, travel

In this chapter, the last in Part One, you assigned a category and value metric to the benefits offered by those features or solutions. As you prepare to fulfill this last step in the information-gathering phase of the ROI model, keep these points in mind:

- When analyzing ROI statements to assign categories and value metrics, try reading the entire row of the value matrix aloud to stimulate thought processes.
- When assigning a category to proposed ROI features/solutions, you must choose from these three options:
  1. Reduce a cost
  2. Avoid a cost
  3. Increase revenue
- A value metric is the unit of measure for the ROI category.
- Avoid using *profit* or *margin* as a value metric.
- Your value metric must be tangible and measurable.
- Your feature/solution can be a service, a product, or a combination of the two.
- If a line item can fit into more than one category, split it into two or more items and add the new categories to the end of your value matrix as separate line items.
- Save your intangible savings for your proposal.

Part Two

BUILDING THE PERFECT ROI MODEL

"Questions are the most effective form of verbal behavior you can use to persuade."

NEIL RACKHAM, from *SPIN Selling*

8

CREATING VALUE STATEMENTS

In Part One, you learned the techniques for assigning data to a number of components within the ROI Value Matrix. These components describe the reasons customers might buy your products or services, the individuals within a prospect's organization most affected by these issues, those individuals' desired outcomes, the solution your products or services offer, and the specific type and measurable benefit of the proposed solution. You have also learned how to assign or identify each of these values and record them in individual lines within the ROI Value Matrix. In this chapter, we discuss writing value statements. All of the information in your value matrix is synthesized into these value statements; the process of writing value statements is the first step in actually building your ROI model.

In Chapter 7, we asked you to read each line of your value matrix out loud. In addition to stimulating your thought processes, we hoped this exercise would help you begin the formulation of a value statement. A value statement should articulate the specific value that your products or services are capable of delivering to your prospects. Figure 8.1 shows an example of data selected from one line of an ROI Value Matrix and the value statement created for that line item.

In addition to synthesizing all of the existing data in a single line of the ROI Value Matrix, value statements serve as the foundation for cre-

---

FIGURE 8.1 VALUE STATEMENT TABLE

Business Issue	Desired Outcome	Feature/ Solution	Category	Value Metric
Debriefs are not a productive use of the reps' or managers' time.	I want to reduce the time managers spend conducting account debriefs.	Solution Selling® Sales Management and GRAF	Reduce cost.	Reduce sales reps' and managers' time conducting account debriefs.

Value Statement	Reduce the cost of sales representatives and managers by reducing the amount of time spent conducting account debriefs

---

ating key pain indicators. Also known as KPIs, these are the questions you will include in your Needs Analysis Questionnaire. You learn more about writing and using KPIs in Chapter 10.

In addition to their use within the ROI Selling process, value statements are helpful to your business in many other ways:

- **In marketing campaigns.** Value statements are versatile marketing tools. They are used throughout marketing literature, advertising campaigns, white papers, public relations activities such as speeches and articles, and trade show handouts.
- **As training tools for investors and new personnel.** Value statements are an effective training tool for your personnel—both sales and nonsales—for teaching exactly what your organization delivers to your prospect base. Investors, in particular, like value statements because, in addition to spelling out the specific value your solution is capable of delivering, the statements present an opportunity to assess and quantify the success of that solution.
- **Within proposals.** One of the most essential sales materials you can develop is a proposal that helps clinch the sale of your products; and value statements play a major role in the development of an effective proposal.

Remember the exercise we outlined earlier in which we knew that nine of hearts was the answer before we asked Jennifer the questions

Value Statements in Marketing Campaigns

Constructware, Inc., developed a four-page glossy brochure filled with materials from its ROI Analyzer tool, which we helped the company develop through our workshop process. Constructware's brochure includes screen prints and a number of value statements. Constructware offers this brochure to prospects as part of an e-mail campaign for a free ROI analysis. According to Gary Greenberger, VP of Sales at Constructware, "We identified many capabilities we could quantify during the ROI build process. We quantified the value we delivered and offered a free assessment to prove it. The program was a great success."

about her card. As you create the value statements, remember to keep your prospects' issues and desired outcomes in mind, and craft the statements to reflect the answers you want to encourage your prospects to provide—answers that will lead to quantifiable results from the implementation of your products' features and solutions.

Key Concepts and Guidelines

As with other components of the ROI Value Matrix, each value statement is unique, but all share certain characteristics. When you write value statements, keep these concepts and guidelines in mind:

- **Validate your value matrix input.** A well-written value statement provides precious insight into your customers' and prospects' issues, pains, and goals and validates the effectiveness of your value-based solution offering.
- **Start your value statements with the ROI category and end with the feature/solution.** We recommend that you start each value statement with one of the three ROI categories. By confidently stating "We reduce your cost of . . . by . . ." or "We help you avoid the cost of . . . by . . .," a value statement offers a powerful message that your prospect will notice.

- **The value statement aligns the value metric with the desired outcome.** Remember, the value metric is the unit of measure that applies to the ROI category. Try to lead with the ROI category and follow with the value metric. For example, for the ROI category of reduce cost, the specific value metric, or unit of measure, might be cost of sale. Therefore, this value statement would open with these words: "We reduce your cost of sale by. . . ."
- **The value statement must meet or exceed your prospects' desired outcome.** Adding the desired outcome to the value statement is a little more complex. The desired outcome expresses the stakeholders' expectations. Throughout the book we have emphasized the importance of capturing all the ROI information about your prospects and documenting it in the ROI Value Matrix. To clearly communicate your prospects' needs and expectations, a value statement should clearly state the business issue you are going to resolve, followed by the particular expectation you are going to meet or exceed. The addition of the desired outcome in the value statement helps prospects better understand your value proposition.
- **The value statement must include a feature/solution.** Your value statement needs to clearly state the feature or solution you offer. Including the feature/solution in the statement lends credibility to your organization.

Compiling Effective Value Statements

To write the most effective value statements, you need to study the existing components of the ROI Value Matrix and practice distilling those components into one powerful statement. The process of writing these statements can be generally described in these four steps:

1. **Evaluate each line of your value matrix.** We recommend that to begin the process of creating ROI value statements, you read each line of the value matrix out loud—from why buy to feature/solution—as though each line is a sentence. If you entered the data as we suggested from why buy to value metric, the value statements should write themselves.

2. **Begin all value statements with the ROI category.** Reduce the cost of . . . , or Avoid the cost of . . . , or Increase revenue. . . .

3. **Relate the value metric directly to the desired outcome.** The desired outcome states clearly what your customer or prospect wants from you; therefore, your value statement should clearly address the customer's stated request. In doing so, your statement should associate the value metric with the desired outcome so the prospect can clearly see the measurable benefit that will achieve his or her stated goal, request, or purpose.

> **T** *i* *p*
>
> When you write a value statement, you shouldn't include any new information in it; the statement should be based on the existing data within the ROI Value Matrix. If you feel the statements need additional data, go back and make sure you've covered all the bases in your existing ROI Value Matrix data.

4. **Include the feature/solution as the resolution.** Finish your value statement with how you are going to deliver the value you are proposing. The feature/solution you listed in your value matrix identifies the data you need to list here to complete the value statement.

Examples in the following sections describe each of these steps in more detail.

Using an Abbreviated Table When Writing Value Statements

In the sample ROI Value Matrix shown in Figure 8.2, we break each line down to help you create the associated value statement. In Figure 8.3, we show the data and value statement displayed in the table format you saw earlier in Figure 8.1. This abbreviated table format enables us to focus our attention strictly on the value matrix components that are integral to the value statement. You might want to consider using an abbreviated table like this when building your value statements.

FIGURE 8.2   VALUE MATRIX—SALES TRAINING PROGRAMS—VALUE STATEMENTS

Why Buy?	Business Issue	Stakeholder	Desired Outcome	Feature/ Solution	Category	Value Metric	Value Statement
I want to reduce our cost of sale . . .	because the sales cycle is too long and our costs continue to rise as the deals linger.	VP Sales CFO	I want to reduce the time to revenue and shorten the sales cycle.	Solution Selling Sales Process and Job Aids	Reduce cost.	Reduce the cost of sale.	Reduce your cost of sale by shortening the sales cycle using Solution Selling Sales Process and Job Aids.
I want to increase our revenue per closed lead . . .	because the cost of our marketing programs continues to rise with no increase in close ratio.	VP Marketing VP Sales	I want to increase our close ratios and improve our revenue per lead produced by Marketing.	Solution Selling Sales Process and Pain Sheets	Increase revenue.	Increase revenue per lead closed.	Increase your revenue by increasing your close ratio using Solution Selling Sales Process and Pain Sheets on Marketing-generated leads.
I need to reduce the amount of time spent conducting account debriefs with my sales team . . .	because too much time is taken up weekly for our sales reps and managers doing account debriefs.	VP Sales	I want to reduce the time managers spend conducting account debriefs.	Solution Selling Sales Management, GRAF	Reduce cost.	Reduce account reps' and managers' time (human capital cost).	Reduce the cost of sales reps and managers by reducing the amount of time spent conducting account debriefs using Solution Selling Sales Management and GRAF.

FIGURE 8.3 VALUE STATEMENT CREATION TABLE

Business Issue	Desired Outcome	Feature/ Solution	Category	Value Metric
.... the sales cycle is too long and our costs continue to rise as the deals linger.	I want to reduce the time to revenue and shorten the sales cycle.	Solution Selling Sales Process and Job Aids	Reduce cost.	Reduce the cost of sale.
Value Statement	Reduce your cost of sale by shortening the sales cycle using Solution Selling Sales Process and Job Aids			

Figure 8.3 shows the immediately significant portions of a single line of the value matrix. We used this information table to create a value statement for the first line of the value matrix in Figure 8.2.

In Figure 8.3, the business issue discusses the continuing rise in cost as a deal lingers, leading us to the desired outcome of wanting to reduce the time to revenue and shorten the sales cycle. Each section of the value statement example is a column in the value matrix—an excellent example of how a value statement can write itself.

Writing Statements That Align Desired Outcomes to Category and Value Metric

By the time you are ready to write value statements, you have already entered an ROI category and value metric for each line in your value matrix. In some situations, however, these elements (ROI category and value metric) don't line up with the desired outcome. Sometimes the ROI category and the value metric are derivatives of another line; sometimes they are split into multiple line items. We find the extra effort of looking at each line and determining the value statement a worthwhile task that will pay many rewards as you build your ROI model. Figure 8.3, for example, deals with an increase in revenue, but the desired outcome in this example is not clear for the purposes of defining the value statement.

The desired outcome in Figure 8.4 states that our customers want an increase in close ratio but doesn't obviously state that customers want to increase revenue, reduce a cost, or avoid a cost. Our objective throughout this process is to document the truth about your products or services so there is little room for guessing. Sometimes, the revenue category you choose can be a function of particular product attributes you want to emphasize. In this case, the creator of the ROI Value Matrix wanted to focus on helping her customers reduce the marketing cost per closed sale.

To correct this statement, we need to include the value metric and do additional analysis of the desired outcome. Remember, to create value statements you want to use all of the data you entered into your ROI Value Matrix. As part of that analysis, ask yourself, based on the listed desired outcome, "What ROI category are we trying to achieve?" Use the answer as the basis for creating the value statement. We are not telling you to go back and rewrite your value matrix; we are, however, telling you to build the value statement on your interpretation of the facts you collected when creating the ROI Value Matrix.

FIGURE 8.4 VALUE STATEMENT TABLE

Business Issue	Desired Outcome	Feature/ Solution	Category	Value Metric
The cost of our marketing program continues to rise with no increase in close ratios.	I want to increase our close ratios and improve our revenue per lead produced by marketing.	Solution Selling Sales Process and Pain Sheets	Reduce cost.	Reduce marketing cost per closed lead.
Value Statement	Reduce your marketing cost per closed sale by increasing your close ratio using Solution Selling Sales Process and Pain Sheets on leads generated by marketing			

Summary

By synthesizing specific customer issues and pains and articulating the value delivered by your company's products or services, value statements offer multiple benefits to your organization. In addition to serving as a culmination of all previous information in the ROI Value Matrix and forming the first step in actually building your ROI model, value statements are useful in marketing campaigns, in training materials for investors and new personnel, and in proposals. Depending on the quality of information in your value matrix, creating value statements can also be one of the easier tasks in the ROI development process. As we said earlier, if your why buy, business issue, stakeholder, desired outcome, feature/solution, ROI category, and value metric hang together, your value statements will virtually write themselves. Remember these key points from this chapter when writing your own value statements:

- Begin your value statements with the ROI category and end them with the proposed feature/solution.
- Your value statement should directly align the associated value metric and desired outcome.
- The feature/solution should be put forward as the resolution within your value statement.
- Be sure the value statement meets or exceeds the prospect's desired outcome, resolves the prospect's business issue, and gives your prospect a reason to buy from you.
- In the next phase of the ROI Selling process, we are going to build questions to address the value statements, so as you write these statements, remember the nine of hearts!

9

ANALYZING THE
VALUE MATRIX

You should now have a value matrix
with rows documenting approximately 50 value statements. For each
row, you should have columns listing the eight pieces of information you
have identified so far:

1. Why buy statement
2. Business issue
3. Stakeholder
4. Desired outcome
5. Feature/Solution
6. ROI category
7. Value metric
8. Value statement

We are now ready to start shaping all of this information into an ROI
model. (If you are not comfortable with all of the terms listed above and
their relationships to each other, we suggest you review Part One or, at
minimum, the introduction. You must be familiar and comfortable with
the ROI Selling terminology and concepts to be able to create a work-
able, credible ROI model.)

The first step in moving from a value matrix to an ROI model is analyzing the value matrix. Up to this point, we have emphasized an open, brainstorming approach to gathering information and building the matrix to be sure we cast a broad net and captured every possible idea. Now it's time to take a hard look at the data we have gathered and organize it to make our ROI model as concise and compelling as possible. To do this, you will categorize all of the items listed in your ROI Value Matrix into 10 to 15 groups. When you have combined the value statements into groups and reviewed all of the statements within each group to exclude duplicate or weak statements, you will use the remaining categorized statements as the basis for creating key pain indicator questions. These questions become the content of the Needs Analysis Questionnaire (you learn more about these elements of the ROI model in Chapters 10 and 11). Figure 9.1 illustrates the analysis process.

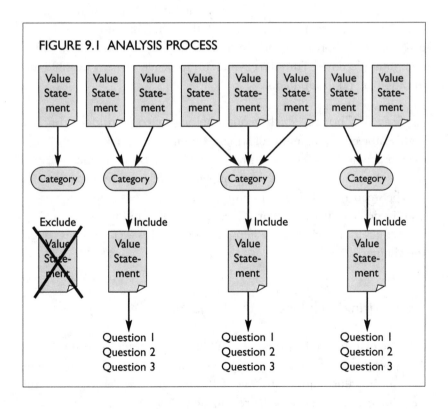

FIGURE 9.1 ANALYSIS PROCESS

N *o t e*

As you read through the remainder of this chapter, be aware that the value matrix analysis process can be very subjective. Therefore, we will not attempt to give you a fixed set of parameters on which to base the decisions required to determine which items you should (or should not) include in your Needs Analysis Questionnaire.

Key Concepts and Guidelines

In this chapter, we provide general information and guidelines for the analysis process that are based on our experiences and those of our clients and customers. These are the three major steps of the analysis process:

Step 1: Group-related items on the matrix. Until now we haven't paid attention to sequence or grouping in the matrix, so it is time to pull related items together. Assuming you have the typical number of value matrix rows (50 or so), your goal will be to pull them into 10 or 15 groups of related items.

Step 2: Eliminate duplicates. Duplication hurts the credibility of your ROI model because it can give prospects the impression you are double-dipping by counting one ROI item multiple times. Therefore, you want to be alert to any possible duplication as you group items.

Step 3: Choose which groups belong in your model. This is a highly subjective judgment for which you must rely on your knowledge of your products and customers to determine the areas in which you can deliver the greatest value. If you grouped your 50 or so value statements into between 10 and 15 groups, our experience suggests you will narrow that list down to between 8 or 12 groups for inclusion in your model.

We describe each of these steps in more detail as we proceed through the chapter.

Categorizing Each Line of the Value Matrix

The first step in the process of building your questions for the Needs Analysis Questionnaire is analyzing your data and categorizing each line item in the value matrix into one of 10 to 15 groups. These groups will help you better understand the relationships between the business issues you have defined. Also, by grouping the line items in your value matrix, you will avoid repeating items and doubling up on the value your products or services deliver.

Review each value statement and decide what group it falls into. Add a column to your value matrix headed "Group" to document this decision. The groups you define are likely to be arbitrary based on the industry for which you are building the ROI model. Examples of groups we have seen companies use in the past include: Finance, Operations, Services, Maintenance, and Technology. Some software companies choose to be more specific and group value statements by module. For example, Hewlett-Packard started by grouping its value statements into two categories: hardware and software; the company then subdivided software into operating system and application. Remember, the objective of this step of the analysis process is to distill your value matrix into a smaller set of categories that will support the flow of your Needs Analysis Questionnaire, facilitate meaningful summarization of results on your ROI Financial Dashboard, and highlight potential duplicates.

Figure 9.2 illustrates grouping value matrix rows for a company that helps other businesses plan and execute large meetings and conferences— a skill set that is outside the core competency of many organizations.

For the first line in Figure 9.2, we assessed the ROI category and value metric and quickly determined that this group should be reduction in Marketing Department time. In this example, the group happens to be the same as the value metric. In this case, it seems obvious, but it will not always work out that way. On the second line in Figure 9.2, the value metric and category give us all the information we need to categorize the line item. The value metric and category explain that there is an opportunity for cost avoidance in the form of avoiding higher facility and transportation costs during corporate meetings. Therefore, we grouped this line item into travel expenses. Finally, the third line tells us without looking further than the category and value metric that there is an opportunity for us to pay inflated charges for on-site food expenses during our meeting, for which we created a third category called on-site food expenses. Once again, we used the value metric to help us determine this grouping. The point of this example is to encourage you to look at the value metrics within the groupings and put the duplicates together. And there will be duplicates! You learn to deal with these in the next section.

FIGURE 9.2 VALUE MATRIX GROUPS

Why Buy?	Business Issue	Desired Outcome	Category	Value Metric	Group
We do not have time to plan a big conference . . .	because Marketing is too busy to plan and develop a large conference.	We want to just write one check and be done with it.	Reduce cost.	Marketing department time	Productivity for marketing department time
We want the best prices we can get for booking a meeting at the resort . . .	because with no experience we would end up overpaying for the use of the facilities.	Want to get a better price than we could negotiate on our own for the facilities.	Avoid cost.	Higher facility and transportation costs	Travel expenses
We need help selecting the conference menus . . .	because over- or under-ordering food is an expensive mistake.	We need someone who has experience in ordering the right meals and correct portions.	Reduce cost.	Overages in amount of food ordered/ delivered	On-site food expenses

Eliminating Duplicates

Grouping your value statements into categories has given you a head start in identifying and eliminating duplicates. Take this opportunity to delete any rows that repeat information and value already included in another value statement. Then consider whether each statement is capable of standing on its own. This means that when you look at the value statements in a particular group or category, you must consider whether any of the statements should be combined with one or more of the others to create a single set of questions for the Needs Analysis Questionnaire. More times than not, you will have several value statements that are similar or return the same value. For example, automation generally reduces labor cost, but if several value statements reduce labor cost, we recommend that you consider combining them into one set of questions. Otherwise you may double-dip on the value delivered.

This next example (Figure 9.3) provides you with some additional information on how to handle duplicates.

Figure 9.3 displays three different why buy statements, all of which share the same group. The reason for this is that the value metric in all three lines is essentially a time or labor reduction for the Marketing Department. Value metrics that are exactly the same or very similar are generally an indication that the associated value statements belong in the same group.

The first line in this example is about planning a large conference, whereas the second and third lines have to do with executing the plan and conducting the conference. All three lines indicate that the delivered benefits are measurable by the same value metric—a reduction in the Marketing Department's time or labor.

Deciding Which Line Items to Include

For your ROI model (and any other sales tool) to have maximum impact, it must be focused on your customer's stakeholders' areas of greatest pain and potential return. If you throw too much detailed information at your prospects, you run the risk of losing the most important items in the mix. In this final step of the analysis process, you must determine which of the groups and items are the strongest candidates for

FIGURE 9.3 VALUE MATRIX GROUPS—MEETING AND EVENT PLANNING

Why Buy?	Business Issue	Desired Outcome	Category	Value Metric	Group
We do not have time to plan a big conference . . .	because Marketing is too busy to plan and develop a large conference.	We want to just write one check and be done with it.	Reduce cost.	Marketing department time	Productivity for marketing department
We need help creating the slide deck presentations . . .	because they are being produced by so many different sources that we need a coordinator to manage them.	Want a central control from outside the company to force compliance with our standards.	Reduce cost.	Marketing department's labor to build and maintain the slide decks	Productivity for marketing department
We need someone to liaise with the hotel on signage, room layout, and all other room logistics . . .	because it must be correct for the presenters—Marketing doesn't have the time.	A single source contact that will manage all issues with the conference	Avoid cost.	Marketing department's time dealing with hotel issues	Productivity for marketing department

inclusion in your ROI model. Your goal is to narrow the categories and the value statements within them to include only those on which you can base questions you will use to gather information from your prospects and drive the calculation of the estimated value your products or services can deliver. The process for the decision is quite simple. Focus on one group at a time and review each of the value statements in that group.

You probably have 30 to 50 lines in your value matrix. The goal of this exercise is to narrow that list to 15 or fewer lines. Why 15 and not 20 or more? Because you do not have to sell every feature of your solution to prove you can deliver value. As you analyze each value statement within the category, decide the following:

- Under which groupings do we deliver the most value?
- Which items within each group deliver the most value? (Hint: Look at your value statements, as they might help you answer this question. The key phrase you want to focus on is "the most value.")

Use the value statements that best promote that value to formulate the questions in your Needs Analysis Questionnaire. Remember to select the value statements in each category that drive the most value based on your knowledge of the value delivered by your products or services. Remember, this is a subjective exercise in which your knowledge of your products or services plays an essential role.

N *o t e*

We have already mentioned that this process is very subjective. Therefore, we suggest you read through this chapter first and then return to your value matrix and begin the analysis process, using the data we are providing as a guideline for creating your questions.

T *i p*

The analysis process is fairly simple but requires independent thinking, meaning that you must put aside your biases regarding product features and benefits and view them as objectively as possible. If there are line items in your value matrix you don't understand, we suggest you contact a product or service expert and get a thorough explanation of why it is in the value matrix and what issue it resolves.

Summary

Your value matrix contains a wealth of valuable information about your prospects' issues, pains, and goals, the underlying business issues, the stakeholders who care most about those issues, and the ability of your products or services to deliver value. Analyzing, organizing, and consolidating that information makes the tasks you must perform in the next chapters to build your ROI model much easier. Let's review the key points in this chapter:

- You analyze the value matrix so as to group items into categories, to eliminate duplicate items, and to determine which items to include in your ROI model.
- This analysis is an important first step in building the key pain indicators that will be used in the Needs Analysis Questionnaire. Building the questions for your Needs Analysis Questionnaire is truly the magic in what we do in the ROI Selling process.
- Once you have grouped each line of your value matrix, you then have to analyze each value statement within the category and decide which groups deliver the most value and which items within each group deliver the most value. Look at your value statements to help make this determination.
- You must be prudent in the selection process. Therefore, your product experience will prove to be invaluable as you determine the value matrix items to use in the Needs Analysis Questionnaire.

10

DEVELOPING KEY PAIN INDICATORS

A key pain indicator (KPI) is a statement in the form of a question that describes a primary issue, pain, or goal your customer or prospect experiences. KPIs restate the value statements you created in Chapter 8 as leading or probing questions. If your value statement reads, for example, "Reduce your cost of sale by shortening the sales cycle using . . . ," your KPI would simply be: "Is your sales cycle too long?" KPIs are designed to encourage your prospects to describe the pain they feel as a result of the issues originally noted in business issue statements. The nine of hearts example you read about in Chapter 1 demonstrates how KPI questions work—you want to design these questions to guide your prospects to the answers you're seeking. The KPIs form the basis of the questions you'll include in the Needs Analysis Questionnaire that you learn to create in the next chapter.

Key Concepts and Guidelines

In Chapter 9 you combined your value matrix line items into categories called groups. You then narrowed these groups so they contained only the most compelling line items, which will be addressed in your Needs Analysis Questionnaire and ROI model. Now you are ready to develop

KPI questions for that short list of the most painful business issues your products or services can address—where you can deliver the greatest value. As you develop your KPIs, keep the following key concepts in mind:

- **ROI begins with a KPI.** KPIs are the questions that will help both you and your prospect identify the prospect's pain, issue, or goal.
- **You have two ears and one mouth.** Using KPIs in your early contacts with a prospect helps stimulate conversations that lead to a better understanding of the prospect's business issues. Once you have asked the KPI question, listen for the response. Your prospect's response to the KPI will likely lead you to the next set of detailed needs analysis questions you have to ask to quantify your prospect's pain, issue, or goal and the value your solution can deliver.
- **Use the prospect's pain to help formulate solutions.** As you collect pain-based data, you are gathering important information that will help educate you about the issues your products or services can resolve for your prospects. KPIs form the basis on which you can calculate and communicate the pain-reducing value you are capable of delivering through your products or services.
- **Make the hair on the back of their necks stand up.** It is very important for your customer or prospect to "feel" the pain you are trying to resolve. Formulate your KPI questions so that stakeholders cringe when they consider the issue that drives the question. People don't buy unless they feel pain.
- **Value justification versus cost justification.** Using KPIs to lead the sales process is an opportunity to establish the baseline that you *and* your competitors must be measured against. This technique is called *value justification.* When you formulate questions for the Needs Analysis Questionnaire in Chapter 11, remember that your questions must focus on justifying the value your solution is capable of delivering rather than justifying the solution's cost.

N *o t e*

Jimmy Touchstone, of Solution Selling, says, "You want your customer or prospect to ask you 'What is the value I am going to receive?' not 'What is the cost of your product?' Like Jimmy, we strongly emphasize value justification over cost justification."

Creating KPIs

Creating key pain indicators is a simple exercise; as mentioned earlier, a KPI is a restatement of your value statement in the form of a question. Figure 10.1 displays several value statements and the key pain indicators we created for each of them.

Begin the process of creating KPIs by referring to the narrowed list of value statements you created in Chapter 9. Draw a line down the center of a sheet of paper to create two columns, as shown in Figure 10.1, and then list the value statements in the left column. In the right column, create a KPI question for each of these statements. If you want to, you can go back later and complete this exercise for every statement in your original value matrix.

Remember that your KPI should encourage a prospect to feel the pain. It is critical that there be a direct relationship between the value statement and the pain defined by the KPI you're developing. You will learn the importance of this relationship in Chapter 13, "Designing the ROI Needs Analysis Questionnaire Interface."

Using Questions to Drive Specific Answers

As we've stated earlier, KPIs are designed to drive prospects toward specific answers—valuable solutions you can provide through your company's products or services. To better understand this process, think

---

FIGURE 10.1 KPI DEVELOPMENT TABLE

Value Statement	Key Pain Indicator
Reduce your cost of sale by shortening the sales cycle using . . .	Is your sales cycle too long? Doesn't it cause your cost of sale to rise?
Increase your revenue by increasing your close ratio on leads generated by marketing programs using . . .	Do your marketing programs help to increase your close ratios?
Reduce sales reps' and managers' cost of time associated with conducting account debriefs using . . .	Do weekly account debriefs take too long?

N *o t e*

If you are part of an organization that is conducting an ROI workshop, we recommend that you complete this exercise on your own. The workshop is intended to be a brainstorming session in which you want to use group interaction to gather as many good ideas as you can. This process, however, is best performed by an individual who understands the entire ROI development process and is proficient in designing questions that produce the right answers. A group will only confuse matters and cause a delay in producing the final ROI model.

about the nine of hearts exercise we used in Chapter 1. We started by asking Jennifer a single question, which led to a series of additional questions following a logical sequence based on her responses. We offered diamonds, spades, clubs, and hearts, knowing that no matter what Jennifer chose, our response would lead her back to the nine of hearts. Remember, we then offered high hearts, middle hearts, and low hearts, once again narrowing her choices to the one we wanted her to select. And finally, we limited her choice to the eight, nine, or ten of hearts. If Jennifer would have chosen the eight or ten, I would have simply asked, "What does that leave?" and thus would have led her to the only choice left: the nine of hearts! Figure 10.2 illustrates Jennifer's choices as we narrowed each response to lead her to the nine of hearts.

You use KPIs in your sales process in a similar manner. Follow each KPI question by pressing on with your needs analysis questions to discover the details about that pain. By preparing the KPI questions, you are in

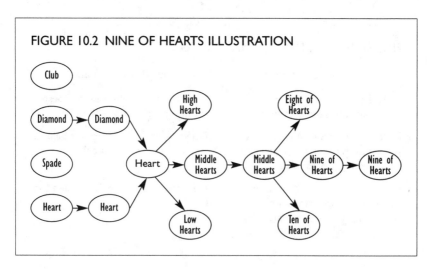

FIGURE 10.2 NINE OF HEARTS ILLUSTRATION

essence providing a script that both helps your salespeople and ensures that they follow a consistent, effective information-gathering process.

Summary

Developing KPIs helps ensure that you accurately identify the issues, pains, and goals your prospect experiences. By using KPIs during the sales process, you are establishing the evaluation criteria against which your company—and, potentially, your competition—must be measured. Craft your KPIs carefully, remembering these important points you learned in this chapter:

- KPIs are signals formed by restating value statements in the form of a question.
- You have two ears and one mouth; KPIs can help you use them in that proportion as you use them to gather critical information about your prospect's issues, goals, and pains.
- KPIs are developed to be used at the beginning of the sales process—not the end!
- KPIs establish the value justification criteria used in the sales process.
- Be sure your KPIs cause the hair on the back of stakeholders' necks to stand up—people must feel the pain to make a change.
- Use your KPIs to formulate questions that will drive your prospect toward the value you offer as the feature/solution of your ROI model. The nine of hearts exercise is a metaphor for creating the questions that drive the pain.

11

CREATING NEEDS
ANALYSIS QUESTIONS

In Chapter 10, you learned to restate value statement issues as questions called key pain indicators, or KPIs. These questions are used to help your prospects connect directly with the pain (a problem, an unreached goal, or other business issue) you propose to resolve with your products or services. In this chapter, you learn to create needs analysis questions. When prospects tell you they feel one of the pains you are probing for with your KPI, you follow up with needs analysis questions relevant to those KPIs. Needs analysis questions form the basis of the Needs Analysis Questionnaire (you learn about creating the questionnaire in Chapter 13). The objective in creating the Needs Analysis Questionnaire is to gather measurable information you can use to create an ROI algorithm that estimates the value your products or services are capable of delivering. You learn how to create these algorithms in Chapter 12, "Building the ROI Calculations."

Needs analysis questions help you do the following:

- Gather quantifiable data for an ROI measurement
- Establish the current level of pain
- Educate prospects by helping them think through the tangible impact of their needs and issues

- Establish a measurement criteria for the 360 Degree ROI Value Assessment
- Lay a foundation for competitive selling (we will not be column fodder!)

Most of the information you need to develop needs analysis questions is implicit in your value matrix. In this chapter, you learn how to break the business issue down into components to extract this information. After you've accomplished that step, you're ready to write the questions. We provide you with a template to help break down each line of your value matrix and create your questions. As we proceed through the chapter, we present a number of examples showing you how to use this template and illustrating the process of creating needs analysis questions. We'll also show you how to review and group the questions you've written, weed out any duplicates, and be certain that your needs analysis questions contribute to an effective Needs Analysis Questionnaire. Finally, we show you how to use the needs analysis questions to measure the status quo, or current level of pain—an important step in developing an effective Needs Analysis Questionnaire and ROI model.

Key Concepts and Guidelines

Effective, well-written needs analysis questions gather measurable and quantifiable information that can be used to calculate the estimated value your product or service is capable of delivering. Remember these points when developing your own needs analysis questions:

- **Needs analysis questions educate your prospects.** The content and organization of your questions and questionnaire educate your customers and prospects while you use the document to gather information.
- **Needs analysis questions drive consistent data gathering.** Companies with large sales forces and/or distribution channels use their Needs Analysis Questionnaires to drive consistent data gathering by all distribution channel partners and sales representatives. If you are responsible for managing multiple sales resources, a well-

crafted set of questions ensures that you are gathering the same data from everyone who sells your products and services.

- **Use the questionnaire to define the current situation.** Always remember that your needs analysis questions must ask specifically about a prospect's current situation. There is no way for you to prove the value your products or services provide in the future unless there is agreement on the baseline or starting point, which is the current situation.

- **Gather enough detail to drive the calculations.** Depending on the quality of information available to your prospect, you may have to ask multiple questions to reach the data you need. For example, if your prospect doesn't know his company's current cost per sale, you may need to ask more detailed questions such as: "What are your total sales expenses per year?" and "How many sales do you close in a year?" so you can calculate the cost per sale for the prospect.

- **A well-crafted question adds to your credibility.** Your needs analysis questions drive a credible ROI model. No matter what sales methodology your company uses (Solution Selling®, Miller Heiman, KLA Group, TAS, or others), a series of well-thought-out, quantifiable questions adds to your credibility with prospects and helps ensure your success in increasing revenue, shortening the sales cycle, and reducing your cost of sale.

Developing Effective Needs Analysis Questions

Preparation is the key to success in developing the questions for your Needs Analysis Questionnaire. This is where the time you spent creating your value matrix pays off, and the quality of that information has a huge impact on the quality of your ROI model. Therefore, the information you entered into the value matrix up to this point must be absolutely solid, credible, and reliable. That means your why buy and business issue statements must reflect real pains and issues that your prospects experience, the stakeholders must be affected by these issues and have the ability to make or influence purchase decisions, and your product or service must offer a feature or solution that meets or exceeds expectations for the desired outcome with existing functionality. If any of these requirements are in question for any of the items remaining in

How One Company Uses the Needs Analysis Questionnaire

Great Plains Software has a distribution channel of more than 2,000 resellers. Great Plains is also known for its world-class support. Sometimes the sheer size of its reseller channel can create a great deal of havoc for the Great Plains personnel responsible for supporting the distribution network. Great Plains personnel told us that they were getting a large number of requests from their channel partners for assistance on sales opportunities. The data they were getting from the partners, however, was often incomplete, irrelevant, and definitely inconsistent. We analyzed the situation and recommended that Great Plains develop a set of questions that channel partners would be required to complete before Great Plains would release any resources to help the partner. We developed a Needs Analysis Questionnaire that Great Plains could distribute to its channel and direct sales force. The questionnaire consists of several high-level value statements that describe the value Great Plains Software is capable of delivering. Each value statement is followed by a set of questions that partners and reps use to gather quantifiable data about their prospects. As the reseller or sales rep completes the Needs Analysis Questionnaire, the ROI model calculates summary results and displays them in both numeric and graphic formats. Developing and deploying this Needs Analysis Questionnaire has helped Great Plains drive consistency in its data-gathering efforts and has improved the effectiveness of both direct and channel sales personnel.

your value matrix, either correct or eliminate those items. The entire premise of building a credible ROI model is based on the truthfulness and accuracy of your input and responses. One error or exaggeration can destroy the validity of the entire model in the eyes of your prospects.

Your needs analysis questions must also be relevant to the subject matter and limited in their nature so that you don't waste a prospect's time. Important considerations for developing needs analysis questions include:

- How is the question phrased?
- Which stakeholder does the question target?
- What is the relevance of the question?
- What will the answer (or response) tell me?

Each question you use in your Needs Analysis Questionnaire will be evaluated by your prospects for its validity. Your prospects are also likely to wonder whether the needs analysis questions you ask are in fact describing a feature or solution offered by your products. For example, when we ask our prospects, "Does your customer turnover exceed 5 percent annually?" most of our prospects understand that we are implying that our programs will help reduce customer turnover.

A First Look at the Process

The question creation process is very straightforward. Begin with the narrowed list of groups you created in Chapter 9. For each of the items within those groups, complete these four steps:

1. Review the value metric and establish the type of ROI you are going to calculate—for example, a reduction in labor cost or an increase in productivity.
2. Think about the measurable data you need in order to calculate that type of ROI. For example, calculating a reduction in labor cost will almost certainly require the annual labor cost for a particular position or trade as one input item. When you see the word *time* or *labor* in the value metric field, you can be pretty sure that the calculation will require the total cost (also known as the *burdened cost*) of the relevant employee, meaning the cost of the employee's salary, benefits, and other overhead. Analyze each type of ROI for which you'll be creating calculations, and try to determine all of the information you'll need for those calculations.
3. Look at the business issue column and establish the issue, pain, or goal on which you are going to base your calculation of value delivery. For example, the statement ". . . because we don't have time to figure out the issue on our own" tells you that you need to ask about the current cost of the time the prospect loses trying to "figure out" issues.
4. Compose the questions based on the first three steps.

As we noted earlier, you may have to determine if it is necessary to create an additional calculation for your prospects because they may not have the numbers you need readily available. When your prospects don't track costs or revenues at the level of detail required for the ROI calculations, you may need to create questions that will help you and the prospects with the calculation. For example, you may need to know the hourly burdened cost rate of personnel to calculate a reduction in labor cost, and your prospects may track only annual salary. You then have to ask for the annual salary, the burden rate (usually a percentage of the annual salary), and possibly the standard number of working hours per year for someone in that position and do the calculations yourself to derive the burdened rate. Situations like this are not uncommon when building ROI models.

Developing Questions to Address Business Issues

Figure 11.1 is an example from one of our workshops with Rockwell Automation; the items in this example are related to support agreements.

In Figure 11.1, the value metric for all of the line items is the same: human capital. Therefore, we have placed all of these items within the same group, which we designated as engineering staff time. When we created the needs analysis questions designed to drive the value offered by the proposed product or service, we developed questions that address the business issues of all of these items as a single group. The resulting series of five questions looks like this:

1. How many hours per month are spent trying to figure out the issues in-house?
2. What is the average annual full-time equivalent (FTE) cost for staff involved in the analysis?
3. How many staff members are affected by a downtime event?
4. What is the average annual FTE cost for staff affected by downtime events?
5. How many of these events occur every year?

As you can see, these five questions cover the data we need for all three of the business issue statements listed in Figure 11.1. The table shown in Figure 11.2 lists these questions alongside the business issues they address.

FIGURE 11.1 VALUE MATRIX—ROCKWELL AUTOMATION—QUESTIONS

Why Buy?	Business Issue	Desired Outcome	Category	Value Metric	Group
We need technical expertise . . .	because we don't have the time to figure out the issues on our own.	We want live, instant support.	Reduce cost.	Human capital	Engineering staff time
We need fast response . . .	because if we don't get instant support, our staff is "dead in the water."	We want live, instant support.	Reduce cost.	Human capital	Engineering staff time
We want system level support . . .	because it is too time consuming to figure out system-level issues ourselves.	We want to reduce the amount of time our engineers spend trouble-shooting system-level issues.	Reduce cost.	Human capital	Engineering staff time

FIGURE 11.2 BUSINESS ISSUE–DRIVEN QUESTIONS

Business Issue	Questions to Drive Value
. . . we don't have the time to figure out the issue on our own.	• How many hours per month are spent trying to figure out the issue in-house? • How many staff members are involved in trying to figure out issues when they occur? • What is the average annual FTE cost for staff members involved in the analysis?
. . . if we don't get instant support, our staff is "dead in the water."	• How many hours per month are spent trying to figure out the issue in-house? • What is the length of the average downtime per event? • How many staff members are affected by the downtime? • What is the average annual FTE cost for staff members affected by downtime events?
. . . it is too time consuming to figure out system-level issues ourselves.	• How many hours per month are spent trying to figure out system-level issues in-house? • What is the average annual FTE cost of personnel trying to figure out system-level issues?

Using the Needs Analysis Questionnaire Development Template

To assist you in creating the questions for your Needs Analysis Questionnaire, we have developed a template, shown in Figure 11.3, to gather all the data you need. The Needs Analysis Questionnaire development

> **T i p**
>
> One important element of a well-crafted question is the appropriate use of terminology from a prospect's industry. When talking about finance, for example, it can be impressive to understand and use the term *DSO*, which stands for days sales outstanding, and is an important measurement of cash flow and accounts receivable management for many companies. Every industry has terms and acronyms—you must understand and use those that are important in your market when you are talking to and questioning prospects.

FIGURE 11.3 NEEDS ANALYSIS QUESTIONNAIRE DEVELOPMENT TEMPLATE

Business Issue	Component of Issue	Questions
(A)	**(D)**	**(E)**
Feature/Solution	**Value Statement**	
(B)	**(C)**	

---

template is divided into five sections. You complete the first three sections (A, B, C) by entering data directly from your value matrix. During the analysis process, your list of value statements should have been narrowed to approximately 10 or 12 items; you need to create a template for only those 10 or 12 items. If you wish to come back later and add other items, feel free to do so. We have clients who have requested this as part of a training exercise.

The information in sections B and C is used primarily for reference when developing your questions. We encourage you to have a complete picture of the situation you are trying to resolve when developing the needs analysis questions.

In section D of the template, enter the components—the measurable attributes—of your business issue statement. Typically, components are one of the following:

- Time
- Wages
- Cost of an acquisition or service

Section E of the template holds the questions themselves.

We realize that completing this template represents an extra step in the question development process, but our experience in building ROI models with many other companies has proven the value of this approach to creating needs analysis questions.

Tom Hayes is the president of Piuma, Inc. Piuma develops and sells accounting systems to small and medium-sized businesses. Tom competes with Quick Books and other budget-priced accounting systems. When we met with Tom, he told us he developed a list of 138 line items Piuma did better than its competitors. Before working through the ROI Selling development process, Tom believed people bought in his market based on price first and then features, in that order. Tom's goal before he implemented ROI selling was to price- or cost-justify his product with a list of 138 features he had defined. Tom's team would lead with price and then justify with features. We began the ROI build process by having Tom and his staff list the top 25 reasons people buy budget-based accounting systems. As Tom worked through the process with his team, he quickly realized he needed to focus on only 12 or 13 items. There was so much value in some of the areas of his system that he didn't have to promote 138 different features.

As head of a small company, Tom was able to assess his pricing, selling method, marketing materials, and Web site very quickly and implement the newly found magic of ROI Selling based on the value his company is capable of delivering. We checked back with Tom recently to get an update on his progress, and he told us that his sales increased more than 50 percent in the first month after our ROI workshop as a result of implementing ROI Selling.

Studying Sample Question Templates

To better understand the process of identifying components for the template, take a look at a series of examples. In each of these examples, follow the order that data is entered into the template, and you should gain a clear understanding of how these components were identified for use in ROI calculations. Figure 11.4 shows the first of these examples.

In Figure 11.4, we determine what the components are going to be by breaking apart the business issue statement: ". . . because the [sales cycle] is too long and [our costs] continue to rise as the [deals linger]." The three bracketed phrases or words in the business issue statement are the components of the business issue we include in our template;

FIGURE 11.4 SAMPLE ISSUE PLACED WITHIN NEEDS ANALYSIS
QUESTIONNAIRE DEVELOPMENT TEMPLATE

Business Issue (A)	Feature/ Solution (B)	Value Statement (C)	Components of Issue (D)
. . . because the sales cycle is too long and our costs continue to rise as the deals linger.	Solution Selling Sales Process and Job Aids	Reduce your cost of sale by shortening the sales cycle using Solution Selling Sales Process and Job Aids	• Sales cycle • Cost of sale • Average sale amount

these components are the measurable items from which we formulate
our questions and determine the potential value delivered.

Working with these three components, we created three needs analysis questions to help us determine the current cost of this prospect's pain, issue, or goal:

1. What is the length of your current sales cycle?
2. What is your current cost of sale?
3. What is the revenue on your average sale?

The components and abbreviated forms of these questions are shown in the template sample in Figure 11.5.

Each question we created in this example requires an answer that we can use to calculate value and measure our successes in the future. Once

FIGURE 11.5 COMPONENTS AND PRELIMINARY QUESTIONS
FOR A SAMPLE BUSINESS ISSUE STATEMENT

Business Issue (A)	Components of Issue (D)	Questions (E)
. . . because the sales cycle is too long and our costs continue to rise as the deals linger.	• Sales cycle • Cost of sale • Average sale amount	• How long? • How much? • How much?

The Cost of Short-Term Pain

We cannot emphasize enough how necessary it is for your customers and prospects to see and feel the cost of not buying from you on a daily, weekly, or monthly basis. Always try to break costs down using this principle. Short-term pain is much easier to sell.

One of our clients shared this story about short-term pain with us. He was following up on a referral for his product and met with the prospect company's president. The president shared a need for help on a project but mentioned, "I am leaving on vacation for a week and want you to follow up with me when I return." After the vacation, the salesman diligently called the president and dropped by his office to discuss his project. After repeated attempts, he finally met with the president weeks after his return from vacation and found that the president's priorities had changed. He didn't seem to feel the pain anymore.

Why didn't he feel the pain? Our theory is the pain still exists but has been replaced with other "more pressing" issues. The lesson in this story is the extreme importance of quickly identifying and communicating the cost of not buying a solution from you. Ask yourself, "How much will it cost this prospect daily, weekly, or monthly not to buy from me?" By answering this question, you are creating a compelling reason for your prospect to buy from you.

we have captured the revenue information, sales cycle, and cost of sale, we can calculate the daily cost of sale for every opportunity that is lingering out there. In other words, our calculations reveal the daily cost of not closing a sale—a very powerful calculation.

Identifying the components of the business issue statement helps you quantify the underlying pain, issue, or goal your prospects face in their day-to-day business. Once you have identified the pain, you can calculate the cost of not buying from you. Each component you define must include measurable items. Let's take a look at another example, illustrated in Figure 11.6.

Follow the same instructions as you did in the previous example and break apart the business issue statement as follows: . . . because the [cost] of our [marketing programs] continues to rise with no increase in [close ratios].

FIGURE 11.6 BUSINESS ISSUE AND COMPONENTS LISTED IN
QUESTIONNAIRE DEVELOPMENT TEMPLATE

Business Issue (A)	Feature/ Solution (B)	Value Statement (C)	Components of Issue (D)
. . . because our cost on marketing programs continues to rise with no increase in close ratios.	Solution Selling Sales Process and Pain Sheets	Increase your revenue by increasing your close ratio using Solution Selling Sales Process and Pain Sheets on Marketing-generated leads	• Marketing budget • Number of programs • Number of total leads • Close ratio from leads generated

The five questions that evolved when we identified the components
of the business issues statement are these:

1. What is your annual marketing budget?
2. How many lead-generation programs do you support with this
   budget?
3. How many leads came out of the programs supported by this
   budget?
4. How many sales did you produce from those leads?
5. What is your close ratio on the leads generated from these
   programs?

The relevant portions of the Needs Analysis Questionnaire development template for this example are shown in Figure 11.7.

At the risk of stating the obvious, notice that each of these questions
is designed to produce quantifiable answers. They all require a response
that we will use to calculate the value we expect to deliver to get our customers and prospects to the goal expressed in the value statement.

Let's review one more example of how to create the questions for
your ROI Needs Analysis Questionnaire. In the next example, we follow
the same steps as in the previous examples to identify the components
of the business issue statement: . . . because [too much time] is taken up

FIGURE 11.7 TEMPLATE COMPONENTS WITH PRELIMINARY
QUESTIONS

Business Issue (A)	Components of Issue (D)	Questions (E)
. . . because the cost of our marketing programs continues to rise with no increase in close ratios.	• Marketing budget • Number of programs • Number of leads • Number of sales • Total close ratio from leads generated	• How much? • How many? • How many? • How many? • Close ratio?

weekly for our [sales representatives] and [managers] doing account debriefs.

Three questions resulted from our analysis of the business issue statement, as shown in Figure 11.8:

1. How much time is being spent weekly doing account debriefs?
2. What is your annual cost for sales representatives?
3. What is your annual cost for managers?

All of these examples illustrate one of the most important points to keep in mind when developing your needs analysis questions: Each business issue statement must drive a certain number of components; that number will vary depending upon what the business issue is and how it

FIGURE 11.8 BUSINESS ISSUE, COMPONENTS, AND
PRELIMINARY QUESTIONS LISTED IN QUESTIONNAIRE
DEVELOPMENT TEMPLATE

Business Issue (A)	Components of Issue (D)	Questions (E)
. . . because too much time is taken up weekly for our sales representatives and managers doing account debriefs.	• Time doing debriefs • Sales reps • Managers	• How long? • Sales rep cost? • Manager cost?

is stated. The components then form the basis for the needs analysis questions, as we have shown in this chapter's examples.

Measuring the Status Quo with Needs Analysis Questions

As you complete each needs analysis question, ask yourself these important questions:

- Can I measure the status quo with these questions?
- Will these questions enable me to compare the status quo to the value I expect to deliver?

If the answer to either question is no, then you must develop additional questions that will enable you to calculate the current situation and compare the projected results.

Also, remember that the preliminary questions drive additional questions. The sample Needs Analysis Questionnaire development template in Figure 11.9 shows the results of our work with Great Plains Software, in which we discussed the issues, pains, and goals associated with

---

FIGURE 11.9 NEEDS ANALYSIS DEVELOPMENT TEMPLATE

Business Issue (A)	Components of Issue (D)	Questions (E)
There is a decline in contract renewals because they are not being processed in a timely manner, and customers are not renewing.	• Contract renewals • Time to process renewals • Number of customers not renewing	• Total number of contracts? • Current time to process a renewal? • Percentage of contracts not renewing?

Feature/ Solution (B)	Value Statement (C)
Automated contract renewal software	Avoid the cost of hiring additional personnel to manage contract renewals.

managing maintenance agreements and contract renewals. The questions we developed in this example are designed to examine a decline in contract renewals and how Great Plains software can help customers or prospects reduce the decline—perhaps even increase their renewals and revenue. The breakdown of this business issue statement looks like this: There is a decline in [contract renewals] because they are [not being processed] in a timely manner, and customers are [not renewing].

In this example, we have defined three components:

1. Contract renewals
2. Time to process renewals
3. Number of customers not renewing

In this example, the questions created to address the business issue component contract renewals did not produce enough information for us to arrive at the personnel cost result expressed in the value statement, "Avoid the cost of hiring additional personnel to manage contract renewals." In Figure 11.10, we have added several questions to calculate the existing state of contract renewal processes and costs at this prospect's organization.

The three additional questions we formulated to calculate the status quo must now be added to our original questions to understand the true cost of contract renewals. Figure 11.11 illustrates the addition of our original "pain" questions from Figure 11.9 to the new set of status quo questions from Figure 11.10.

A lot of things are happening in Figure 11.11. We started out defining the current process and then moved to quantify the current cost of

---

FIGURE 11.10 CURRENT PROCESS COST BREAKDOWN TO DEMONSTRATE STATUS QUO

Current process . . .   Cost breakdown:
- Number of personnel performing manual contract renewals?
- Annual cost per staff member?
- Amount of time spent weekly performing contract renewal activities?

FIGURE 11.11 COST BREAKDOWNS WITH ORIGINAL QUESTIONS

Current process . . .	Cost breakdown:
	• Number of personnel performing manual contract renewals?
	• Annual cost per staff member?
	• Amount of time spent weekly performing contract renewal activities?
Pain . . .	• Total number of contracts?
Cost of	• Percentage of nonrenewals?
nonrenewals	• Amount of time to process a renewal (hours)?

---

this prospect's issue, pain, or goal. As you build your questions, keep in mind these two points:

1. Always ask questions to define the current situation.
2. Try to quantify the cost of the current situation—the status quo.

Next, define the prospect's cost going forward. Your prospects may realize the current cost of their issue but rarely will they realize how that cost multiplies as time passes. In Figure 11.12, we added some additional questions to help quantify our prospect's future cost.

The questions we added help us calculate the future cost of doing nothing. Each time this prospect adds a new contract to his or her portfolio of agreements, additional resources are required to manage the renewal. The additional questions are:

- Average annual value of contract?
- Projected growth for additional year's calculation?
- Additional staff required to manage the anticipated growth?

These additional questions provide the data required to calculate the cost of doing nothing—the status quo. In addition to establishing the status quo, these questions also anticipate the cost going forward if the status quo continues—in other words, the cost that will accrue if the prospect doesn't buy our application to automate its contract renewal

FIGURE 11.12 NEEDS ANALYSIS QUESTIONS REGARDING THE
COST GOING FORWARD

Current process . . .	Cost breakdown:
	• Number of personnel performing manual contract renewals?
	• Annual cost per staff member?
	• Amount of time spent weekly performing contract renewal activities?
Pain . . .	• Total number of contracts?
Cost of	• Percentage of nonrenewals?
nonrenewals	• Amount of time to process a renewal (hours)?
Pain . . .	• Average annual value of contract?
Going	• Projected growth for contracts in the future . . .
forward	1 year, 2 years, etc.?
	• Staff required to manage growth (can be calculated).

process. Remember, short-term pain relief is good for creating a sense of urgency, but constant pain (ongoing cost) is a powerful means of justifying the value of a purchase decision.

We realize this kind of detailed analysis requires a lot of work to achieve what might seem such a simple goal. However, when preparing Needs Analysis Questionnaires for situations such as these, working through the details is absolutely vital to the credibility of your ROI model. Your prospects and customers will demand objectivity and credibility.

Summary

As we mentioned in the introduction to this chapter, the objective in creating the questions for your Needs Analysis Questionnaire is to gather measurable information you can use to create an ROI algorithm that estimates the value your product or service is capable of delivering. In Chapter 12, "Building the ROI Calculations," we discuss the mathematics behind the questions we have created here. We encourage you to understand the question-building process thoroughly before forging ahead to develop the algorithms. As you move further into the ROI model-building process, you will find the process confusing and difficult if you don't thoroughly understand the concepts on which the questions within the Needs Analysis Questionnaire are built. After you have read this chapter and reviewed the examples it contains, we suggest you return to the beginning of this chapter and work through our examples one more time if you are still having difficulty with this concept. Pay close attention to the relationships that were created between the items entered in the ROI Value Matrix.

Once you feel comfortable with our examples, we suggest you use the Needs Analysis Questionnaire development template to create questions based on data from your own value matrix. As you do so, remember these important points from this chapter:

- Preparation is the key to success.
- The data within the value matrix must be the unequivocal truth.
- Define the components of each business issue statement that your prospects face on a daily basis.
- Extend the components to create measurable questions.
- Always define the current situation—the only way you will be able to measure your success; define the current situation by asking questions that help drive an understanding of the current cost and the pain it will cause in the future.

12

BUILDING THE ROI
CALCULATIONS

In Chapter 11, we told you how to create 30 to 50 needs analysis questions based on the refined list of value statements remaining in your matrix. In this chapter, you learn how to build the ROI calculations that enable you to use the answers to those questions for determining the potential value your products or services are capable of delivering. This is where all of your efforts in building a solid ROI Value Matrix pay off. The ROI calculations translate the answers to your needs analysis questions into a compelling model of the ROI that your prospects can receive as a result of using your products and services. As such, the ROI calculations serve as the foundation for credibility when building an ROI model.

Each of your needs analysis questions is designed to elicit quantifiable (numeric) responses that can be used to calculate potential value. At the same time, not all of the calculations you create will directly express that value. In Chapter 11 we discussed creating calculations to assist in gathering data that are needed to support other calculations. If you'll recall, we cited an example about your prospects' tracking labor costs by *annual* salary and burden, whereas your ROI formula calls for *hourly* wages, including burden. This requires at least one additional calculation to divide annual labor cost by the average number of hours worked in a year. Finally, there are times when you want to insert summary calculations to simplify a complex mathematical equation. For example, you may have collected labor costs for various tasks or positions and need to summarize them as part of your ROI calculation. The calculations you are going to build vary widely.

The results of your calculations generally make up the estimated value delivered section of the Needs Analysis Questionnaire. Figure 12.1 is a sample Needs Analysis Questionnaire, including several calculated fields, sample data, and results.

Notice how the sample makes it clear which fields are entered and which are calculated. The Needs Analysis Questionnaire serves the dual function of helping you gather information and produce a preliminary display of results for your prospects. Showing clearly the information you recorded and the calculations you performed to arrive at the result will help your prospects buy into the potential ROI you are presenting. Don't hide calculations; you don't want your prospects wondering, "Where did that number come from?" Keep this in mind as you work through this chapter to build the mathematical equations and capture all of the steps taken to reach a calculated field.

Building the ROI calculations can be one of the most challenging parts of creating your ROI model. As we stated early in the book, you don't have to be a mathematician to create the ROI model or build these calculations, but if you aren't familiar with Microsoft Excel or a similar spreadsheet program, you'll find it helpful to draw on the resources of someone with that expertise. Our customers tell us that personnel from the finance department are often a good resource for this information.

> **T** *i p*
>
> Before you begin building the calculations, we recommend that you go back and record all the ROI Value Matrix information you have in a single spreadsheet if you haven't already done so. Be sure you include the business issues, desired outcome, category, value metric, value statement, and group, along with the needs analysis questions you created in Chapter 11. Having all this data in one place makes it easier to formulate the questions, develop the math, and build a value matrix you can use elsewhere in your organization.

Key Concepts and Guidelines

Although difficult to build, calculations are the heart and soul of creating an ROI

FIGURE 12.1 SAMPLE NEEDS ANALYSIS QUESTIONNAIRE WITH ROI CALCULATIONS

Increase revenue by increasing the number of leads closed with leads generated from marketing programs

What is your annual marketing budget for lead generation?	$5,000,000
How many lead-generating marketing programs do you support annually?	125
Calculated cost per lead-generation program:	$40,000
How many leads are generated from the marketing programs?	1,400
Calculated cost per lead:	$29
What is your close ratio on the leads generated from marketing programs?	10%
Calculated number of leads closed:	140
Average revenue per sale: (from above)	$285,000
Calculated annual revenue from leads generated from marketing programs:	$39,900,000
Calculated annual marketing cost per CLOSED lead:	$35,714

The typical ROI Selling customers increase their close ratio by 10%–20%.

Estimated impact ROI Selling will have on close ratios:	10%
New close ratio: (current close ratio + estimated increase)	1.10%
Calculated additional number of leads to become customers:	15.4
Average revenue per sale: (from above)	$285,000
New calculated annual revenue from marketing department lead-generation programs:	$44,289,000
New calculated cost per closed lead:	$32,175

Calculated annual revenue increase from improved close ratio:	$4,389,000
Calculated annual cost avoidance from leads generated by marketing:	$550,000

model. Be overly cautious as you work through the process. You must understand all of the calculations you use, and your logic must be rock solid and easy to explain to prospects. The following key concepts and guidelines help you stay focused on building accurate and credible calculations:

- **Assume your prospects know little about the details.** This should serve as your first rule of thumb. Don't assume that your prospects understand all of the fine details of the data you have assembled.
- **Simple is always better.** Your prospects should not have to be math wizards to understand the calculations or the values derived from them. You want the results of your ROI model to contain straightforward information your prospects can readily grasp and buy into. Look for ways to simplify your equations.
- **Always calculate the status quo first.** As another rule of thumb, always quantify the cost of your prospect's existing pain. To truly quantify the value of the solution offered by your products or services, you'll need to know the cost of *not* using that solution.
- **The credibility of your ROI model is at stake.** It is critical that the mathematics used in your ROI model are correct. Any error detracts from the credibility of your entire model.

Understanding ROI Calculations and Mathematics

If you followed all the steps outlined in previous chapters—without skipping anything—the mathematical calculations will definitely be easier to create. If you failed to follow our suggestions and skipped ahead . . . you may have your work cut out for you. There are many examples in this chapter to draw from, so be patient and study those examples carefully to work through areas where you're stuck.

Gathering Basic Data to Create Basic Calculations

Figure 12.2 displays the value matrix line item for a sales training program that we have used in many of the previous chapters, in which a prospect wants to use our product to reduce the cost of sale.

FIGURE 12.2 VALUE MATRIX TABLE WITH ROI QUESTIONS

Why Buy?	Business Issue	Stakeholder	Desired Outcome	Category	Value Metric	Value Statement	ROI Questions
I want to reduce our cost of sale . . .	because the sales cycle is too long and our costs continue to rise as the deals linger.	VP Sales	I want to reduce the time to revenue and shorten the sales cycle.	Reduce cost.	Reduce the cost of sale.	Reduce the cost of sale by shortening the sales cycle.	• What is your average sale amount? • How many deals do you close annually? • What is your current cost of sales percentage? • How long is your sales cycle?

Again, the first rule of thumb is to assume that your customers or prospects know very little about the details of what is needed to calculate the value you will deliver. With this in mind, you need to create an ROI model in which you have applied your expertise and the data developed in your ROI information-gathering activities (discussed in Part One) to supply the required formulas. KPIs and value statements are the basis for the value you intend to deliver. Begin with the key pain indicator you developed in Chapter 10. The KPI for Figure 12.2—"Is your sales cycle too long?"—addresses the goal expressed in the value statement for the item: *"Reduce the cost of sale by reducing your sales cycle."*

The first question we created in Figure 12.2 asks for the average sale amount. There are times when a customer or prospect won't know this figure. In those situations, you need to know which questions to ask to get the basic data and then calculate the number based on the answers you receive. For example, you might ask these questions to gather the basic data needed to calculate the average sale amount: What is your annual revenue from product sales? How many deals make up your annual revenue figure? With these two figures you can calculate your prospect's average revenue per sale by dividing annual revenue by the number of deals that make up that revenue.

The next question in Figure 12.2 calls for your prospect's current cost of sales percentage. Remember, we are trying to reduce the cost of sale by shortening the sales cycle. Once again, you need to create a calculation that figures the cost of sale per deal closed (the cost of sale percentage is a figure most CFOs have handy). Creating this calculation is very simple:

Dollar value of average size deal closed × Cost of sale percentage

Finally, the last question asks about the sales cycle. We need to make an additional calculation to narrow the total cost per sale to the daily cost per sale. We have mentioned the importance of breaking pain down to a constant. Expressing pain on a recurring daily basis makes for a more compelling story than a single annual figure. Therefore, what we are going to do is divide the total cost per sale by the number of days in the sales cycle. This figure is the status quo—the prospect's current cost per sale on a daily basis. Each day a sale does not close, the prospect's company experiences this cost. Remember that the key to this value statement is to reduce the sales cycle—fewer days in the cycle mean lower cost (not to mention the less quantifiable benefit of getting the deal "off the street" so it doesn't fall to the competition).

These calculations are the first step in developing the estimated value your products or services are capable of delivering. All of the questions and calculations involved in this example are shown in Figure 12.3.

This figure displays the set of quantifiable questions that could be used to calculate the key pain indicator; in this case, the KPI is the pain your stakeholders are feeling as their deals continue to linger in the sales process. In this example, the cost of unclosed deals is $333 per day. If you want to get your prospect's attention, take this calculation one step further and multiply the daily cost times the number of deals the prospect must close annually to reach the $50,000,000 annual revenue figure. ($333 × 500 deals = $166,000). This figure is probably unrealistic in that it is not likely all of those sales would be active at the same time, and the number will certainly decline as the 500 deals close during the course of the year. (Another way to approach this would be to ask the VP of Sales how many deals are typically active at any given point and multiply the daily cost by that number.) These calculations clearly illustrate that the aggregated daily cost of sale is higher for companies that do the majority of their business in the last quarter of the year than it is for companies that spread out their sales over all four quarters.

FIGURE 12.3 CALCULATIONS TABLE—COST PER CLOSED DEAL

Components/Questions	Value/Calculation
Annual revenue?	$50,000,000
Number of deals to achieve your annual revenue?	500 deals
Calculate average deal size:	$50,000,000 ÷ 500 = $100,000
Number of days in your sales cycle?	120 days
Your cost of sale percentage?	40% cost of sale
Calculate your cost per closed deal:	$100,000 (avg. deal) × 40% = $40,000
Calculate your daily cost per sale:	$40,000 ÷ 120 days = $333 per day cost per closed deal

Calculating the Status Quo and the Impact of Change

Figure 12.4 shows a Needs Analysis Questionnaire development template completed on the basis of the business issue statement, "... the cost of our marketing programs continues to rise with no increase in close ratio."

This example includes the opportunity for several calculations that can demonstrate the value of the proposed solution. Remember the second rule of thumb you learned earlier in the chapter: *Always calculate the status quo first.* To provide your prospects with a complete understanding of their pain, it is necessary to quantify the existing pain for them. Just as we did in the previous example by showing the daily cost (pain) of having deals linger, in this example we are going to calculate the marketing cost per closed lead and the impact a low close ratio has on it. This example demonstrates that each time a deal does not close, there is a marketing cost that is simply written off and must be absorbed into the cost of sale for deals that do close.

To determine this current or existing cost, we divide the total marketing budget by the number of closed deals. This example is a real-life one and should hit home in most organizations that have a marketing

---

FIGURE 12.4 NEEDS ANALYSIS QUESTIONNAIRE DEVELOPMENT TEMPLATE—MARKETING PROGRAM COSTS

Business Issue (A)	Components of Issue (D)	Questions (E)
... because the cost of our marketing programs continues to rise with no increase in close ratio.	• Marketing budget • Number of programs • Number of leads generated • Close ratio from leads generated	• What is your annual marketing budget? • How many lead-generating marketing programs do you support annually? • How many leads are generated from the marketing programs?

Feature/ Solution (B)	Value Statement (C)	
Solution Selling Sales Process and Pain Sheets	Increase revenue by increasing your close ratio on marketing-generated leads.	• What is your close ratio on the leads generated from marketing programs?

department spending money to generate leads. You'll notice that the questions shown in the example in Figure 12.4 are reflected in the questions and calculations shown in Figure 12.5.

Notice in Figure 12.5 that even though the cost per raw lead generated by marketing programs is $3,571, it jumps to $35,714 per closed deal after you factor in the close ratio on marketing-generated leads. This table quantifies the prospect's current situation—the prospect's status quo. We now have a baseline against which we are able to compare the impact we can have on the prospect's business. If we increase the prospect's close ratios, the prospect's revenue will increase and the cost per closed lead will decline (see Figure 12.6).

This table demonstrates the value of doubling the close ratio from that shown in Figure 12.5; with the closed leads doubled, the average value of the 280 leads also doubled and the marketing cost per closed sale declined by 50 percent. The difference represents the reduction in marketing cost per closed deal. Notice that in this case the company is not spending less on marketing but is producing more results for the same outlay. Therefore, the ROI category for marketing might be cost

---

FIGURE 12.5 CALCULATIONS TABLE—COST PER CLOSED LEAD

Components/Questions	Value/Calculation
Annual lead generation budget:	**$5,000,000**
Number of lead-generation programs you support annually with this budget?	**125 programs**
Calculate the average cost per program:	$5,000,000 ÷ 125 programs = **$40,000 cost per program**
Number of leads generated by marketing programs?	**1,400 leads**
Calculate the cost per raw lead:	$5,000,000 ÷ 1,400 leads = **$3,571**
Annual close ratio on leads generated by marketing?	**10% close ratio**
Calculate the number of closed leads:	1,400 leads × 10% = **140 closed deals**
Average sale amount?	**$285,000** average sale
Calculate the value of those 140 leads:	$285,000 × 140 leads = **$39,900,000**
Calculate the marketing cost per lead to generate the above revenue:	$5,000,000 ÷ 140 closed leads = **$35,714**

FIGURE 12.6 CALCULATIONS TABLE—COST PER CLOSED LEAD WITH HIGHER CLOSE RATIO

Components/Questions	Value/Calculation
Annual lead-generation budget:	**$5,000,000**
Number of lead-generation programs do you support annually with this budget?	**125 programs**
Calculate the average cost per program:	$5,000,000 ÷ 125 programs = **$40,000 cost per program**
Number of leads generated by marketing programs?	**1,400 leads**
Calculate the cost per raw lead:	$5,000,000 ÷ 1,400 leads = **$3,571**
Annual close ratio on leads generated by marketing?	**20% close ratio**
Calculate the number of closed leads:	1,400 leads × 20% = **280 closed deals**
Average sale amount?	**$285,000** average sale
Calculate the value of those 280 leads:	$285,000 × 280 leads = **$79,800,000**
Calculate the marketing cost per lead to generate the above revenue:	$5,000,000 ÷ 280 closed leads = **$17,857**

avoidance—the prospect was able to increase the number of sales and revenue without increasing marketing expense.

Calculating Annual Costs

Figure 12.7 is a summary of our business issue statement: ". . . because too much of our sales representatives' and managers' time is taken up doing weekly account debriefs."

Figure 12.8 shows the questions and straightforward calculations that quantify the costs of the Figure 12.7 business issue. The questions and calculations break down this prospect's annual cost of performing account debriefs. Read through these questions and calculations carefully and compare them with the information supplied in the example shown in Figure 12.7 to understand the process we used to build this set of ROI calculations.

FIGURE 12.7 COMPONENT DEVELOPMENT TABLE— MARKETING PROGRAM COSTS

Business Issue (A)	Components of Issue (D)	Questions (E)
. . . because too much of our sales representatives' and managers' time is taken up doing weekly account debriefs.	• Time doing debriefs • Sales reps • Managers	• How long do they spend weekly doing account debriefs? • What is your annual cost for sales representatives performing account debriefs? • What is your annual cost for managers performing account debriefs?
Feature/ Solution (B)	**Value Statement (C)**	
Solution Selling Sales Management, GRAF	Reduce the cost of sales representatives and managers by reducing the amount of time spent conducting account debriefs.	

Summary

As we stated earlier in this chapter, building the ROI calculations may seem like the most difficult part of the ROI Selling process. We realize that the information you've learned in this chapter may be a little overwhelming at first; but take your time and work through each of the examples and tables shown in the chapter to fully understand the logic we used to arrive at these calculations. If, after walking through these examples, you are still uneasy about the calculations, go back to the beginning of this chapter and work through the examples once again. Once you understand the logic used in these examples, you'll find the process of building ROI calculations is much easier than you think. Remember these important points from this chapter:

- Assume nothing—calculate as much as possible for your customer or prospect.
- Use the business issue statements and the value statements, desired outcomes, and other components defined in the ROI Value

FIGURE 12.8 CALCULATIONS TABLE—COST OF ACCOUNT DEBRIEFS

Components/Questions	Value/Calculation
Number of quota-carrying sales personnel?	80 salespeople
Average annual cost per salesperson?	$75,000 per salesperson
Average amount of time spent weekly preparing and conducting account debriefs?	45 minutes
Calculate annual amount of time spent preparing and conducting account debriefs:	(80 salespeople × 45 minutes) × 52 = 187,200 minutes
Convert minutes to hours:	187,200 ÷ 60 minutes in an hour = 3,120 hours annually spent on account debriefs
Calculate hourly cost of sales personnel:	$75,000 ÷ 2,080 working hours in a year = 36.06 per hour
Calculate annual cost for sales personnel for account debriefs:	3,120 hours × $36.06 per hour = **$112,507 annual cost**
Number of sales managers performing account debriefs?	4 sales managers
Annual cost per sales manager?	$125,000 annual cost per sales manager
Average amount of time spent weekly preparing and conducting account debriefs?	60 minutes
Calculate annual amount of time spent preparing and conducting account debriefs:	(4 managers × 60 minutes) × 52 weeks = 12,480 minutes
Convert minutes to hours:	12,480 ÷ 60 = 208 hours
Calculate hourly cost of sales manager:	$125,000 ÷ 2,080 = $60.10 per hour
Calculate annual cost for sales manager for account debriefs:	208 hours × $60.10 per hour = **$12,500 annual cost**
Total annual cost for account debriefs:	$112,507 + $12,500 = $125,007

Matrix and the ROI Needs Analysis Questionnaire development template to decide the mathematical formulas required to show the value you can deliver.

- Always calculate current cost of doing nothing—this becomes your starting point when comparing deliverable value.
- If possible, calculate future costs a prospect will accrue if no action is taken.

13

DESIGNING THE ROI NEEDS ANALYSIS QUESTIONNAIRE INTERFACE

The Needs Analysis Questionnaire interface graphically represents in a spreadsheet program (such as Excel or Lotus) the questions and calculations you learned to devise in Chapter 11. As you use the interface to add data to the questionnaire, the formulas you developed in Chapter 12 calculate and display the quantifiable benefits deliverable by your company's product or service. The questionnaire's interface should be clean, easy to read, simple to use, and should display your data in an effective and compelling format.

Your Needs Analysis Questionnaire contains the following data, which you learned to gather and create in Chapters 8 through 12:

- **Value statements.** These statements articulate the specific value that your products or services are capable of delivering to your prospects. At this stage, you have grouped the value statements and eliminated duplicates to produce a finite list of the highest-impact items.
- **Key pain indicators.** KPIs are questions that you use to find the areas of pain your customers are experiencing.
- **Needs analysis questions.** You use these questions to follow up on your key pain indicators and collect the specific measurable data that drives your ROI model.

- **Calculations.** You use these mathematical formulas to transform the data you collect from your prospects into a projection of the ROI the prospects will realize from using your products or services.

With this information in hand, you are ready to start building your Needs Analysis Questionnaire interface. Your sales team will use the questionnaire to gather and present the information to your prospect. The interface with which the data is presented and calculated is the "public face" of your Needs Analysis Questionnaire, which consists of five primary components:

1. General information
2. KPI identification
3. Needs analysis questions
4. Estimate of impact you will have on current situation
5. Estimate of value you intend to deliver

No matter which sales methodology you use, you will be able to employ the Needs Analysis Questionnaire to guide you in gathering customer or prospect data to create and present an ROI model.

In this chapter, we show you how to create the Needs Analysis Questionnaire interface to present your ROI data in a compelling, easy-to-understand format. We also show you how to create a customized opening tab for your spreadsheet that is used to identify your prospect and present the prospect's KPIs. In later chapters we discuss how to create the other parts of the ROI model, including the ROI Financial Dashboard (used to summarize data from the Needs Analysis Questionnaire, as you learn in Chapter 14) and the 360 Degree ROI Value Assessment form (discussed in Chapter 15). The design and layout of all of these components of the ROI model helps you ensure ROI Selling success. The Needs Analysis Questionnaire is perhaps the most important, however, because it supplies the data that drives your entire model, and because it will be the first exposure your prospects have to your ROI materials.

Key Concepts and Guidelines

The objective of this chapter is to take the information you have developed in Chapters 8 through 12 and arrange it logically in a spreadsheet to be used to collect data from, and present feedback to, your prospects. Each of the concepts and guidelines listed here helps to ensure your layout and design are consistent, simple to use, and—of course—logical:

- **Design the interface to match the flow of your ROI Selling process.** Your layout should follow your sales process. In most sales cycles you will gather general information from your prospects, identify their business issues, and determine how you can help resolve their pain with features of your product. Figure 13.1 illustrates the flow your Needs Analysis Questionnaire should take.

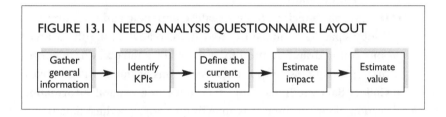

FIGURE 13.1 NEEDS ANALYSIS QUESTIONNAIRE LAYOUT

- **Reduce the question count.** When building a Needs Analysis Questionnaire, it is important to be careful with the amount of data you are requiring for data entry, because there is a limit to the number of questions your prospects will be prepared to answer. We recommend you limit the number of questions to 45 or fewer.
- **Show all calculations.** We strongly recommend that you display the results of each calculation as an inset line on your document. Displaying your calculations makes your ROI model easier to understand and more credible. We offer several examples of this technique later in the chapter.
- **Support your calculations with data from credible sources.** Research should include annual reports, customer Web sites, in-house databases, corporate research firms like Hoovers, and other third-

party sources (you read about all of these later in this chapter). Supporting your data with research adds credibility to your calculations and helps you reduce the number of questions you ask by presenting compelling data that need only be confirmed, rather than supplied, by your prospect.

- **Set the standard with impact statements.** An *impact statement* is used to estimate the value you expect to deliver. It has two components:
  1. Statement of fact: For example, "According to Gartner Group, online collaboration reduces labor costs by X percent," or "Our research indicates typical ROI Selling customers reduce their cost of sale by 5 to 25 percent."
  2. Variables: Variables are data entry fields into which you insert an appropriate value that estimates the impact for a prospect's situation based on the above statement of fact. For example, "Based on the information we have, we estimate your reduction in cost of sale will be X" (where X represents the appropriate variable).
- **Design your interface to be visually compelling and effective.** Use double-spacing to make the text more readable; highlight areas you want to draw attention to; use bold or italic text where appropriate; and enclose important calculations or statements in boxes.
- **Collect data you'll use more than once in a general information section.** Some of the needs analysis questions produce data that is used in more than one calculation. Examples include such data as annual revenues, number of sales personnel, and so on. Collect the information from these questions in a section titled General Information, so your prospect won't have to reenter data in multiple sections of the questionnaire.

Understanding the Process of Interface Design

The first step in designing a Needs Analysis Questionnaire interface is to lay out the questions and determine the pertinent calculations that will help drive the value estimates you propose to deliver. The interface layout and design utilize each of the components you have built in Chapters 8 through 12. The following is a summary of the steps involved in creating a Needs Analysis Questionnaire. After the summary we walk through each of the eight steps in greater detail.

1. **Open a new spreadsheet file.** Start with a clean spreadsheet and give it a name that helps you later identify the file. Each component of the ROI model (KPI input, Needs Analysis Questionnaire, Financial Dashboard, 360 Degree ROI Value Assessment) is going to be built in this new file.

2. **Create general information questions first.** Review all of the questions you created in Chapter 11 and identify duplicates (questions that calculate value delivered on more than one value statement). List duplicated questions in the general information section of the Needs Analysis Questionnaire. Figure 13.2 shows an example of a user interface for a general information section.

FIGURE 13.2 GENERAL INFORMATION SECTION WITH USER DATA ENTERED

General Information	
Enter your annual revenue for product sales only: (DO NOT include service revenue)	$60,000,000
Enter the number of management personnel managing your sales force:	10
Enter the average number of quota-carrying sales personnel:	650
Enter the average annual quota for sales personnel:	$1,000,000
Enter the average percentage of quota-carrying sales personnel who achieve quota annually:	50%

---

3. **Enter the first value statement.** At the top of the spreadsheet, enter a value statement from the list you created (see Chapter 8 for information on creating this list). The value statement sets the tone and direction for all of the questions that follow, so you may want to set it apart in a shaded background, special font, or other highlighting format. See Figure 13.3 for one example of formatting for this element.

4. **Enter the needs analysis questions.** Below the value statement, enter the needs analysis questions you created for this value statement (refer to Chapter 11). In Figure 13.3, we have boxed these questions with the relevant value statement.

FIGURE 13.3 THE FIRST STAGES OF THE NEEDS ANALYSIS
QUESTIONNAIRE INTERFACE

Reducing your cost of sale by shortening the sales cycle

What is your annual revenue?

How many sales make up the above revenue?

What is your cost of sale percentage?

How long is your current sales cycle? (days)

---

5. **Add calculations to quantify the current situation and support and expand the value statement.** In Figure 13.4, we have added ROI calculations on an inset line following some of the questions. These value-based calculations add credibility to your ROI model by graphically displaying current costs and projected benefits.

FIGURE 13.4 NEEDS ANALYSIS QUESTIONNAIRE WITH VALUE-
BASED CALCULATIONS

Reducing your cost of sale by shortening the sales cycle

What is your annual revenue?	$50,000,000
How many sales make up the above revenue?	500
Calculated average sale amount:	$100,000
What is your cost of sale percentage?	40%
Calculated cost to close each opportunity:	$40,000
How long is your current sales cycle? (days)	120
Calculated cost per day for outstanding sale:	$333.33

6. **Add the impact statement to drive your prospects to a conclusion.** The impact statement clearly states what savings your prospects can expect to receive from using your proposed solution and offers an estimated percentage range for that savings, as shown in Figure 13.5. For example, both components of an impact statement in a Rockwell Automation Needs Analysis Questionnaire might read: "A typical Rockwell Automation customer achieves reductions of 2 percent to 10 percent in system downtime after implementing the service maintenance system. Enter the estimated reduction in system downtime." These estimates are based on the prospect's answers to your questions, published prospect data, data from similar prospects, and research analysis from independent firms and third-party references.

FIGURE 13.5 IMPACT STATEMENT SHOWING THE SAVINGS PERCENTAGE A TYPICAL CUSTOMER ACHIEVES

Reducing your cost of sale by shortening the sales cycle

What is your annual revenue?	$50,000,000
How many sales make up the above revenue?	500
Calculated average sale amount:	$100,000
What is your cost of sale percentage?	40%
Calculated cost to close each opportunity:	$40,000
How long is your current sales cycle? (days)	120
Calculated cost per day for outstanding sale:	$333.33

A typical ROI Selling customer reduces its sales cycle by 2% to 10%.

Enter the estimated reduction in sales cyle using ROI Selling: 5%

---

7. **Add the final calculations to show specific savings for your client based on the estimated impact your solution will have on the client's issue.** These calculations show your client or prospect the projected savings based on the aggregate of previously listed values and the impact statement, as shown in Figure 13.6.

FIGURE 13.6 ESTIMATED VALUE DELIVERED BASED ON IMPACT ESTIMATIONS

Reducing your cost of sale by shortening the sales cycle

What is your annual revenue?	$50,000,000
How many sales make up the above revenue?	500
Calculated average sale amount:	$100,000
What is your cost of sale percentage?	40%
Calculated cost to close each opportunity:	$40,000
How long is your current sales cycle? (days)	120
Calculated cost per day for outstanding sale:	$333.33

A typical ROI Selling customer reduces its sales cycle by 2% to 10%.

Enter the estimated reduction in sales cyle using ROI Selling:	5%
Calculated reduction in sales cycle: (days reduced)	6
New calculated average days in sales cycle:	114
Estimated reduction in cost of sale using ROI Selling:	$1,000,000

---

8. **Add a product benefit statement.** As the last step in this process, you may want to attach a paragraph, called the product benefit statement, describing the solution you are offering to resolve the KPIs and deliver the value statement. We list this step as optional, because some of our customers prefer to present the product benefit statements as part of their proposal. These customers feel that presenting these statements within the Needs Analysis Questionnaire might be giving away too much information at this stage of the ROI sales process. Figure 13.7 is an example of a benefit statement integrated into our Needs Analysis Questionnaire; in this example, the product benefit statement is placed directly beneath the value statement.

FIGURE 13.7 BENEFIT STATEMENT ADDED TO NEEDS ANALYSIS QUESTIONNAIRE

Reducing your cost of sale by shortening the sales cycle

ROI Selling tools are used to gather the vital information needed to calculate many financial metrics. The calculations include not only the standard CFO metric (e.g., NPV, IRR, ROI, etc.) but also the cost of not purchasing. This unique calculation includes a start-up factor to reduce the risk of your customer's not buying from you.

What is your annual revenue?	$50,000,000
How many sales make up the above revenue?	500
Calculated average sale amount:	$100,000
What is your cost of sale percentage?	40%
Calculated cost to close each opportunity:	$40,000
How long is your current sales cycle? (days)	120
Calculated cost per day for outstanding sale:	$333.33

A typical ROI Selling customer reduces its sales cycle by 2% to 10%.

Enter the estimated reduction in sales cyle using ROI Selling:	5%
Calculated reduction in sales cycle: (days reduced)	6
New calculated average days in sales cycle:	114
Estimated reduction in cost of sale using ROI Selling:	$1,000,000

Although the first few steps of this process—opening the spreadsheet and creating the general information section—need little explanation, the remaining steps can be more challenging. The following sections explain steps 3 through 8 of the above process in more detail.

Adding the Value Statement

As described in Chapter 8, value statements summarize the entire value proposition of each row of your value matrix. The value statement establishes the baseline against which your success will be measured and establishes the criteria on which your prospect will be focused throughout the sales process. All of the questions and calculations that follow support the value statement shown in the header. As mentioned earlier, because this is such an important element in the questionnaire's interface, you may want to highlight the statement by putting it in a box, presenting it in bold text, adding a shaded background, or using other graphical elements to make the statement more visually prominent and compelling.

Adding the Needs Analysis Questions

In the rows below the value statement, add each of the detailed needs analysis questions you've chosen to use for this value statement. Figure 13.8 shows an example of the questionnaire with the value statement and needs analysis questions in place.

FIGURE 13.8 THE FIRST STAGES OF THE NEEDS ANALYSIS QUESTIONNAIRE INTERFACE

Powerful programming software tools to reduce programming costs and increase revenue from faster operation start-up

Enter the average amount of time (hours) spent per person monthly programming PLCs:	30
Enter the number of personnel involved in the programming process:	3
Enter the hourly burdened cost of personnel involved in the programming process:	$34.00

The simple layout shown here can be used throughout your development process. Notice how we shaded the value statement and the data entry fields to draw attention to the values we need to collect from the prospect to calculate potential ROI. As we noted earlier, these graphic enhancements draw the user's attention to the vital information first.

Adding Calculations to Quantify the Current Situation

In Figure 13.9 we have expanded the questionnaire to include calculations that quantify the cost of the current situation. These initial results represent the current situation, or status quo, against which your projected ROI will be measured. They support the critical requirement of assessing and illustrating the current situation when calculating the estimated value your products or services can deliver.

Study this figure carefully, paying particular attention to the manner in which the calculations support a logical flow in the questioning process. Also notice how all calculated values are boxed to draw the reader's attention. Clearly displaying all of the calculation results adds to your model's credibility and makes it easier for your customers and prospects to follow the logic you've used to arrive at your conclusions. When prospects can see and follow the

T *i p*

Throughout your ROI Needs Analysis Questionnaire interface, you will create many calculated fields like the boxed cells shown in Figure 13.9. Be sure to protect these fields in your spreadsheet so they cannot be manipulated or changed. This protects the integrity of your model by preventing users from altering formulas.

FIGURE 13.9 NEEDS ANALYSIS QUESTIONNAIRE WITH VALUE-BASED CALCULATIONS

Powerful programming software tools to reduce programming costs and increase revenue from faster operation start-up

Enter the average amount of time (hours) spent per person monthly programming PLCs:	30
Enter the number of personnel involved in the programming process:	3
Enter the hourly burdened cost of personnel involved in the programming process:	$34.00
Calculated annual rate:	$70,720
Calculated estimated annual cost of programming PLCs:	$36,720

logic, they accept the results of your ROI model more readily. In addition, when the results of your calculations appear on the screen while you are entering data, they are much easier to explain to prospects.

Adding an Impact Statement

Once you have documented the current situation, add the impact statement to your model. Once again, an impact statement has two components, the first being a declaration of fact from one of the following sources:

- Customer impact surveys or studies
- Reports from industry analysts (e.g., Gartner, PriceWaterhouse Coopers, Aberdeen, or other industry analysts specific to your product or service)
- 360 Degree ROI Value Assessment results from other customers (you learn more about conducting these assessments in Chapter 15).

In Figure 13.10 we have added the first component of an impact statement to our developing Needs Analysis Questionnaire interface. In this example, the purpose of the impact statement is to lead the prospect to a conclusion that Rockwell Automation can indeed help the prospect reduce costs, increase revenue, or avoid other costs.

Remember that you must be able to support the statements of fact within your impact statements with research. The quality of data from your own customer surveys is typically better than research from third-party research organizations because it tends to be specific to your market and the manner in which customers use your products and services. We sometimes hear that customer impact surveys or studies can be difficult to obtain, because the data are not always readily available in the customer organization. Our experience shows that with appropriate tools, such as a 360 Degree ROI Value Assessment, you can question your customer base and help customers estimate the results they've achieved from the implementation and use of your company's products or services. Most customers will oblige you with estimates of the value you've delivered if you approach them in an organized and logical manner. As

---

FIGURE 13.10 THE FIRST COMPONENT OF THE IMPACT
STATEMENT IS A STATEMENT OF FACT

**Powerful programming software tools to reduce programming
costs and increase revenue from faster operation start-up**

Enter the average amount of time (hours) spent
per person monthly programming PLCs: 30

Enter the number of personnel involved in the
programming process: 3

Enter the hourly burdened cost of personnel involved
in the programming process: $34.00

Calculated annual rate: $70,720

Calculated estimated annual cost of
programming PLCs: $36,720

**Rockwell Automation customers have saved up to 40%
in programming time.**

---

you learn in Chapter 15, the 360 Degree ROI Value Assessment information is highly valuable for a number of purposes, one of which is as data
to be used in support of impact statements.

Third-party research groups are another important source of supporting data for your Needs Analysis Questionnaire impact statements.
Gartner Group, Meta Group, PricewaterhouseCoopers (PWC), and
many others have produced studies complete with statistics on a wide variety of industries and products; their studies are available through many
sources. The Internet is an extremely powerful research resource that is
at your fingertips. Use a quality search engine and retrieve as much
background data as you can to support your impact statement. We are
partial to http://www.dogpile.com because it includes data from many
sources and not just the ones that pay to be listed.

On the next line, enter the percentage of savings based on the expectation outlined in your impact statement that your customer or
prospect can expect to receive from your product or service, as shown in
Figure 13.11. This information represents the second component of
your impact statement.

FIGURE 13.11 THINK OF THIS AS THE SECOND LINE OF THE IMPACT STATEMENT.

Powerful programming software tools to reduce programming costs and increase revenue from faster operation start-up

Enter the average amount of time (hours) per person, per month spent programming PLCs:	30
Enter the number of personnel involved in the programming process:	3
Enter the hourly burdened cost of personnel involved in the programming process:	$34.00
Calculated annual rate:	$70,720
Calculated estimated annual cost of programming PLCs:	$36,720

Rockwell Automation customers have saved up to 40% in programming time.

Enter your estimated savings from using tag-based programming:	40%

If your prospect doesn't feel that his or her company fits "the norm" and that your estimates aren't representative of his or her business, ask the prospect to supply the estimated benefit. Ask the prospect: "Do you agree there will be some sort of value delivered? Is there an opportunity for you to realize either a cost reduction, cost avoidance, or revenue increase?" In most cases the response will be yes. With that in mind, ask the prospect: "What is your estimate of potential savings? And please be conservative!" By turning the model around and enabling your prospect to estimate the value to be received from your product, you are giving the prospect ownership of the answer and increasing the likelihood that the prospect will buy into the

T *i p*

To obtain customer buy-in for the results produced by the ROI model, make sure key data quantifying projected results, like the percentage variable shown in Figure 13.11, come from the customer or prospect.

result. Don't be concerned about the impact of encouraging your prospect to be conservative in this estimate. When you have an opportunity to test your model, you will find that no matter what number you place in the impact statement field, a value is returned and ROI is generated. In addition, your real purpose is to have the prospect buy into the ROI model itself. Once you have a prospect supplying data for the model, you're on the home stretch.

Calculating the Savings

Now add the final set of calculations to show the potential value delivered using this model. In Figure 13.12, we are going to calculate the amount of cost savings a Rockwell Automation customer will receive as a result of using tag-based programming to reduce programming time.

FIGURE 13.12 CALCULATION OF ESTIMATED BENEFIT

Powerful programming software tools to reduce programming costs and increase revenue from faster operation start-up

Enter the average amount of time (hours) per person per month spent programming PLCs:	30
Enter the number of personnel involved in the programming process:	3
Enter the hourly burdened cost of personnel involved in the programming process:	$34.00
Calculated annual rate:	$70,720
Calculated estimated annual cost of programming PLCs:	$36,720

Rockwell Automation customers have saved up to 40% in programming time.

Enter your estimated savings from using tag-based programming:	40%
Potential cost reduction in programming time:	$14,688

Adding a Product Benefit Statement

The final step in building your Needs Analysis Questionnaire interface is adding a product benefit statement. Benefit statements should
spell out which features of your product or service will accomplish the
value statement—an optional step as mentioned earlier. About half of
our customers include benefit statements in their ROI models; others
believe that benefit statements have more impact in proposals. We believe this statement offers an opportunity for you to explain "how" your
product or service is going to meet or exceed your prospects' expectations, resolve their business issues, and give them a reason to buy from

---

FIGURE 13.13 NEEDS ANALYSIS QUESTIONNAIRE INTERFACE
WITH PRODUCT BENEFIT STATEMENT IN PLACE

**Powerful programming software tools to reduce programming
costs and increase revenue from faster operation start-up**

Tag-based programming: Use of tag-based addressing means that your
memory mirrors your application. It allows you to create and maintain
separate documentation for data table layout, eliminate the need to select a
logical address (just create the actual name like "tank rate" and "flow rate"),
eliminate the need to create documentation for many objects, and reduce the
need to "lookup."

Enter the average amount of time (hours) spent per person monthly programming PLCs:	30
Enter the number of personnel involved in the programming process:	3
Enter the hourly burdened cost of personnel involved in the programming process:	$34.00
Calculated annual rate:	$70,720
Calculated estimated annual cost of programming PLCs:	$36,720

**Rockwell Automation customers have saved up to 40%
in programming time.**

Enter your estimated savings from using tag-based programming:	40%
Potential cost reduction in programming time:	$14,688

you . . . now! Therefore, we generally encourage using benefit statements in the ROI model; if you use the statement in the questionnaire, place it at the top of the screen immediately below the value statement, as shown in Figure 13.13.

Building a Sample Needs Analysis Questionnaire Interface

To further illustrate the techniques involved in building a Needs Analysis Questionnaire interface, we work through a sample set of questions related to ROI selling. In this exercise, we build an ROI Needs Analysis Questionnaire that contains both a revenue increase and a cost reduction. Our model demonstrates the reduction of a prospect's marketing cost per closed lead and the increase of the prospect's total revenue through an improved close ratio.

Figure 13.14 shows the needs analysis development template for this value statement: "Increase revenue by increasing the number of leads generated from marketing programs that we close." In this example, we use only the four questions shown in Section E of this template to calculate the potential value delivered. However, you'll see there are 11 addi-

FIGURE 13.14 SAMPLE NEEDS ANALYSIS DEVELOPMENT TEMPLATE

Business Issue (A)	Components of Issue (D)	Questions (E)
. . . because the cost of our marketing programs continues to rise with no increase in close ratio.	• Marketing budget • Number of programs • Number of leads generated • Close ratio from leads generated	• What is your annual marketing budget? • How many lead-generating marketing programs do you support annually? • How many leads are generated from the marketing programs?
Feature/ Solution (B) Solution Selling Sales Process and Pain Sheets	**Value Statement (C)** Increase revenue by increasing the number of leads generated from marketing programs that we close.	• What is your close ratio on the leads generated from marketing programs?

tional calculations we make using the collected data to help the prospect better understand the value we expect to deliver.

When we add the value statement from Section C of Figure 13.14 and the four questions from Section E, the Needs Analysis Questionnaire initially looks like the example shown in Figure 13.15.

FIGURE 13.15 NEEDS ANALYSIS QUESTIONNAIRE WITH VALUE STATEMENT QUESTIONS IN PLACE

Increase revenue by increasing the number of leads closed with leads generated from marketing programs	
What is your annual marketing budget?	$5,000,000
How many lead-generating marketing programs do you support annually?	125
How many leads are generated from the marketing programs?	1,400
What is your close ratio on the leads generated from marketing programs?	10%

T *i p*

As you learned earlier in this chapter, when data needs to be shared between two or more value statement areas, it is best to create a general information section and gather the data once. This will enable you to default the data into the calculations when they are needed later.

In Figure 13.16, we have added calculations to help us define the current situation. These calculations include:

- Marketing program cost per lead generated
- Current number of leads generated by marketing programs and closed by sales

You'll notice that this example also displays "calculated cost per lead-generation program"; though this information is irrelevant to this example, we display the calculation because it is used elsewhere in the program.

FIGURE 13.16 NEEDS ANALYSIS QUESTIONNAIRE WITH FIRST CALCULATIONS IN PLACE

Increase revenue by increasing the number of leads closed with leads generated from marketing programs

What is your annual marketing budget for lead generation?	$5,000,000
How many lead-generating marketing programs do you support annually?	125
Calculated cost per lead-generation program:	$40,000
How many leads are generated from the marketing programs?	1,400
Calculated cost per lead:	$3,571
What is your close ratio on the leads generated from marketing programs?	10%
Calculated number of leads closed:	140

In Figure 13.17 we added three additional figures to calculate these status quo costs:

- Average revenue per sale (taken from the general information section)
- Calculated annual revenue from leads generated from marketing programs
- Calculated marketing cost per closed lead

The calculations for revenue and cost are the baseline figures used to quantify the current situation. We can use this portion of the interface to show our prospect what his or her current cost and revenue are from a marketing lead-generation program.

Next we need to define the impact statement and calculate the savings based on the impact our products or services can make on the prospect's key pain indicator (KPI). Figure 13.18 shows how this is expressed in the form of an expected percentage increase in the prospect's close rate resulting from use of the ROI Selling product.

FIGURE 13.17 NEEDS ANALYSIS QUESTIONNAIRE

Increase revenue by increasing the number of leads closed with leads generated from marketing programs

What is your annual marketing budget for lead generation?	$5,000,000
How many lead-generating marketing programs do you support annually?	125
Calculated cost per lead-generation program:	$40,000
How many leads are generated from the marketing programs?	1,400
Calculated cost per lead:	$3,571
What is your close ratio on the leads generated from marketing programs?	10%
Calculated number of leads closed:	140
Average revenue per sale: (from above)	$285,000
Calculated annual revenue from leads generated from marketing programs:	$39,900,000
Calculated annual marketing cost per CLOSED lead:	$35,714

This example also illustrates the important concept of clearly displaying all of your calculations. We inset and draw boxes around all calculated fields to draw attention to the fact they are calculations we performed. We also state that the data in these fields are "calculated." And remember to protect these calculation cells, too, to prevent them from being altered.

Also notice that the example in Figure 13.18 only required us to ask four questions—a vital part of building a successful ROI Selling campaign. Ask only for the data that is necessary to perform the calculations required to estimate the value you can deliver.

FIGURE 13.18 NEEDS ANALYSIS QUESTIONNAIRE WITH ESTIMATED BENEFIT OF ADOPTING THE PROPOSED SOLUTION

Increase revenue by increasing the number of leads closed with leads generated from marketing programs

What is your annual marketing budget for lead generation?	$5,000,000
How many lead-generating marketing programs do you support annually?	125
Calculated cost per lead-generation program:	$40,000
How many leads are generated from the marketing programs?	1,400
Calculated cost per lead:	$3,571.43
What is your close ratio on the leads generated from marketing programs?	10%
Calculated number of leads closed:	140
Average revenue per sale: (from above)	$285,000
Calculated annual revenue from leads generated from marketing programs:	$39,900,000
Calculated annual marketing cost per CLOSED lead:	$35,714

The typical ROI Selling customers increase their close ratio by 10%–20%.

Estimated impact ROI Selling will have on close ratios:	10%
New close ratio: (current close ratio + estimated increase)	1.10%
Calculated additional number of leads to become customers:	15.4
Average revenue per sale: (from above)	$285,000
New calculated annual revenue from marketing lead-generation programs:	$44,289,000
New calculated cost per closed lead:	$32,175
Annual revenue increase from improved close ratio:	**$4,389,000**
Annual cost avoidance from leads generated by marketing:	**$550,000**

Assembling a Start Screen

When we create a new ROI spreadsheet, we also add another tab to the spreadsheet file. This tab, which we call a *start screen*, is used as a cover sheet to the spreadsheet, displaying customer identification information and the prospect's KPIs. Figure 13.19 is an example of a start screen containing eight KPIs we developed for a company called Sales Performance International. The KPIs listed here include many of the issues faced by SPI's customers.

We suggest you build a hyperlink on each KPI that will take you to the position on the Needs Analysis Questionnaire that addresses this issue. Refer to your spreadsheet "Help" for assistance on how to create hyperlinks.

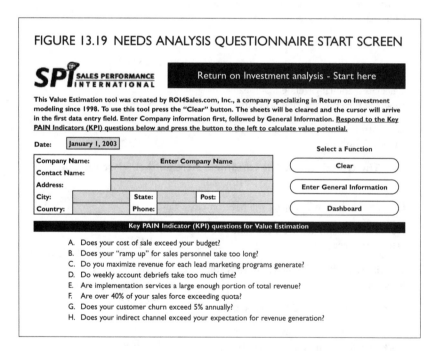

FIGURE 13.19 NEEDS ANALYSIS QUESTIONNAIRE START SCREEN

SPI SALES PERFORMANCE INTERNATIONAL

Return on Investment analysis - Start here

This Value Estimation tool was created by ROI4Sales.com, Inc., a company specializing in Return on Investment modeling since 1998. To use this tool press the "Clear" button. The sheets will be cleared and the cursor will arrive in the first data entry field. Enter Company information first, followed by General Information. Respond to the Key PAIN Indicators (KPI) questions below and press the button to the left to calculate value potential.

Date: January 1, 2003

Select a Function

Company Name:	Enter Company Name
Contact Name:	
Address:	
City:	State:	Post:
Country:	Phone:

Clear

Enter General Information

Dashboard

Key PAIN Indicator (KPI) questions for Value Estimation

A. Does your cost of sale exceed your budget?
B. Does your "ramp up" for sales personnel take too long?
C. Do you maximize revenue for each lead marketing programs generate?
D. Do weekly account debriefs take too much time?
E. Are implementation services a large enough portion of total revenue?
F. Are over 40% of your sales force exceeding quota?
G. Does your customer churn exceed 5% annually?
H. Does your indirect channel exceed your expectation for revenue generation?

Summary

You may have found the information in this chapter to be somewhat complex. Remember, however, that there is no right or wrong way to build a Needs Analysis Questionnaire—the questionnaires we have helped our customers develop address a wide range of products and services, and vary considerably in form and content. We are confident that if you follow our model and modify it to meet the profile of your customers, products, and services, the result will be a compelling ROI model that your entire organization will adopt and use to generate more sales and build stronger customer relationships. As you build your own Needs Analysis Questionnaire interface, keep these important points from this chapter in mind:

- Your Needs Analysis Questionnaire interface presents the ROI components you learned to create in Chapters 8 through 12.
- Create a general information section to collect information that is shared between needs analysis questions for multiple value statements.
- Head each page of your Needs Analysis Questionnaire with a value statement.
- Limit the number of questions to 45 or fewer.
- Always display your calculations.
- Highlight, shade, or bold the data you want to draw attention to and use double-spacing to make the interface data easier to read and understand.
- Earn credibility by supporting your calculations with data from recognized, reliable sources: customer impact studies, 360 Degree ROI Assessments, and third parties, such as Bitpipe.com, Gartner, PricewaterhouseCoopers, or META, for example.

14

THE ROI FINANCIAL DASHBOARD

The ROI Financial Dashboard is a financial summary page. It indicates the returns on investment you have calculated for each key pain indicator (KPI) in your value matrix combined with a set of financial metrics that a decision maker or influencer can understand and use to compare and evaluate his or her options for purchase. The ROI Financial Dashboard delivers a compelling presentation of the calculations from the Needs Analysis Questionnaire in a single page. As such, it is an important sales tool that plays a prominent role in the presentation and proposal stages of your sales process, which are discussed in Chapter 16, "ROI in the Sales Process."

To build your ROI Financial Dashboard, you summarize the ROI data you collected and calculated in the Needs Analysis Questionnaire and add information about your prospect's investment and implementation period to calculate the following figures:

- Return on investment (ROI) percentage, which is your prospect's accumulated net benefit over a specific period of time, divided by the initial cost.
- Net present value (NPV), which is the dollar value of your prospect's expected return expressed in today's dollars. NPV essentially translates the dollars your prospect expects to realize in the

future into current value by applying a factor for inflation or other variables. This calculation is useful for comparing the investment you plan to make today against returns you will receive in the future. NPV is often called the P&L (profit and loss) on a project.

- Internal rate of return (IRR), or the rate of return your prospect will receive from his or her investment in your product or service, expressed such that the NPV of future cash flows from the investment are zero.
- Payback period, or the time it will take your prospect to recoup the investment.
- Potential cost of waiting (often called the opportunity cost) is the daily, weekly, or monthly cost your prospect will experience as a result of *not* purchasing your product or service.

In addition to these figures, the ROI dashboard may contain other elements, including calculations of start-up costs and discount rates and factors. You learn more about each of these figures and elements later in the chapter as well as how to use them effectively in creating your own ROI Financial Dashboards.

We recommend presenting your dashboard information in a graphical format. The easiest way to build the dashboard is to create an additional tab or section within the spreadsheet you have already created for your Needs Analysis Questionnaire. The elements of the ROI Financial Dashboard are typically contained within three major sections, each having a distinct purpose:

1. *The financial summary and metrics section* summarizes the impact of the investment on company cash flow. This section also offers some "what if" opportunities, derived by manipulating the discount factor and investment figures. Both figures impact the NPV and IRR.

2. *The KPI summary* recaps your prospect's issues, pains, and goals as identified and recorded in the Needs Analysis Questionnaire. The person in your prospect's organization who reads and analyzes the dashboard may not have participated in all of the dialogue and analysis phases of the ROI assessment. Therefore, you need to summarize both the financial impact of the investment

as well as the key pain indicators you identified in your discussions with other stakeholders.

3. *Graphs* display an overview picture of the pain, investment, and potential return. You don't need to be a financial analyst to understand and explain the ROI dashboard. The content of this easy-to-read and simple-to-design ROI Financial Dashboard can be learned very quickly. To illustrate this concept and provide ideas as you think about the design of your dashboard, a sample ROI Financial Dashboard is shown in Figure 14.1.

FIGURE 14.1 ROI FINANCIAL DASHBOARD

Return on Investment

Return by Category

Financial Dashboard Summary	
ROI Selling Investment:	**$300,000**
Savings from Cost Reductions:	**$200,000**
Savings from Cost Avoidances:	**$300,000**
Savings from Revenue Increases:	**$212,159**
Estimated Savings:	**$712,159**
Financial Dashboard Summary Metrics	
Return on Investment Percentage:	237%
Payback Period: (Months)	8.1
Factor: 8% Net Present Value:	**$332,784**
Internal Rate of Return:	137%
Start-up 90 After payback period,	**$51,168**
Factor: Days monthly cost to wait:	
Key PAIN Indicators	
Reduction in cost of sale:	$85,000
New account rep time:	$75,000
Cost per lead:	$89,000
Revenue per lead:	$120,159
Account debriefs:	$65,000
Increase service sales:	$63,000
Customer life cycle:	$90,000
Channel partners:	$125,000
Total value estimation from KPIs:	**$712,159**

Key PAIN Indicators

The ROI Financial Dashboard is a powerful communication tool you and your company's sales personnel can use to graphically present the value delivered as a result of the purchase of your product or service to your prospects. We urge you to use the dashboard in your proposal and presentation materials to illustrate and explain the value that will be produced by the prospect's investment. CFOs comparing investment options will appreciate this one-page summary of their company's key pain indicators and investment opportunity data. Using the ROI Financial Dashboard gives you a unique advantage in that you are providing this level of detailed, verifiable ROI information for your prospect during the sales process.

N *o t e*

According to a survey by *CIO Insight* magazine, depending on the size of the company, CFOs review the business potential of information technology (IT) investments on 62.9 percent to 73.5 percent of purchases. The ROI dashboard includes several standard ROI calculations that CFOs frequently use in their investment analyses.

Key Concepts and Guidelines

The following key concepts and guidelines will assist you in developing the ROI Financial Dashboard:

- **Sell the financial metrics of the ROI Financial Dashboard.** To ensure that your points hit home with your target audience, it is important that you make an effort to understand and convey how significant and valuable the financial metrics are to the CFO and other key decision makers evaluating your proposal.
- **Keep your design simple.** Simple is always best. We have included examples throughout this chapter and at the end of the book for you to emulate as you build your own ROI Financial Dashboard model.
- **Let the spreadsheet do the work.** Most spreadsheet programs have built-in financial analysis capability; they have, for example, standard formulas that calculate NPV and IRR for you. Utilizing the power of the spreadsheet program and taking advantage of its financial calculations saves effort and improves the accuracy of your

ROI Financial Dashboard. If you aren't proficient with formula functions within your spreadsheet program, you may want to call on your company's financial staff to help develop the dashboard.

Building the ROI Financial Dashboard

As mentioned earlier, you create the ROI Financial Dashboard as an extension of your ROI model. At this point your ROI model spreadsheet should include tabs or sections for the Needs Analysis Questionnaire and a start-screen tab that contains your key pain indicator questions. To start building your dashboard, add an additional tab to your ROI model spreadsheet titled "Financial Dashboard."

The first step is summarizing the results of the data collected from your prospect in the Needs Analysis Questionnaire. Our most effective ROI Financial Dashboards contain 11 elements. The following table lists those 11 ROI dashboard elements and summarizes where the information for each originates. We explain each of these elements in more detail in the following sections.

Element	Source
1. Key pain indicators summary	Summarized KPI descriptions and projected ROI from Needs Analysis Questionnaire
2. Category charts, investment versus cost charts	Graphical displays of information collected and calculated on the dashboard
3. Investment input	Prospect's cost, either entered into dashboard or interfaced from a pricing spreadsheet or application
4. Net present value (NPV)	Calculation using standard spreadsheet NPV formula and based on projected ROI and entered NPV factor
5. Internal rate of return (IRR)	Calculation using standard spreadsheet IRR formula

6. Return on investment (ROI) percentage calculation

Calculation based on total projected ROI, investment, and payback period

7. Payback period

Amount of time required for prospects to recoup their investment, generally including a start-up factor for product implementation

8. Discount rate/factor

Data entry field on dashboard supplying a variable used in NPV calculation

9. ROI category summary (reduce cost, avoid cost, increase revenue)

Summarization of ROI by category based on data from Needs Analysis Questionnaire

10. Start-up factor (time it takes to implement solutions)

Data entry field on dashboard used in calculation of payback period

11. Cost of waiting (ongoing cost of not purchasing from you)

Calculation on dashboard showing cost per time period (day, week, month, year, etc.) of not purchasing your products or services

Although it is not necessary to include all of these elements, you should include as many as you can in your summary spreadsheet. The more of these data you include in your ROI Financial Dashboard, the more effective the dashboard's presentation will be. The following sections discuss each of these 11 elements in more detail and offer techniques for creating these elements in your own ROI Financial Dashboard.

Summarizing Key Pain Indicators

The first step in creating your ROI Financial Dashboard is building a table that summarizes the prospect's KPIs. You learned in earlier chapters that a KPI identifies a primary issue, pain, or goal your prospect experiences and takes the form of a restatement of the business issue as a question of pain. Gather your key pain indicators from the start screen

U se A n a l y s i s   t o   S u p p o r t
F i n a n c i a l   B e n e f i t s

Bob Kantin is the president of SalesProposals.com and author of several books, including *Sales Proposals Kit for Dummies* and *Strategic Proposals: Closing the Big Deal*. Bob recently shared his thoughts with us on the importance of demonstrating financial benefits to prospects:

> To a buyer, a financial benefit means either less cost, cost avoidance, or more revenue (or a combination of them all). Financial benefits represent the hard value part of your value proposition because you can measure financial benefits in dollars and cents. You use the financial benefits subsection of your proposal to show your prospect how your product or service reduces or avoids costs or increases revenues—in other words, how it lets the company take advantage of its improvement opportunity. You must make the financial benefits realistic and accurate and support them with an easy-to-understand, unquestionable financial analysis. I believe ROI Selling does this.

you created in Chapter 13. The objective now is to create a summary table on which your prospect can quickly see the return for each KPI and the total estimated value for all of the KPIs.

When you build your KPI summary table, you are presenting the value your product or service is going to deliver. This summary will ensure you have a complete view of the key pain indicators your product or service can resolve. Based on the ROI Selling methodology explained in Chapter 16, your summary table may include KPIs that don't apply to this particular prospect. By listing all possible KPIs on your ROI Financial Dashboard, you are telling the customer or prospect that you are building an ROI model that is as comprehensive as possible in order to focus on the prospect's primary issues. Also, reviewing the KPI summary, including items that were not identified as pains during the sales process, can lead your prospect to realize he or she might be facing some of these other issues in his or her own business.

Figure 14.2 is a sample KPI summarization table for ROI Selling.

FIGURE 14.2 KPI SUMMARY TABLE

Key PAIN Indicators	
Reduction in cost of sale:	$0
Reduce cost of getting new sales reps productive:	$20,769
Revenue increase factored for quota achievers:	$138,462
Reduce annual lead-generation cost:	$0
Revenue increase from increased close ratio:	$0
Reduce the amount of time spent on account debriefs:	$256,250
Increase revenue by selling more services:	$0
Increase revenue by moving reps above quota:	$0
Increase revenue from less customer turnover:	$125,000
Increase revenue from indirect channel:	$0
Total value estimation from KPIs:	**$540,481**

Dan Bizub—CPA, financial consultant, accountant for Medical Associates, and an expert we use for advice on our dashboard designs—tells us: "When I am having a discussion regarding the cost and benefit of a purchase with a vendor, it needs to be a learning experience for both of us. When I looked at the ROI Financial Dashboard, I particularly liked the KPI listed at the bottom [the KPI summary]; it helped me understand the business issues we face."

Using Charts to Graphically Convey Data

The ROI Financial Dashboard confirms the saying "A picture is worth a thousand words." CFOs and other financial personnel may be accustomed to reviewing columns of numbers and zeroing in on the important data. As a salesperson, you want to illustrate the impact of the ROI analysis as vividly as possible with charts and graphs. We like to present several different slices of the financial data graphically in the ROI Financial Dashboard.

When it comes to charting data, Microsoft Excel is incredibly flexible. But don't let all of that flexibility encourage you to create complex or hard-to-read charts. Keep your charts and graphs simple. Stick to standard chart types like pie charts and bar charts. The cost versus investment

T *i p*

Chart locations can vary, but be sure all the data fits on one page. Your ROI dashboard should not be more than one page in length.

chart our clients use is typically a vertical bar chart that displays the difference between the cost and benefit. We also include a pie chart of the ROI categories (cost avoidances, revenue increases, and cost reductions). Examples of these charts are shown in Figure 14.3.

We present the ROI categories chart in terms of the percentage each category makes up of the total savings. In other words, X percent is cost reductions, Y percent is cost avoidances, and Z percent represents revenue increases. Make sure your prospect reviews these charts carefully, however, because sometimes people zero in on cost reductions and dismiss the value delivered by cost avoidances and revenue increases. Solid customer data helps you show your customers that these two can be as great as, or greater than, cost reductions.

The final chart we suggest on the ROI Financial Dashboard is a KPI summary chart—a vertical bar chart representation of the data in your KPI summary table. Use a different color on each of the bars so that each KPI stands out on its own (see Figure 14.4).

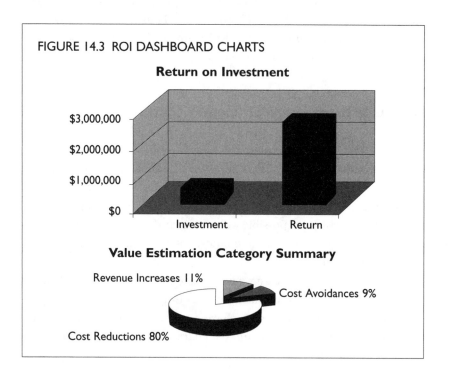

FIGURE 14.3 ROI DASHBOARD CHARTS

Return on Investment

Value Estimation Category Summary

Revenue Increases 11%

Cost Avoidances 9%

Cost Reductions 80%

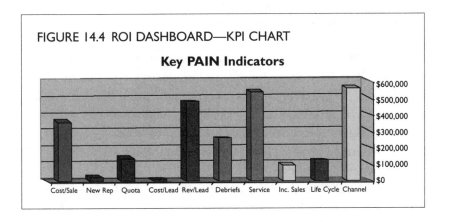

FIGURE 14.4 ROI DASHBOARD—KPI CHART

Key PAIN Indicators

Creating an Investment Line

Our ROI models almost always include an investment line. The investment is the cost to your prospect for your products or services. You can either feed the investment figure into your dashboard from a pricing module or simply enter it into the field.

If you want to get fancy and build a "quoting" tool that includes price lists, maintenance, service costs, and the like, you can interface this tool's data into the investment line field on the financial dashboard. Other options you have are to add multiple investment lines to include other expenses associated with purchasing your product or service—for example, maintenance, consulting, hardware, or software. If you choose to just enter a number into the investment field, we suggest you include backup data detailing what this investment figure is composed of in your proposal presentation. Figure 14.5 shows how we present the investment figure as the top line of the ROI Financial Dashboard summary.

FIGURE 14.5 FINANCIAL DASHBOARD WITH INVESTMENT LINE

Financial Dashboard Summary	
Investment:	$2,500,000
Savings from cost reductions:	$7,230,009
Revenue increase opportunities:	$1,007,980
Savings from cost avoidances:	$ 800,000
KPI value estimation summary:	**$9,037,989**

Calculating the Net Present Value (NPV)

NPV is the amount of your prospect's expected return expressed in current dollars. This helps the prospect compare the dollars he or she invests today against savings that will occur in the future. The calculation is simply the sum of the present value of the net benefits for each year minus the initial costs of the project. If the project has a positive NPV, then it generated more cash than it required in funding. If the NPV is negative, then the project generated a loss. Microsoft Excel makes the calculation of NPV very easy for you by including an NPV function in its standard set of formulas.

We create a subsection on the ROI Financial Dashboard screen that includes NPV as part of the dashboard metrics. Grouping all of the financial metrics together makes it much easier for the reader of the document to decipher the data. See Figure 14.6 for an example of how we group the financial metrics on the ROI Financial Dashboard.

Remember that NPV doesn't really tell you when savings are going to occur. In other words, it calculates the profit and loss but doesn't consider the time frame within the payback period. Savings could occur monthly, annually, or, sometimes, at the end of the project.

Calculating the Internal Rate of Return (IRR)

The internal rate of return (IRR) is the rate of return your prospects receive on their investment—the percentage rate you must apply to the

---

FIGURE 14.6 FINANCIAL DASHBOARD—SUMMARY FINANCIAL METRICS

Financial Dashboard Summary Metrics			
Return on investment percentage:			123%
Payback period: (months) (factored for sales process)			12.7
Factor:	8%	Net present value: (NPV)	$73,457
Internal rate of return: (IRR)			23%
Start-up:	90	Monthly cost of not purchasing:	$10,248

annual benefits for the NPV of the investment to equal zero. In other words, to determine IRR, you must discount the benefits until they equal the cost. This calculation enables you to compare investment opportunities and decide—based on risk and return—which is the best investment. For example, Figure 14.7 compares four separate investment opportunities with various investment requirements and IRR results.

Notice that the most expensive item has the highest IRR. The CFO needs to decide whether, even with an IRR that is this high, he or she believes the project is worth the $750,000 cost. The use of IRR enables the CFO to look at each project fairly, regardless of the investment amount.

Once again, Microsoft Excel makes it easy for you to add this information to your ROI Financial Dashboard. IRR is one of the standard formulas included in Microsoft's Office product. CPA Dan Bizub, our financial consultant, makes this observation regarding the IRR percentage: "If you can find an investment with a higher return than the IRR percentage, then take it. That is the purpose of the IRR—to compare different investments."

Calculating the Return on Investment (ROI) Percentage

ROI percentage is the most common calculation used when building ROI models. The percentage represents the accumulated net benefit over a fixed period of time divided by a prospect's initial cost. The results are always displayed in a percentage format and qualified by a fixed period. For example, if your prospect's benefit is $25,000 over one year and the investment is $20,000, the calculation is as follows: $25,000 ÷ $20,000 = 125%.

FIGURE 14.7 INTERNAL RATE OF RETURN TABLE

Investment Opportunity	Investment	Internal Rate of Return
New software project	$450,000	25%
New crane	$750,000	55%
New dump trucks	$300,000	35%
New tool truck	$350,000	40%

Calculating the Payback Period

The payback period is the time (usually months or years) it takes to recoup a prospect's investment. The traditional calculation is simply cost divided by investment. For our purposes we multiply the payback period times 12 months to *annualize* our results for consistency within our model.

We have discussed the concept of payback period and its affect on the credibility of our model with many CFOs. Practically every CFO told us that payback periods that are too short are not believable. Some over-enthusiastic salespeople try to present payback periods that are less than the amount of time it takes to implement the solution. It is clear that you hurt the credibility of you ROI model when you include an unrealistic payback period. To counter this objection, we suggest you factor your payback period with the number of days it takes to implement your solution. We identify this figure as the start-up factor on our models.

The start-up factor is a period (typically, a period of days) that identifies how long it takes before your customer fully enjoys functional use of your product or service. Some companies call this factor the *implementation and deployment period* for the product or service. The start-up factor affects both the cost of waiting and the payback period. It shifts the estimated return beyond the typically calculated payback period. Figure 14.8 demonstrates how the payback period can shift when recalculated using the start-up factor.

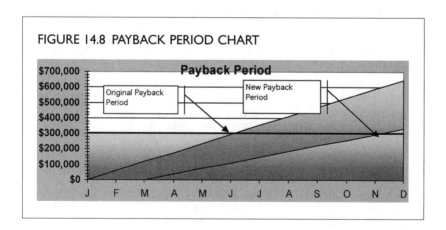

FIGURE 14.8 PAYBACK PERIOD CHART

Again, the start-up factor must be taken into account for your ROI model to be credible and convincing. It is important to understand the difference between the traditional calculation of the payback period and the one we use in this book.

Establishing the Discount Rate

In order to compute NPV you have to discount future benefits and costs. The discounting reflects the time value of money; benefits and costs are worth more if they are experienced sooner rather than later. For your model to reflect this simple but important fact, all future benefits and costs should be discounted. The higher the discount rate, the lower the present value of future cash flows. For a typical investment, with costs concentrated in early periods and benefits following in later periods, raising the discount rate reduces the NPV. We refer to the discount rate as the factor.

Figure 14.9 is an example of how we group together all of the financial metrics on the ROI Financial Dashboard.

FIGURE 14.9 FINANCIAL DASHBOARD—SUMMARY METRICS

Financial Dashboard Summary Metrics			
Return on investment percentage:		362%	
Payback period: (months)		9.3	
Start-up/Implementation period:	180		
Monthly cost of waiting after start-up period:		$701,552	
Discount rate/Factor:	4%		
Net present value: (NPV)		$5,952,283	
Internal rate of return: (IRR)		262%	
Current annual cost of status quo:		$25,946,347	
Purchase delay: (days)	30		
Daily/Total delay cost:		$117,938	$3,538,138

ROI category summary. Each potential saving in your model is already attributed to one of the three ROI categories: cost reductions, cost avoidances, or revenue increases. An important part of the creation of your ROI Financial Dashboard is the summarization of each of the categories within your current proposal. Summarize the savings by category for presentation on the financial dashboard, including your charts and graphics. Figure 14.10 is an example of how we group the savings categories together on our financial dashboard.

We have discussed our ROI model and financial dashboard with several accountants who compare purchase options as part of their responsibilities. Their consensus is that cost avoidance has one of the greatest impacts on the model because it clearly identifies a cost that will occur if the prospect does not act. Therefore, don't be shy about including cost avoidance items on your dashboard. If you worked through the ROI Selling process with the stakeholders, these figures stand up to scrutiny.

FIGURE 14.10 FINANCIAL DASHBOARD SUMMARY—
ROI CATEGORIES SUMMARIZED

Financial Dashboard Summary			
Investment:		$2,500,000	
Savings from cost reductions		$7,230,009	
Revenue increase opportunities:		$1,007,980	
Savings from cost avoidances:		$800,000	
KPI value estimation summary:		$9,037,989	
Financial Dashboard Summary Metrics			
Return on investment percentage:		362%	
Payback period: (months)		9.3	
Start-up/Implementation period:	180		
Monthly cost of waiting after start-up period:		$701,552	
Discount rate/Factor:	4%		
Net present value: (NPV)		$5,952,283	
Internal rate of return: (IRR)		262%	
Current annual cost of status quo:		$25,946,347	
Purchase delay: (days)	30		
Daily/Total delay cost:		$117,938	$3,538,138

Demonstrating the Cost of Waiting

The cost of waiting is a calculation used to identify the cost of not purchasing. Some call this field the opportunity cost or opportunity loss. It is displayed as a daily, weekly, or monthly figure (see Figure 14.11).

Cost of waiting is based on the following parameters:

- Investment
- Estimated annual return
- Payback period
- Start-up factor

Recall that we always want to define the prospect's "current situation" as a basis for comparison with the projected savings. To calculate the cost of waiting, follow these four steps:

1. Return to your Needs Analysis Questionnaire and accumulate all of the current situation cost figures.
2. Refer to your ROI Financial Dashboard's investment figure, and subtract that figure from the estimated annual return. We call the balance the benefit figure.
3. Next, calculate the payback period—(Investment/Estimated value delivered)*12 to annualize—and add the start-up factor to it.
4. Finally, divide your benefit figure by the new payback period and you get the monthly cost of waiting.

FIGURE 14.11 COST OF WAITING

Financial Dashboard Summary Metrics		
Return on investment percentage:		120%
Payback period: (months) (factored for sales process)		13.0
Factor: 8%	Net present value: (NPV)	$46,708
Internal rate of return: (IRR)		20%
Start-up: 90	Monthly cost of not purchasing:	$6,965

Figure 14.12 breaks the cost of waiting calculation into a step-by-step table with sample data.

In this figure, the investment is $300,000 and the expected return is $712,159. First we subtracted our investment of $300,000 from the expected return of $712,159 to get the benefit value of $412,159. Next, we calculated the traditional payback period and added the start-up factor to it. The result of that calculation was 8.1 months. Finally, we divided the benefit value by the payback period to arrive at the monthly cost of waiting. The table in this figure demonstrates how factoring in the start-up factor costs can change these figures. Taking the start-up period into account is more realistic and practical, and it adds credibility to your ROI model.

FIGURE 14.12 COST OF WAITING TABLE

Item	Description	Example
Investment	Original investment from ROI Financial Dashboard	$300,000
Estimated annual benefit	Total estimated savings from ROI Financial Dashboard	$712,159
Start-up factor	Time it takes to get the project up and running and ready to measure	90 days or 3 months
Benefit value	Subtract investment from estimated annual benefit	$712,159 – $300,000 = $412,159
New payback period	Recalculation of the payback period to include the start-up factor	($300,000 ÷ $712,159) × 12 months = 5.1 months + 3 months start-up = 8.1 months payback period
Monthly cost of waiting	Divide benefit value by payback period	$412,159 ÷ 8.1 = $51,168

Designing an Effective ROI Financial Dashboard Interface

We have discovered that there is no right or wrong way to present the data on your ROI Financial Dashboard. The dashboard examples in this chapter and in Appendix B are based on designs that have proven very successful in actual client presentations. You should feel free to use your own ideas and develop your own designs. Just remember that you should include as many of the 11 elements discussed in this chapter as possible.

The user interface for your ROI Financial Dashboard must reflect simplicity, elegance, and class. It is imperative that your calculations are correct. We feel we must repeat this phrase once again louder: YOUR CALCULATIONS MUST BE CORRECT! Test them, retest them, and test them once more for good measure. The validity of your value estimation tool is under constant scrutiny. If one calculation is wrong, you and your company run a serious risk of being eliminated from consideration—one of the reasons we have repeatedly stressed the importance of clearly displaying the results of all calculations.

Adding color to your ROI Financial Dashboard also contributes a great deal to the success of your presentation. Use color to identify the input cells, such as investment, discount rate (factor), and start-up. Highlight the estimated savings and the total value estimation from KPI savings to draw attention to the value you are going to deliver. Each chart should include a color relationship to its corresponding number in the tables to help your prospect associate the data with the charts.

Summary

The ROI Financial Dashboard will become one of your most potent weapons in the sales process. Make sure you invest appropriate time and effort to ensuring that it is compelling, accurate, attractive, and easy to understand. As you move forward with ROI Selling, the financial dashboard will play a major role in developing your 360 Degree ROI model and creating persuasive proposals that help you close deals. If you are still unclear about how to develop an ROI Financial Dashboard, read the following summary and then return to the beginning of the chapter to review the examples one more time:

- There is no need to become a financial analyst to explain an ROI Financial Dashboard; the document should be simple and easy to read and interpret.
- Use the format and design for the ROI Financial Dashboard that works best for your presentation and style, but be sure to include as many of the 11 critical elements as possible.
- At a minimum, your ROI Financial Dashboard should include sections for KPIs, charts, and financial summaries.
- Be sure to take advantage of your spreadsheet program's built-in financial analysis calculations, such as NPV and IRR.
- Don't focus only on cost reductions as ROI benefits; cost avoidance and revenue increases can be equally or more important.
- Use cost avoidance to help people feel the pain of waiting.
- Use color to highlight and draw attention to details you want to emphasize, such as savings, and on entry cells to draw attention to input that is needed.
- Make your ROI Financial Dashboard a prominent component in your sales presentations and proposals.
- Be sure to triple-check your calculations to guarantee their accuracy—use your corporate CFO to help you in the design, presentation, and verification of your accuracy.

15

360 DEGREE ROI SELLING

Up to this point, we have worked through the process of gathering information for and developing a compelling ROI model to help you become more effective in the sales process, shorten your sales cycle, and generate more revenue from new sales. This chapter wraps up Part Two, by explaining how to build a 360 Degree ROI component into your ROI model. In Part Three we tell you how to integrate your ROI model into your existing sales methods, automation tools, and marketing programs. This chapter bridges the ROI development topics discussed in Parts One and Two and the deployment suggestions in Part Three.

The 360 Degree aspect of ROI Selling turns the information you developed during the sales process into a tool you can use to proactively manage customer relationships after a sale. You and your customer use the 360 Degree Value Assessment Summary Dashboard, which you learn to create in this chapter, to measure the results your products and services have actually delivered to your customers against the expectations created during the sales process. In essence, 360 Degree ROI is a program designed to measure the actual value delivered after a sale.

During a sale, you can increase your credibility by presenting a sample value assessment summary dashboard to your prospect and explaining that, as part of the closing process, you and the prospect will set a specific date in the future to review results and measure the value actually delivered to this new customer. During this follow-up visit, you use the 360 Degree ROI Value Assessment Summary Dashboard to gauge your prospect's success and highlight any areas where your product or service isn't working as well as it could be, so you can determine ways to improve performance in these areas. Figure 15.1 is an example of one of our value assessment summary dashboards for ROI4sales; this example incorporates each of the key points you'll learn about in this chapter.

This proactive approach to customer satisfaction can also drive your success in future sales opportunities. You learn more about your customer base and its use of your products or services in addition to building relationships that will help you with other opportunities in the future. Other benefits you can realize from deploying 360 Degree ROI after the sale include these:

- Building customer loyalty and retention by demonstrating your commitment to your customers' success. In other words, you too have some "skin in the game."
- Creating opportunities for additional revenue from existing customers. Countless studies have demonstrated that it is much less expensive to sell to a customer you already have than it is to sell to a new customer.
- Proactively managing the customer relationship by identifying and resolving issues before they reach the boiling point.
- Avoiding "scope creep," which can result from changes in your customers' expectations after the sale. The 360 Degree ROI program maintains focus on the key pains and benefits that drove the selection of your products or services.
- Gathering valuable data for use in future sales processes and for directing product development.
- Further differentiating yourself during a sale by showing your commitment to tracking and proving the results your products or services deliver.

In Chapter 16 we explain how to leverage 360 Degree ROI at the beginning of the sales cycle and throughout the sales process. Although Chapter 15 is based on the principles and examples you have learned thus far in *ROI Selling*, the information we present can be used with other ROI

FIGURE 15.1 360 DEGREE ROI VALUE ASSESSMENT SUMMARY DASHBOARD

Value Assessment Summary Dashboard

Goal vs. Return

Statistics Center	
Original date:	January 1, 2003
Current date:	August 13, 2003
Days between analysis:	224
Initial investment:	$1,000,000
Expected return:	$2,756,178
Return to date:	$3,337,834
Financial Goal Achieved	
ROI percentage:	121%
ROI to date:	334%

Key PAIN Indicator	Original Baseline Goal	Current	Percent of Baseline Achieved	Goal Status
Cost of sale reductions:	$960,000	$791,034	82%	Warning
Lead generation cost reductions:	$38,178	$87,280	229%	Goal achieved
Marketing lead generation program revenue:	$1,008,000	$1,889,520	187%	Goal achieved
Revenue increase from more sales reps above:	$400,000	$265,000	66%	Warning
Revenue increases from additional channel sales:	$350,000	$305,000	87%	Warning
Summary total>>	$2,756,178	$3,337,834	121%	Goal achieved

models and/or sales processes. Therefore, we encourage you to take advantage of the ideas and concepts laid out in this chapter even if you are using an ROI model you developed using some other methodology.

Key Concepts and Guidelines

These key concepts behind 360 Degree ROI selling can help you as you build your own 360 Degree ROI Value Assessment tool and program:

- **Go beyond the survey.** For years, companies have surveyed their customers to gather valuable performance information, using the information to establish value-based pricing and in advertising or competitive promotional programs. The 360 Degree ROI program is different from a traditional survey because it relates directly and specifically to the value assumptions that were developed during the sales process.

- **360 Degree ROI creates a true sales cycle.** The 360 Degree ROI Value Assessments are actually an extension of the sales process into the customer relationship management cycle. The fact that a sale doesn't end when your prospect signs an agreement to purchase your goods or services leads to a "cycle" in which you proactively manage the relationship by returning to your customer periodically to measure the value you have delivered, address any issues, and identify opportunities for additional sales.

- **Use the 360 Degree ROI competitive edge.** A lot of companies are missing the boat on postsale value assessment, so the 360 Degree ROI postsales processes you learn here give you a competitive edge. Make the most of this advantage when talking with your prospects. Make this process of committing to a future date a standard part of your closing activity. Explain how the follow-up is a measurement of the actual ROI your customers will have realized based on the specific data in the ROI value assessment you are developing to help with the customers' product evaluation and selection. Tell prospects how the data is used to feed the impact statements, support the value justification, and prove your commitment to *their* success.

T *i p*

Just how much of a competitive edge does 360 Degree ROI Selling give you? Our own research reveals that only 10 to 15 percent of organizations return to their customer base and measure the value their products and services have delivered.

- **Manage your customers proactively.** By using the concepts described in this chapter, you are proactively managing your customer relationships. The information you gathered in the Needs Analysis Questionnaire during the sales process establishes the measurement criteria by establishing the baseline goals your customers hope to achieve by using your products or services. By establishing measurement criteria up front in the sales process, you can maintain focus on your customers' key pains and issues, and avoid the potentially costly distraction of new questions and issues introduced after a sale. Also, when prospects are focusing on their issues, they are not focusing on price. Finally, you gather valuable information to be used as justification or proof of your impact statements in the Needs Analysis Questionnaire during the due diligence phase of future sales processes.

- **Realize this process is not a selling ploy.** The process is *a true commitment to a customer partnership*. With 360 Degree ROI, you are changing the paradigm between salesperson and prospect. You are committing to a partnership with checkpoints throughout the customer lifecycle to confirm success and identify and address issues.

- **Highlight successes.** Be sure to celebrate every success your customers have realized. Even small victories are worth bringing to your customers' attention. In the press of day-to-day business, complicated by digesting a new set of products and services, these successes might otherwise pass unnoticed. Individuals within a customer's organization who approved or sponsored

N *o t e*

Brian Sommer, vice president of Field Research Services for the Aberdeen Group, says: "Most vendors have figured out how to build the spreadsheet ROI, but few seem to understand what ROI really needs in order to be an effective sales tool. Rarely are [these vendors] willing to put a postsale contract program in place and measure the milestones. Companies need to make ROI a program, not an event." Using ROI value assessments in and throughout your sales process will deliver more sales, higher customer retention, and a program your sales team can commit to.

your product or service will definitely appreciate being provided with hard evidence of tangible success and payback!

- **Focus on issue management.** It is almost inevitable that certain of the ROI components you identify in the sales process perform better than others. When you follow through with a 360 Degree Value Assessment, you can specifically determine which areas are performing to expectations and which need attention. Once you have identified the areas, you are able to assess the issues and reasons for not gaining the success anticipated and act accordingly.

Creating and Using 360 Degree Value Assessments

One of the great things about 360 Degree Value Assessments is that much of the information and structure you need to create them already exists as a result of your use of ROI during the sales process. Therefore, the first steps in preparing for a value assessment should simply involve reviewing and confirming that information.

In Parts One and Two of *ROI Selling*, we taught you how to create an ROI model that consisted of a list of KPIs, a Needs Analysis Questionnaire, and a financial dashboard. Each of these tools will be used to create your new value assessment tool. To begin the process, insert an additional tab into your ROI model and label it "Value Assessment." You can populate most of the information in this tab by copying or referring to entries made to the other tabs of your existing ROI model. (To do this, you need an understanding of how your spreadsheet program handles data collection by referencing a cell in a different worksheet. If you are not familiar with this procedure, consult the spreadsheet help text or a friend or coworker for assistance.)

The six steps for creating and using the 360 Degree ROI Value Assessment are as follows:

1. **Restate and verify the KPI goals.** The first step in creating a value assessment tool is to review and confirm the goal for each KPI you defined on the Needs Analysis Questionnaire (you learned about defining KPIs in Chapter 10, "Identifying Key Pain Indicators"). Each value statement drives a goal that was established in

the Needs Analysis Questionnaire during the questioning process. Capture this goal and document it on your 360 Degree Value Assessment spreadsheet.

2. **Establish the baseline.** Once you have determined the goal for each KPI, you will need to insert the baseline KPI figures from the financial dashboard into your value assessment. Figure 15.2 displays examples of the types of baseline figures you can capture from your financial dashboard.

FIGURE 15.2 FINANCIAL DASHBOARD—KPI SUMMARY/BASELINE FIGURES

Key PAIN Indicators	
Reduction in cost of sale:	$0
Reduce cost of getting new sales reps productive:	$20,769
Revenue increase factored for quota achievers:	$138,462
Reduce annual lead-generation cost:	$0
Revenue increase from increased close ratio:	$0
Reduce the amount of time spent on account debriefs:	$256,250
Increase revenue by selling more services:	$0
Increase revenue by moving reps above quota:	$0
Increase revenue from less customer turnover:	$125,000
Increase revenue from indirect channel:	$0
Total value estimation from KPIs:	**$540,481**

---

3. **Add further supporting data.** You can add a wealth of other supporting data to your value assessment, such as schedules for value assessments, ROI percentage, initial investment versus return-to-date dollars, and so on. See Figure 15.3 for examples of the information we include on our 360 Degree Value Assessment Dashboards.

4. **Compare.** After you have established the baseline and entered the current results from the financial dashboard into your model, you are ready to begin the actual assessment. At this point, you want to assess and compare the impact your product or ser-

FIGURE 15.3 SAMPLE SECTION OF THE VALUE ASSESSMENT SUMMARY DASHBOARD

vice has actually delivered to the customer (see Figure 15.4 for an example). The comparison could be against multiple benchmarks, including the goals you established during the initial needs analysis questioning process and industry standards, using data from sources such as Wire the Market and Ten Dots (http://www.wirethemarket.com and http://www.tendots.com).

5. **Add charts and graphs.** As with the ROI Financial Dashboard, many of your customers will find your 360 Degree Value Assessment more meaningful and easier to read if you integrate graphs and charts into your model.

6. **Analyze assessment results.** As you and your customer review the completed 360 Degree Value Assessment, be prepared to provide the appropriate follow-up attention to the customer's results. As mentioned earlier, it's important to note successes. Not only does this open up the opportunity for further successful sales with this customer, but it gives your customer hard information to affirm that he or she made the right decision by purchasing your products or services. Helping your customers understand and overcome areas where they are not meeting goals and expectations is

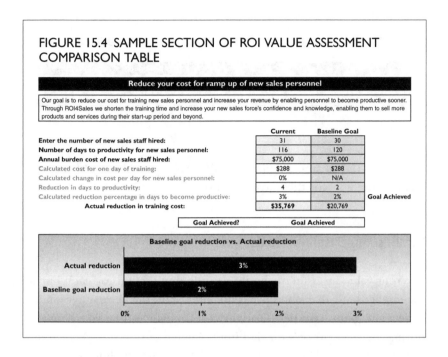

FIGURE 15.4 SAMPLE SECTION OF ROI VALUE ASSESSMENT COMPARISON TABLE

Reduce your cost for ramp up of new sales personnel

Our goal is to reduce our cost for training new sales personnel and increase your revenue by enabling personnel to become productive sooner. Through ROI4Sales we shorten the training time and increase your new sales force's confidence and knowledge, enabling them to sell more products and services during their start-up period and beyond.

	Current	Baseline Goal	
Enter the number of new sales staff hired:	31	30	
Number of days to productivity for new sales personnel:	116	120	
Annual burden cost of new sales staff hired:	$75,000	$75,000	
Calculated cost for one day of training:	$288	$288	
Calculated change in cost per day for new sales personnel:	0%	N/A	
Reduction in days to productivity:	4	2	
Calculated reduction percentage in days to become productive:	3%	2%	Goal Achieved
Actual reduction in training cost:	$35,769	$20,769	

Goal Achieved?	Goal Achieved

Baseline goal reduction vs. Actual reduction

equally important. Use the analysis to identify ways to improve performance going forward.

The following sections discuss each of these steps in more detail.

Defining KPI Goals

In Chapter 10 we discussed creating KPIs, a process that starts with your value statements. Remember, a value statement is the culmination of each line of your ROI Value Matrix. It is designed to help articulate the specific value that your products or services are capable of delivering to your prospects. The goal you want to enter into your value assessment rephrases the value statement you defined in Chapter 8. For example, if your value statement is "Reduce your cost of sale by shortening the sales cycle," then your goal would read "Our goal is to reduce the cost of sale." The goal defines the baseline measurement we are going to use to determine our success.

FIGURE 15.5 VALUE ASSESSMENT HEADER—GOAL DEFINED

Reduce your cost for ramp up of new sales personnel

Our goal is to reduce our cost for training new sales personnel and increase your revenue by enabling personnel to become productive sooner. Through ROI4Sales we shorten the training time and increase your new sales force's confidence and knowledge, enabling them to sell more products and services in their start-up period and beyond.

Figure 15.5 is an example of an ROI Value Assessment header that includes the goal for the current section of the assessment.

Establishing Baseline Goals

Your value assessment should include one section for each impact statement. Beneath each impact statement, show the percentage change in revenue gains, cost decreases, or cost avoidances that you estimated during the sales process for that impact statement on the Needs Analysis Questionnaire. These estimates are the primary baseline goal against which you will measure your customer's results, saying in effect, "Here is the data on which you based your purchase decision, and here are your actual results. How have we done?"

In the ROI Needs Analysis Questionnaire, the impact statement declares the value a typical customer receives from using your products or services. However, it is important to remember that the impact statement may not always be the baseline goal we want to measure for a specific customer. For example, in the previous chapter we built questions for several KPIs related to sales training. The first KPI, "Does your cost of sale exceed your budget?" led to the following impact statement: "The typical ROI selling customer reduces his or her sales cycle by 2 to 10 percent." Although this impact statement would appear to be the baseline measurement criteria, it is not. Reduce the cost of sale is the value metric in this example, and, in this case, it is a better reflection of what we need to measure. Remember, when we built our Needs Analysis Questionnaire, we stated that a reduced time to revenue (sales cycle reduction) will in fact reduce our customer's cost per sale based on the assumption that there is a cost for every day a sale remains unclosed—reduce the number of days and you also reduce the cost. In this instance we are tracking two metrics to determine the baseline goals: cost of sale reduction and sales cycle reduction. Cost of sale has the added benefit of being measurable in dollars.

Adding Other Supporting Data

In addition to measuring the KPIs, it is recommended that you add some of the following metrics to your value assessment documents (usually on the value assessment dashboard or summary page):

- Days between value assessments
- ROI percentage
- Internal rate of return (IRR)
- Initial investment versus project-to-date dollars and percentage returned
- Graphs for investment versus return
- Graphs for KPI baseline goals achieved versus goals not achieved
- KPI graph displaying original dollar goal versus current dollar goal achieved

There is no limit to the amount of information you can add or analyze when creating a value assessment dashboard summary sheet.

Comparing Baseline Figures to Results

Figure 15.6 compares the baseline information from a $60 million software company over the course of one year. The changes in the company's business during that time are reflected in the assessment. Pay special attention to the areas where we achieved a goal. Keep in mind that we do not always meet or exceed our customer's expectation. There are several calculations on the sheet where we did achieve a goal. We reduced both the customer's cost per sale and the length of the sales cycle, but the average sale was somewhat smaller than a year ago. In this type of situation, you and/or your customer may want to analyze the impact of the lower average sale amount on the cost of sale and sales cycle.

FIGURE 15.6 360 DEGREE VALUE ASSESSMENT WITH BASELINE
GOALS FOR COMPARISON

Reduce your cost of sale by shortening the sales cycle

	Current	Baseline	
Enter your annual revenue:	$62,000,000	$60,000,000	
Enter the number of sales that make up annual revenue:	525	500	
Calculated average sale:	$118,095	$120,000	Note: Revenue
Enter your cost of sale percentage:	37%	40%	Goal achieved
Calculated cost to close each opportunity:	$43,695	$48,000	Cost reduction
Enter your current sales cycle: (days)	145	150	Reduced cycle
Calculated/goal reduction in sales cycle:	5	6	
Goal/no. of days reduced in sales cycle:	N/A	144	
Calculated cost per day for outstanding sale:	$301	$320	WARNING
Percentage reduction in sales cycle:	3%	4%	WARNING
Actual reduction in cost of sale:	$791,034	$960,000	WARNING
+/– Baseline cost reduction goal:	($168,966)	<<Warning	

Figure 15.6 shows the baseline goals from our earlier example as they would appear in the value assessment. We constructed this example comparing our original data with current information from our customer.

There are several warning messages in the far right column that draw attention to areas where we did not achieve our goal. Notice that warning messages are applied only to areas where we measure a goal or success criteria. We simply put a note next to the field where the average revenue per closed deal declined.

T *i p*

The warning messages in the margins are "if . . . then" statements in your spreadsheet. You put an instruction in the cell that says, in essence, "If current is less than baseline, display warning."

As with the Needs Analysis Questionnaire and the dashboard, it is very important to clearly display the results of all of your calculations in the 360 Degree Value Assessment. The approach to creating these pages should be the same as the one you used to create the Needs Analysis Questionnaire. Show your math, keep it simple, and stay focused on the goal you are trying to help your customer achieve.

The format used for your value assessment can be as simple as that shown in Figure 15.6. Be sure to include text explaining what your goal is and how it is going to be achieved. This text will help explain the importance of measuring your progress against the original baseline goal from the Needs Analysis Questionnaire when you print the document and present it to your customer.

Adding Graphics

Like the ROI dashboard, the results of your value assessment are a sales tool. Therefore, we suggest you add graphical displays of key data to your design. For example, graph each value statement displaying the baseline goal and the amount achieved. The use of color is also very important to the presentation. Maintain consistency in your color scheme from the Needs Analysis Questionnaire, ROI Financial Dashboard, and ROI Value Assessment tools. As with the ROI dashboard, your value assessment is an analysis tool, and the data it contains should be easy to understand. Simple, well-planned graphs and charts help to accomplish this goal.

Figure 15.7 builds on the information displayed in Figure 15.6 by inserting a text box that describes the features used to drive the expected value. Also, we have inserted a graph displaying the value delivered. The use of color in these graphics enhances the visual appeal and readability of the presentation.

Analyzing the Assessment with Your Prospect

When you address your customers' issues using data gathered during a 360 Degree Value Assessment, you are sending an important message to your customers about your commitment to their success. There are ups and downs in the course of every vendor-customer relationship. The manner in which you identify and address situations that are not going well is what determines the additional revenue from, and lifetime value of, that customer. As you can see from the example in Figure 15.7, we did not fully achieve our goal in this case, but we did return over

FIGURE 15.7 360 DEGREE VALUE ASSESSMENT WITH EXPLANATORY TEXT AND GRAPH

Reduce your cost of sale by shortening the sales cycle

Our primary goal is to reduce your cost of sale. This goal can be achieved
by reducing the sales cycle. Each day a sale does not close,
an accumulated cost is associated with that opportunity.

	Current	Baseline	
Enter your annual revenue:	$62,000,000	$60,000,000	
Enter the number of sales that make up your annual revenue:	525	500	
Calculated average sale percentage:	$118,095	$120,000	Note: Revenue
Enter your cost of sale percentage:	37%	40%	Goal achieved
Calculated cost to close each opportunity:	$43,695	$48,000	Cost reduction
Enter your current sales cycle: (days)	145	150	Reduced cycle
Calculated/goal reduction in sales cycle:	5	6	
Goal/no. of days reduced in sales cycle:		144	
Calculated cost per day for outstanding sale:	$301	$320	WARNING
Percentage reduction in sales cycle:	3%	4%	WARNING
Actual cost reduction in cost of sale:	$791,034	**$960,000**	WARNING
+/– Baseline cost reduction goal:	($168,966)	<<Warning	

$750,000 in cost reduction. This is an opportunity to discuss the project with your customers to determine their level of satisfaction and decide whether additional actions are required to meet their goals.

When you review the 360 Degree ROI Value Assessment results, analyzing areas that may require attention and improvement can lead to revenue-increasing opportunities for your organization. Perhaps a particular customer needs additional products, consulting services, or an upgrade. The review of this customer's current situation and comparison with the original Needs Analysis Questionnaire provides a context and sets a tone for you to drive customer satisfaction and, potentially, additional revenue.

When your customers aren't realizing success, it is important that your organization be prepared to manage the situation. Identifying the issue can be the most critical success factor. Although some customers take the "squeaky wheel" approach, the majority may never let you know that they are not achieving all of the results they expected from your products or services. Companies that fail to pursue a proactive approach of measuring and addressing customer results and satisfaction run the risk of letting dissatisfied customers become ticking time bombs.

Figure 15.8 is a value assessment that uses data from another example we have discussed previously: increasing revenue by increasing your close ratio on marketing-generated leads. In this value assessment, we

---

FIGURE 15.8 360 DEGREE VALUE ASSESSMENT MEASURING TWO BASELINE GOALS

Increase revenue by increasing your close ratio on marketing-generated leads

	Current	Baseline	
Enter your annual marketing budget:	$4,000,000	$4,200,000	Note: Change warning: lead reduction
Enter the number of leads generated annually:	2000	2100	
Average sale calculated from above:	$118,095	$120,000	
Enter your close ratio for leads generated by marketing programs:	5%	4%	Goal achieved
Goal/calculated change in close ratio:	25%	10%	Goal achieved
Calculated/number of leads closed from lead-generated programs:	100	84	
Goal/actual additional sales opportunities closed:	16	8.4	
Calculated revenue for leads generated from marketing programs:	$11,809,500	$10,080,000	
Calculated cost per closed lead:	$40,000	$50,000	Goal achieved
Calculated cost avoidance per closed lead:	$10,000	$4,545	
Actual annual cost avoidance per closed lead:	$87,280	$38,178	
Annual increase in revenue per lead:	$1,889,520	$1,008,000	
Estimated value delivered:	$1,976,800	Goal Achieved	
Percentage of baseline goal:	189%	Goal Achieved	

measure two baseline goals, resulting in both a cost avoidance and a revenue increase simultaneously.

In this example, we have introduced a new element: *percentage of baseline goal*, a key figure in our analysis of both this specific line item and the entire project. The baseline percentage is the percentage by which we are above or below our original estimated savings. Whether it is a cost reduction or revenue increase, the baseline percentage will tell us if we are over or under our baseline goal.

Keep in mind that even if you are only at 50 percent of the baseline goal, you have added value for your customer. In this example, we have achieved 189 percent of the baseline goal, which means we have returned almost double our original estimates. If we had only produced 50 percent of the baseline goal, the customer's return would still have been $504,000. The point: a half-million dollar return is worth noting. When you conduct 360 Degree ROI Value Assessments, you are virtually certain to find that you are over on some items and under on others.

When you build your 360 Degree ROI Value Assessment for each of the value statements, include a summary of baseline percentages to give your customers a very quick, dashboard-like view of your overall performance on the project. In addition, make it easy for your customer to "drill down" into each baseline percentage figure and analyze the current situation versus your original baseline goal.

Figure 15.9 is an example of a 360 Degree Value Assessment table we used to analyze a recent project.

This table (Figure 15.9) is designed around the ROI on a sales training model. In the first column, we listed each of the key pain indicators. Next we listed the baseline goal, followed by the value actually achieved. Then we calculated and displayed the percentage of baseline achieved—the current amount divided by the baseline goal. In the last column, we like to include a status for each of the KPIs. This status can be as simple as "Goal achieved" or "Warning," or it can be complex, displaying more details about the issue or problem. You need good data and a reasonable degree of proficiency in spreadsheet design to add the logic on this line for a complex analysis. Your financial department may be a useful resource to help you develop the logic.

FIGURE 15.9 VALUE ASSESSMENT TABLE

Key PAIN Indicator	Original Baseline Goal	Current	Percent of Baseline Achieved	Goal Status
Cost of sale reductions:	$ 960,000	$ 791,034	82%	Warning
Lead-generation cost reductions:	$ 38,178	$ 87,280	229%	Goal achieved
Marketing lead-generation program revenue increases:	$1,008,000	$1,889,520	187%	Goal achieved
Revenue increase from more sales reps above quota:	$ 400,000	$ 265,000	66%	Warning
Revenue increases from additional channel sales:	$ 350,000	$ 305,000	87%	Warning
Summary total>>	$2,756,178	$3,337,834	121%	Goal achieved

Summary

The concepts and techniques you learned in this chapter can be applied regardless of the ROI model you use to measure value during the sales process. If you followed the ROI Selling model from Chapter 1 forward, then the information in this chapter is simply a repeat with a twist. That twist, of course, is the baseline measurements used to compare the value you have delivered with the customer's starting point and with the goals you established in the sales process.

Here are some reminders of the keys to building a successful 360 Degree ROI Value Assessment tool and program you learned in this chapter:

- Selling does not end when the sale closes—360 Degree ROI helps you capture revenue after the close.
- 360 Degree ROI Value Assessments give you a competitive advantage.

- Use 360 Degree ROI to manage your customer relationships proactively.
- Establish the measurement criteria during the sales process.
- Use the data gathered to support your ROI impact statements.
- The impact statement is not always the baseline goal.
- Use color and warning messages to draw attention to areas where your product or service delivers the most value.
- A picture is worth a thousand words . . . use graphics throughout the assessment.
- Even a modest amount of value delivered is worth measuring and noting.
- Measure success by displaying the percentage of baseline delivered.

INTEGRATING ROI INTO YOUR SALES AND MARKETING PROCESSES

"The absolute fundamental aim is to make money out of satisfying customers."
SIR JOHN EGAN (b. 1939), Jaguar

16

ROI IN
THE SALES PROCESS

By working through Parts One and Two of *ROI Selling,* you have invested a lot of time and effort in developing a compelling ROI model to calculate and display the value your products or services are capable of delivering to your customers. Now comes the good part—putting your model to work. This chapter tells you how to use your ROI Selling model to help increase your effectiveness at each stage of the sales cycle. *The information in this chapter is not intended to replace your current selling methodology.* Instead, use these suggestions to enhance your sales methods by incorporating ROI into your existing process. The ROI value justification concepts and tools we describe in this book can enhance the effectiveness of virtually any sales process or methodology you may have in place today. As you learn in the next chapter, ROI may also be integrated into your Sales Force Automation system (SFA) regardless of what SFA system you use. For these reasons, industry leader Sales Performance International (SPI) has incorporated our concepts and technology into its Solution Selling® suite.

ROI and value justification are becoming must-have components in the selling equation. The ROI Insider on http://www.searchCIO.com states that "more than 80 percent of IT buyers now rely on vendors to help them quantify the value proposition of solutions. In fact, many CIOs [chief information officers] now elevate the ability of vendors to

R *O I* *in* *a* C *h a n g i n g* M *a r k e t p l a c e*

The following insight from Steve Smidler, VP of Marketing with Rockwell Automation, underscores the importance of being able to develop and present a compelling and credible value justification analysis as part of your overall sales process, given the changing rules and roles of business-to-business sales and procurement. Rockwell Automation is a very successful 100-year-old company that develops and sells factory automation equipment to manufacturers. Smidler has this to say in regard to the shift from local to global vendor-customer relationships, with an increased emphasis on services rather than products, where sales are often conducted with executives rather than technical staff:

Can a technical sales force, whose focus has been on the technical buyer, driving toward the perfect set of feature / benefits to meet a specification or a technology strategy . . . be trained to be effective in front of an executive-level audience? In our company, we have found we can make this transformation, and one of the keys to our success is the ROI model that you are learning in this book. For us, we are transforming to a value-selling culture by leveraging industry solutions and long-standing relationships with our technical buyers. We see opportunity in helping technical buyers sell up in their organizations and also helping the executive buyer with P&L responsibility align value-driven, bundled product and service solutions with company financial objectives for revenue growth and cost containment.

To show how we've delivered value in the past, our relationships with technical buyers have helped us gather "proof points" of value delivered. To show how we can deliver value in the present, we leverage the trust our clients have put in us in solving their business problems for the past 100 years. And to show how we can deliver value in the future, we use the ROI model to build a credible case of forecasted value for value-add solutions that fully leverage the products responsible for our historical success.

The results? We trained our best and brightest to sell on value, and we didn't have to hire a new sales force. We shifted the focus from discounting to delivery. When we make calls, we are more interested in understanding our prospects' biggest business problems and how they are measuring success in solving those problems. For the first time in our history, we are aligning our value-driven solutions in the language of ROI our clients are using in the boardroom.

We understand more than ever what it means to be a partner our clients trust with helping them solve their problems. *Our future depends on it.*

proactively justify their solutions to one of the top five most important selection criteria."

My father, a salesman his entire life, taught me a valuable lesson with this saying: "As a salesman, you have two ears and one mouth; use them in that proportion!" He would follow that with this: "If you want to help people in sales, ask them about their problems, and then sit back and listen. People like to talk about themselves and their issues." After all these years, I still think he's right. There are thousands of books, articles, seminars, workshops, and even movies about ways to improve the sales process. And they all have one thing in common with ROI Selling: They recommend that you ask a lot of questions!

What we find missing in the vast majority of these programs, however, is solid guidance on how to develop the questions so that decisions can be made by both the salesperson and the buyer. This is just one way that an objective and credible ROI model separates lightweight ROI marketing ploys from substantive ROI analysis tools.

In this chapter, we discuss seven steps of the typical sales cycle and how best to incorporate the ROI Needs Analysis Questionnaire, ROI Financial Dashboard, and 360 Degree ROI follow-up Value Assessment into that cycle. You learn how to use the ROI information and materials you gather and create in qualifying your prospects, demonstrating solutions, creating and presenting your proposal, and shortening the sales cycle. You also learn how to use the 360 Degree ROI follow-up program to drive increased customer satisfaction and increased revenues from postsale opportunities.

Key Concepts and Guidelines

Important guidelines for incorporating ROI techniques and materials in your sales process, to achieve the most benefit from this program, are listed below. Each concept is a stepping-stone to integrating ROI into every aspect of the sale, including a postsale assessment, as described in Chapter 15, "360 Degree ROI Selling":

- **Use questions to inform both buyer and seller.** Your questions are not merely tools to gather data; they serve to educate buyers as well. Through a detailed questioning process, using the Needs Analysis Questionnaire as a guide, you help customers understand the tangible cost of their current issues, pains, and goals in addition to the benefits they can expect to receive as a result of using your products or services. The ROI Financial Dashboard also helps your customers or prospects understand the specific value of those benefits as well as the cost of waiting. Finally, your Needs Analysis Questionnaire's benefit statement describes specifically how you intend to provide the value you are proposing to deliver. This benefit statement can serve as the "silent salesperson" on the proposal.
- **Use ROI Selling to demonstrate the costs of the status quo.** Using ROI Selling in the sales process helps your prospects understand the cost of doing nothing (status quo), the estimated value your products or services deliver, and how current costs continue to accumulate if they do nothing.
- **Close the sale at the right time.** Using ROI in the sales process helps to reduce your time to revenue and minimizes the risk of losing the sale. The sales process can be analyzed using a bell curve, whose horizontal axis is time and vertical axis is interest; the downside of the curve illustrates the period within the sales process when customers or prospects begin to lose interest. The key to using ROI in the sales process is to close sales as near that point as possible, reducing the time to revenue and increasing the likelihood of successful outcomes. The timing of your use of ROI techniques within the sales cycle is the central idea in this chapter.
- **Allow prospects to tell you the impact.** At a certain point in the selling process, you need to update your ROI model with the esti-

mated impact your products or services have on your prospects' business. The key to this transaction is allowing your prospects to provide you with the estimated percentage to use to calculate the potential savings your products or services provide. This interaction with prospects gives them ownership of the results projected by your model.

- **Drive customer loyalty.** Postsale ROI programs like the 360 Degree ROI Value Assessment promote customer loyalty, reduce your annual customer turnover, and create opportunities to generate more revenue from your customer base.

- **Document decision making.** Some products, especially intangibles like software, are subject to scope creep after the sale. Scope creep describes the phenomenon of customer attention and prioritizes shifting from the goals and objectives that drove the sale to encompass other needs and desires during the product implementation phase. As one vendor put it: "Customers buy based on an 80 percent fit to their needs and then quickly focus on the 20 percent that they knew wasn't there when they bought." With a documented ROI Selling model going into the sale and the 360 Degree ROI Value Assessment program after the sale, you can keep the implementation of your products or services focused on the key requirements and benefits that drove the purchase decision—and you can remind customers of the value they are receiving in fulfillment of their original goals.

- **Create a partnership with prospects.** Mike Mullin of GEAC said it best: "Using ROI in the sales process has changed the paradigm between salesperson and vendor. We are now subject matter experts and clearly show our customers and prospects that we have their best interests at heart. ROI Selling has turned the vendor-customer relationship into a partnership relationship."

- **ROI Selling is value justification, not cost justification.** You must understand the value your products produce to effectively use ROI Selling in the sales process. When selling value, you're taking a positive and proactive approach to selling. When justifying costs, you're taking the reactive approach of "defending" your price and may have already lost the deal. There is a big difference between knowing your products' features and knowing the value they deliver. Understanding the difference between product features and customer value also helps salespeople identify the real decision makers. As Jimmy Touchstone from Solution Selling explains: "You typically know you are not talking to power when customers or prospects focus on how much it costs as opposed to, What is the value I am receiving for this investment?"

R O I S e l l i n g I n c r e a s e s P e r c e i v e d V a l u e

Ted Matwijec is the director of Business Development & Alliances for Arena Software, a Rockwell Company. Ted told us how his company has greatly increased its perceived value with prospects through the use of ROI Selling:

In the past three to four years there has been a known phenomenon in the software industry of high cost overruns of integrating software like Enterprise Resource Planning (ERP) and Supply Chain Management (SCM) by major corporations. This issue has caused customers to rethink their major purchases. You can go to most IT directors today and ask about ERP or SCM implementations and see their eyes roll back in their heads as they describe a sinkhole of money they spent with little or no financial justification. This has caused a backlash in the software industry of some sort. Gone are the days when a client would simply purchase with the view that "adding software" would provide value and bottom-line results.

From our work with ROI Selling, we developed a comprehensive ROI model that showed all the aspects of value our software and services deliver. We knew we needed a sales tool that would help us overcome the myths and fear of purchasing enterprise software. We needed to position our application as a valid solution that would guarantee return.

The results have been outstanding. Our products' and services' business has increased sharply in sales since deploying ROI Selling. Why? The perception by the client is that Arena offers real value with a valid return on investment in a purchase or consulting engagement. We are not a simple purchase anymore nor a potential cost overrun project waiting to happen. We are a true asset that can improve our customers' business by improving their bottom lines.

- **Use ROI to offer risk assessment, not risk elimination.** ROI models don't eliminate risk, but there is less need for value justification with low-risk projects. However, when risk becomes real and important, value justification is used to mitigate the risk by offering several metrics for comparison. For example, in Chapter 13, "Designing the ROI Needs Analysis Questionnaire Interface," you learned the importance of including a valid and credible impact statement on all Needs Analysis Questionnaires. You've also learned that in the ROI Financial Dashboard you should compare your customers' or prospects' current situation to an industry benchmark. Both of these techniques help to relieve your prospects' worry about the risk in a potential investment during the sales process.

ROI Selling and the Seven Steps of the Sales Cycle

Figure 16.1 shows a simple sales cycle chart based on a bell curve. The horizontal axis is time; remember that in the sales process, time is our enemy. We want to keep this line as short as possible. The vertical axis represents the prospect's interest in you, your company, your products, and the sales process. As you and a buyer move through the sales process, time continues to tick away, and you move further down the horizontal time axis.

There is a point in every sales process when your prospects have all the information they are looking for. Up to that point, the prospects' interest has continued to build. The peak of clients' interest usually occurs at the point at which they have seen the product presentations, have the appropriate product literature, and know the price. This is a critical point for a salesperson; if you don't close the sale within a reasonable period after this point in the sales process, you will likely lose the opportunity. Now you need to *shorten the time to revenue.* By utilizing ROI in each step of the sales process, you enhance your chances to close deals sooner and reduce the time to revenue significantly.

To best illustrate ROI in the sales process, we have developed a generic set of steps to represent the sales cycle. Our sample sales process has seven steps leading up to the close:

FIGURE 16.1 THE SALES PROCESS BELL CURVE

Step 1. **Target.** At this stage a company is targeted as a potential prospect. A target must meet your company's defined marketing criteria—that is, have a budget and a motive to buy.

Step 2. **Qualify.** A qualified company is one that must have one or more key pain indicators we identified when building our ROI model.

Step 3. **Meet and greet.** At this stage you meet with the prospect to confirm the KPIs you have identified, establish the current situation with the Needs Analysis Questionnaire, and possibly introduce the 360 Degree ROI concept.

Step 4. **Presentation.** At this stage you present to the prospect a demonstration of what your products and services are capable of delivering based on the responses the prospect has given. You once again confirm the KPIs and establish the impact you'll have on the prospect's business.

Step 5. **Propose.** The stage in which you present a written plan for the sale that includes an executive summary of the key ROI information you've gathered. At this stage you also discuss the ROI Financial Dashboard and confirm the value you expect to deliver.

Step 6. **Due diligence.** Your prospect verifies that you are capable of delivering the value you've proposed by using independent research as well as data you've provided for financial savings comparisons.

Step 7. **Pending sale.** At this stage the legal departments negotiate the final sale and you work out the details of the ROI Value Assessment program with your prospect.

Obviously, in some sales situations there are numerous meetings, multiple presentations, and so on as you move through the various stages. Using these seven stages as an example for discussion, we assume that you move a sale from stage to stage on completing some agreed-on criteria.

In Figure 16.2, we have placed the seven stages (plus the close) over our bell curve graphic to illustrate the point at which your prospect's interest begins to decline. As we work through the examples in this chapter, we discuss the role of ROI in each stage of the sales process and discuss how you can use ROI Selling to shorten the sales process and win more sales opportunities.

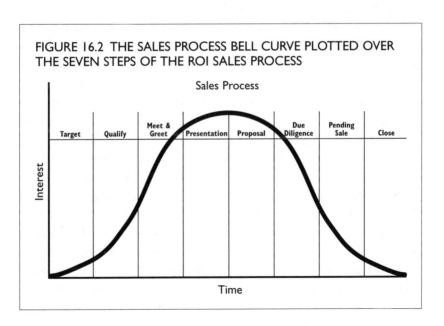

FIGURE 16.2 THE SALES PROCESS BELL CURVE PLOTTED OVER THE SEVEN STEPS OF THE ROI SALES PROCESS

The Target Stage

This is the first step in the sample sales process. Typically, a target is one of a list of companies that your sales personnel will pursue for qualification into their pipeline. For a target company to move on to the qualify stage, it must:

- Meet some minimum marketing criteria; for example, produce a certain amount of revenue, fall into a particular industry, or be on the Fortune 500 list of fastest-growing companies.
- Have a budget that equals or exceeds our minimum cost requirements.
- Have a motive to purchase a product or service like yours.

The following sections discuss these tasks in detail.

Posing Qualifying Questions

To move an account from target stage to qualify stage, you ask a series of qualifying questions derived from your ROI Value Matrix. These questions should be drawn from the general information section of your Needs Analysis Questionnaire, in which you gather information that applies to multiple line items in your ROI model. These questions provide big picture information about your prospects, such as annual revenues, employee head count, and so on, and help you sort through the numerous leads you receive and narrow the targets to those most likely to buy from you.

To qualify a target, you pose a series of qualifying questions based on minimum qualifying criteria. You establish these minimum criteria by simply looking into your own customer base and analyzing the trends in the areas you are using as a basis for qualification. For example, if revenue is an important factor, look at your customer base and determine the low end and high end of the range of revenue your customers produce annually. Set your minimum and maximum criteria based on some relationship to these values; for example, within 20 percent of the range. Here are sample questions companies selling B2B (business-to-business) products might use for qualifying prospective customers:

- What is your annual revenue?
- How many full-time employees do you have?
- Did you have steady growth year-over-year for the past five years?
- Do you sell B2B over your Web site?

If the prospect's responses don't meet the minimum criteria, you don't consider them for qualification into your pipeline. The prospect will either remain a target or be removed from the list altogether.

As you learned in Part One, the foundation for a credible and objective ROI Selling program begins with defining why people buy your products in the first place (why buy statements), what specific issues and pains (business issues) are driving this particular prospect, and the specific results (desired outcomes) stakeholders want as a resolution. You can draw these items from the Needs Analysis Questionnaire to qualify targets during this first step of the sales cycle.

Consider the example of training tools like Solution Selling®, which we refer to frequently in this book. When we worked with Sales Performance International (SPI) to develop an ROI Selling program for Solution Selling, we determined that the following comments indicate the desired outcomes people seek when buying these tools:

- "I want to reduce our cost of sale."
- "I want to increase our revenue per closed lead."
- "I need to reduce the amount of time spent conducting account debriefs with my sales team."
- "Our sales team is discounting too much and we need to show more value."

Determining Whether the Target Meets Minimum Marketing Criteria

Once we determine that a target meets the minimum business criteria, we further qualify the target by using questions from our KPI (key pain indicator) input forms to determine whether the target fits minimum marketing criteria—in other words, whether this target's situation and needs match the range of products or services your company offers. From the four comments listed above indicating reasons to buy sales training tools, for example, we created several KPI questions to use during the target stage to qualify a prospect into our pipeline:

- How long is your sales cycle?
- What is your cost of sale?
- What is your close ratio on marketing-generated leads?
- How much time do you spend weekly on account debriefs?
- What is your average discount per sales opportunity?

Each response needs to be measured against minimum response criteria, and you may want to measure against maximum response criteria also; for example, some opportunities may be too large for you to handle. The table in Figure 16.3 illustrates the concept of minimum response criteria. In the left column are the qualifying questions; across from each question on the right is the minimum response required to consider a target a prospect. Creating this type of table is a useful exercise if you don't already know your minimum and maximum requirements for moving a target to a qualified lead.

This methodology helps you quickly determine whether a target company is a qualified prospect. Your qualifying questions should always be driven by the value you expect to deliver. To effectively accomplish this, it is imperative that you understand the value your company, products, and services are capable of delivering to your customers. Tim Sullivan, VP of Marketing for SPI, points out: "If you are not ready to walk, you are not ready to sell." "Walking" in this context means really under-

FIGURE 16.3 KPI/QUALIFIED CANDIDATE RESPONSE TABLE

Qualifying Question	Minimum Qualified Candidate Response
What is your cost of sale?	At least 30%
What is your close ratio on marketing-generated leads?	No more than 20%
How much time do you spend weekly conducting account debriefs?	No less than one hour
What is your average discount per sales opportunity?	At least 25%

standing the value your products and services deliver. ROI Selling gives your salespeople the confidence to ask the right person the right questions at the right time in the sales process.

Gathering General Needs Analysis Data

The process of questioning your targeted prospects is about establishing their "pain points" through directed questioning. As you qualify your targets, you are educating them at the same time you are gathering information regarding their business issues and KPIs. Determining what questions to ask and when and how to ask them contributes to qualifying targets and to positioning your company and products for the overall sales cycle.

T *i p*

Use this first stage of the sales process to separate real prospects from "tire kickers." We find one simple question, such as "Help me understand why you are looking for a product like ours," serves this purpose. Serious buyers should be able to provide a much more detailed response to this question than does someone who says, "Oh, I just want to keep up-to-date with what is on the market."

Ask yourself why this customer or prospect *wouldn't* buy from you. Is the answer because you aren't the cheapest or because you don't add more value than the competition? The answers to these questions describe two types of buyers:

- The first is the *price shopper,* one who buys based on lowest price. Our recommendation is to stay out of price-shopper deals because everyone loses!
- The type of buyer you want to do business with is the *value buyer.* Price may be important to value buyers but only from the standpoint of asking themselves what value is delivered for the price they're paying. If value buyers don't purchase from you, in most cases either the prospects don't agree that the KPIs you have defined are issues or they don't feel the pain. This is why you build your KPIs from the business issues defined in the ROI Value Matrix you created in Part One. Your questions should make your prospect *feel* the pain or issue.

Brent Jackson, an account manager with CrossAccess, told us that he enjoys having the KPI discussion with his customers and prospects. Brent said he "wants to see the hair stand up on the back of their necks." That is how he knows he hit a nerve and can help these people with their true pain. Brent further explains: "Bonding is a big part of the questioning process. I make the interview an educational experience for both of us. I am learning about a prospect's pain, and at the same time the prospect is learning about our capabilities to resolve the pain or issue."

The Qualify Stage

The qualify stage is the second step in the selling process, in which we identify a prospect's key pain indicators. You use the Needs Analysis Questionnaire throughout the qualify stage to gather information and assess the value your products and services can deliver to this opportunity. The responses you receive to your questions help you decide whether this prospect is worth pursuing. This step of the sales cycle involves these three phases:

1. Identify key pain indicators
2. Ask KPI questions
3. Quantify current situation with needs analysis questions

Identifying KPIs and Asking KPI Questions

To identify and confirm prospects' key pain indicators, we interview prospects and ask if they are experiencing the KPIs we have identified in our ROI Selling model. The source for those KPIs is our business issue statements (see Part Two, Chapter 10).

The interview process during the qualify stage should be conversational. There is no need at this point to formally introduce the fact you want to conduct an ROI with the Needs Analysis Questionnaire. Our experience shows that by simply identifying the KPIs and confirming the needs analysis questions, you are establishing the foundation you need to build a partnership relationship—not merely a vendor-salesperson relationship. Keep in mind that at the same time you are qualifying your customers or prospects, they are evaluating *their* options. Your questions will help them decide these questions:

- Are you prepared and professional?
- Do you know what you are talking about?
- Do you know and understand their business?
- What can they learn from you?
- Do they want to deal with you?

Remember that in the example we used earlier to illustrate the target stage, we gathered the prospect's current cost of sale, close ratios, and the amount of time spent on account debriefs. We now use KPI questions to confirm the pain point and help the prospect "feel" his or her pain. Every time you ask your customer or prospect a KPI question and receive a yes or other positive response, you are emphasizing the prospect's pain point. The table in Figure 16.4 illustrates several business issue statements from the sales training programs example and the KPI questions we wrote in association with those issues.

Figure 16.5 illustrates how you begin with a KPI question. If the response from your prospect is positive (yes), then you move on to asking the needs analysis questions that relate to that KPI. If the response is negative (no), then you move on to the next KPI question.

FIGURE 16.4 BUSINESS ISSUES/KPI QUESTIONS

Business Issues/Sales Training Programs	Qualifying KPI Questions
. . . because the sales cycle is too long and our costs continue to rise as the deals linger.	• Is your cost of sale too high?
. . . because the cost of our marketing programs continues to rise with no increase in close ratios.	• Is your close ratio high enough on marketing-generated leads?
. . . because too much time is taken up weekly for our sales representatives and managers doing account debriefs.	• Do your weekly account debriefs take longer than you would like?

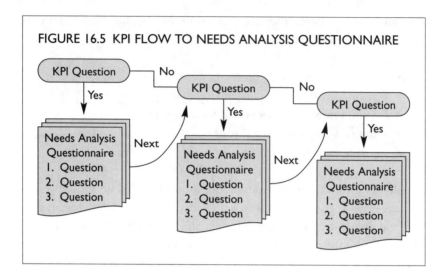

FIGURE 16.5 KPI FLOW TO NEEDS ANALYSIS QUESTIONNAIRE

The key to a quality interview and qualification program is developing questions that drive prospects to the features you defined when building the ROI Value Matrix. Using our sales training example, we identified three KPIs:

- Is your cost of sale too high?
- Is your close ratio too low on marketing-generated leads?
- Is your staff wasting time on account debriefs?

As we learned in Part Two, each KPI leads to a series of questions that we can use to gather additional information to help us calculate the current level of pain and the potential value we are capable of delivering. Each question you ask must return a quantifiable answer that you can use in the ROI Needs Analysis Questionnaire. Figure 16.6 illustrates how we link the KPI to a set of questions written to produce quantifiable results.

Assessing the Current Situation

The qualify stage is one of the most vital steps in the sales process. The KPIs and needs analysis questions help you determine whether a particular prospect is worth pursuing and also give you a basis for demonstrating knowledge and professionalism leading to enhanced cred-

FIGURE 16.6 KPI TO KPI QUESTIONS LINK

KPI	KPI Questions
• Cost of sale is too high.	• What is your current cost of sale? • How long is your current sales cycle?
• Close ratio is too low.	• What is your current close ratio on marketing-generated leads? • How many marketing programs generate leads annually? • What is the annual marketing-lead generation budget?
• Weekly account debriefs take too much time.	• How much time is spent weekly on account debriefs? • Annual cost for sales representative and manager?

ibility throughout the sales cycle. The exchange of information at this stage is primarily used to identify a prospect's pains, issues, and goals, establish the current level of pain the prospect is experiencing, and gather critical information for your ROI model.

Jim Kanir, VP of Sales at Unify, tells us: "Sometimes those quantifiable type of questions make prospects squirm. They don't want to admit to themselves (or others) the high level of pain they are currently experiencing as it relates to a business issue or KPI." We have repeatedly stressed the importance of calculating the current situation to your success in building an ROI model. Every value you expect to deliver based on the ROI model starts with the cost to the prospect of the current situation.

Meet-and-Greet Stage

Meet and greet is the third stage in our sample sales process. This is the stage in which you meet your prospect either face-to-face or via a teleconference to accomplish the following items:

- Confirm data you've gathered regarding KPIs
- Introduce ROI and the concept of 360 Degree ROI Value Assessments
- Introduce the importance of impact statements

Confirming Your Needs Analysis Data

Start by confirming the KPIs identified during the target and qualify stage with such a statement as, "We discussed the following issues you are experiencing. . . ." Also, verify the data gathered to support the KPI calculations and identify any additional pains, issues, or goals this customer or prospect may endure. Once again, this is the conversation that leads to the introduction of the ROI model and the 360 Degree ROI Value Assessment.

Introducing the ROI Model and 360 Degree ROI

This is also the stage in which we recommend that you introduce your ROI model and the 360 Degree ROI to your prospects. Introducing this program is an excellent opportunity to set your company apart from the competition and prove to your customers or prospects their value to you and your organization. In our conversation with Aberdeen VP Brian Sommer, he pointed out that "customers feel they are important during the sales process, when executives visit and discuss their value and all their plans. Once the opportunity closes, the executives

---

P a r t n e r i n g   w i t h   P r o s p e c t s

After implementing ROI Selling at GEAC, we discussed that company's model and its success with General Manager Mike Mullen. He tells us the following:

> When you use ROI models to drive your sales process, you are now a strategic partner with your prospects. You are helping them define the value they need and want from an application to reduce their cost and potentially increase their revenue. When you go on their site to meet them face-to-face, this will become evident. You will be treated more like a partner, consultant, or subject matter expert in their space.

(Remember, you should also be armed with industry averages and research data prospects want to know about and compare their business to.)

move on, and the customer is now left with only the account manager. Therein lies the disintegration of the relationship." By making a value assessment program part of your sales process, you are preserving and reinforcing your relationship with your customers by establishing a plan for future meetings and follow-up. When you introduce the 360 Degree ROI methodology, you are beginning the process of managing your prospects proactively.

Introducing the Importance of Impact Statements

It is critical during the meet-and-greet stage to show a sample ROI model with the impact statements already filled in. These statements define results produced for other customers and encourage the current customer to think about quantifying his or her own potential returns. It also enforces the importance of gathering quality data that you'll use in the presentation step of the sales cycle. You must know what product features you need to present to resolve your prospect's issues and estimate the impact you'll have on the prospect's KPIs. The questions you ask at this meeting are vital, not only to the success of your presentation or demonstration, but also to your proposal and, ultimately, to your client's success after the sale. Be sure you are presenting the right questions to the right stakeholders. The exercise of establishing a stakeholder for each why buy, business issue, and desired outcome you went through when building the ROI Value Matrix (Part One, Chapter 4) will help you further understand the importance of this point.

Presentation Stage

The presentation stage is the fourth step in the sales process. Use your presentation to demonstrate your ability to resolve your prospect's pains, issues, and goals as defined on the Needs Analysis Questionnaire, and establish the impact your products or services will have on the KPIs defined. Your presentations can be a product demonstration or something as simple as a Microsoft PowerPoint slide show. The point of the presentation is to show your prospect that your products or services are capable of delivering the value you're estimating.

ROI plays a dual role in the presentation stage. First, it is an opportunity to collect and confirm the final pieces of data needed to complete your Needs Analysis Questionnaire, including establishing goals for the ROI categories you have defined on the KPIs. Second, it is an opportunity to pinpoint the greatest value you have to offer and obtain your prospect's buy-in by updating the impact statement.

Delivering the Presentation

Up to this point you have been asking questions that drive value. Now you will shift your focus to presenting the value you intend to deliver based on the responses the prospect has given you to date. We suggest that prior to the presentation you take your prospect through the questions and answers you have completed thus far. This will help secure buy-in to the KPIs and will also ensure you are presenting the right materials.

Several approaches can be taken when bringing up the concept of impact statements and their affect on the ROI model. One method is to make it clear that after the presentation you and the prospect will jointly update the impact statements on the ROI model. Another approach our salespeople have taken when presenting the ROI model is to just collect the answers to the Needs Analysis Questionnaire without showing the calculations. If you choose this approach once you have all the data, estimate the impact based on historical 360 Degree ROI data from other customers (discussed in Chapter 15) and present the final completed ROI model to your prospect for discussion. We prefer the up-front method, whereby you discuss the impact prior to the presentation and then complete the impact statement field with the prospect's input.

During a presentation, don't be tempted to show "cool" features unrelated to the ROI value your prospects are expecting. It is crucial for your success to keep driving prospects to the areas where you offer the most value. By doing this you are establishing the measurement against which all other vendors will be evaluated.

Adding the Impact Statement

As part of the buy-in process, you are going to establish goals (impacts) for your customer or prospect to achieve when using your products or services. Our sales training example demonstrates how the training program helps to reduce the cost of sale by reducing the sales cycle. During the presentation step in this example, we would confirm that the prospect's goal is to reduce the sales cycle and establish a measurable goal for the amount of reduction the prospect is trying to achieve.

This action will come naturally if you have introduced your ROI model in an earlier stage. This is the question your prospect is expecting: "Our typical customers reduce their XXX by X percent to Y percent. Based on the presentation we just saw, what sort of a goal do you want to establish in the ROI model to measure the value you expect us to deliver?" This question commits the prospect to participation in building the ROI model and estimating the value expected to be received. Keep in mind that if you subscribe to the 360 Degree ROI model, you are also committing to measuring what you delivered at some point in the future.

The Proposal Stage

Step five in our sample sales process, the proposal stage, is when everything finally comes together. Our friend Bob Kantin from SalesProposals .com tells us: "A winning proposal helps the buyer make an informed decision." Including compelling ROI data is a great way to create a winning proposal, so it astonishes us how often return on investment is not included in proposals. An executive summary including ROI in your proposal will tie together the investment, benefit, and expected return. The proposal stage of the sales cycle involves these phases:

- Summarizing the KPIs
- Including "current cost of pain information" as a baseline
- Presenting and explaining the ROI Financial Dashboard
- Restating your impact statements

As you put together the investment figures or pricing, it is necessary to go back and review the agreed-on value you are expected to deliver (your impact statement). This review should include what we like to call a litmus test. Ask yourself the following questions: (1) *Are the figures realistic?* and (2) *Are the goals attainable?* Sales methodology vendors typically call this process a preproposal review—an opportunity to take one last look at the investment, value, expectations, layout, and design.

Summarizing the KPIs

Your ROI information within the proposal (KPIs, Needs Analysis Questionnaire, and ROI Financial Dashboard) must include your prospect's answers to questions and the agreed-on impact statements or baseline goals. We recommend you include a paragraph or two explaining the process you undertook to obtain and confirm the answers that are included in the documents.

Current Situation–Critical

The current situation defines the level of existing pain your prospect is feeling. It is important to state clearly that you are resolving the current pain or issue. The use of benefit statements (explained in Chapter 11) helps your proposal to explain how you intend to resolve the pain, issue, or goal. Finally, remember that the impact you are proposing is based on a cost reduction, cost avoidance, or revenue increase compared with the prospect's current situation, as documented through the needs analysis questions. Therefore, it is critical that your stakeholders understand the current cost of their pain, which in turn drives home the cost of not buying from you. You must continue to focus on *their* issues, pains, and goals—not on *your* features and benefits.

Presenting the ROI Dashboard

Bob Kantin tells us that "proposals should follow an 80/20 rule: 80 percent of the wording is the same for most customers; the remainder is buyer specific." The value justification data created during the Needs Analysis Questionnaire process is a key element in the buyer-specific data you should include in your proposal. The first section of your proposal should be your "recommendation report," a report made up of the value statements defined by your prospect's KPIs. Your report should also use information from the Needs Analysis Questionnaire to describe the prospect's current situation.

The strength and credibility of your model is further enhanced by including and explaining widely accepted financial metrics from the

ROI Financial Dashboard, such as net present value (NPV) and internal rate of return (IRR), payback period, and, of course, the projected return on investment (ROI) percentage. Be sure to explain these figures and their impact on the value you expect to deliver. At ROI4Sales, we include a calculation in our proposals called the "cost of waiting." We calculate the cost of waiting by using the investment figure, start-up factor, payback period, and the estimated value delivered, all of which are explained in Chapter 14, "The ROI Financial Dashboard."

We also recommend that your proposal include charts and graphs that illustrate where the savings are coming from and a payback period chart based on months. We surveyed hundreds of companies that have requested ROI white papers through our Web site and found that their customers are requiring them to prove a payback period of 18 months or less; the majority, 73 percent, in 12 months or less. Thus, whenever possible, we suggest you try to keep your payback period to less than 18 months.

Restating the Impact Statement

Throughout this stage we have emphasized the use of each of the ROI Selling tools you created in Part One. The culmination of your work comes down to this one point: What will the impact of your solution be on your prospect's business? You must make it clear that a typical customer of yours gets these returns, or, using third-party data, that companies implementing comparable products experience a return of X percent. As a result of purchasing your solution, therefore, your prospect can expect a similar return. Remember to state your sources for the impact statements; in other words, if you used a white paper or a study from Aberdeen, Gartner, or PWC, don't forget to quote the source for credibility.

The ROI presentation you make must be believable and objective. We have heard of salespeople showing ROI as high as 2,000 percent in their models and proposals. This is simply not believable. Several of our clients have asked us how much return is too much. We recommend that you use realistic financial savings comparisons. Do your research on the industry norms, and adjust your model and recommendations accordingly. We suggest companies like Aberdeen, Gartner, or Pricewaterhouse-Coopers for some of those general industry figures. You may also opt for Internet-based research firms like Bitpipe.com, ITPapers.com, or Itools.com. The U.S. government also does a tremendous amount of research that can be used for comparisons or benchmarks. Entering "US Government research" and a keyword relating to your industry into an Internet search engine should get returns on most subjects. Obviously, the research you require will depend on the product or service you sell. Using surveys to poll your own client base and determine an average value returned on each of the KPIs you have defined up front can provide valuable benchmark data.

Shortening the sales cycle is one of the primary benefits our customers expect from their use of ROI Selling. We emphasize the late stages of the sales process because this is the point at which sales are at the highest risk of going south. Our experience and research show that more deals are lost to "no decision" than are lost to competitors. As you can see from the bell curve shown earlier in the chapter, the possibility of closing the opportunity begins to fade as soon as you have presented your proposal. The work you have done thus far in collecting the data and presenting the ROI model will, by showing your prospect the cost of waiting or doing nothing, help you shorten the sales cycle and reduce the number of opportunities you lose to "no decision."

In summary, a winning proposal that includes valid, objective, and credible ROI data and benchmarks helps you differentiate yourself from your competition. By presenting your data in a format that is easy to understand, educational, informative, and definitive in terms of value delivered, you will close more business in a shorter period of time.

The Due Diligence Stage

In step six, the due diligence stage, your prospect verifies that you are capable of delivering the value you estimated in the proposal and ROI model. As part of this stage, you want to provide your customer or prospect with the data you used to confirm the impact statements listed in your proposal. You can provide your prospect with stories and case studies, existing customer contact information, and additional examples of how you measured your successes with existing customers.

By committing to a proactive value assessment program, you are forcing your organization to gather performance data that will help prove the value a typical customer receives when using your products and services. This commitment and follow-through often allows customers and prospects to reduce the amount of time they spend validating your impact statement claims. After all, they too will become part of the impact statement statistics you used to sell them. Remember, when you conduct a 360 Degree ROI, the data is yours and can be used for analysis, marketing programs, advertising programs, and internal product assessment programs (see Chapter 18, "ROI Marketing").

One way to shorten the time to a sale's closing is to help your prospect feel the heat of waiting to buy. Every day that passes without a decision to buy from you, your prospect is losing potential savings—and you may be losing to the status quo. The *cost of waiting* figure helps your prospect understand that the longer the due diligence stage continues, the more value he or she is losing.

Your work to this point is the foundation for proving your value justification to a customer during this step in the sales process. The data you provided for financial savings comparisons is critical for reducing the time to revenue. A credible and objective ROI model used at this stage is what separates the winners from the "we-came-in-second" group. Always remember to make your prospects feel there is a cost to waiting by comparing the pain of their current situation with the returns they could be enjoying through using your products or services.

Using Follow-up to Verify Customer Satisfaction

Siebel Systems for years advertised customer satisfaction statistics to prove its successes in CRM deployment. It took the follow-up assessment very seriously because part of the compensation for everyone in the company was dependent on the results of these customer value assessments (including Tom Siebel himself). Although the follow-up survey was more focused on proving customer satisfaction results than on measuring the value Siebel delivered, the program was an effective way of gathering measurement data. Siebel continues to publish the results of this survey in its annual report.

Pending Sale Stage

The pending sale stage is step seven, our final step before the close and the stage when the legal departments take over. Therefore, this is a good place to strongly caution you against embellishing the value you can deliver. Be sure you have confirmed the numbers you produced through a thorough litmus test and try to err on the conservative side. Remember that any figure entered into the impact statement field displays value, so you don't have to overextend your estimates. This stage is also a good time to work out the details of the 360 Degree ROI Value Assessment follow-ups for after the sale.

ROI after the Sale–360 Degree ROI

Your return on investment work isn't over when the sale closes. In Chapter 15, "360 Degree ROI Selling," you learned the details of designing and using the value assessment forms in an after-the-sale follow-up program with your clients. Our research and experience show that companies prefer to revisit the impact of their purchase at intervals of six to nine months and again at the end of the payback period (assuming the payback period is beyond six or nine months). However, there is no hard-and-fast rule on the best time to conduct your follow-up assessments. We do recommend that you follow up more than once.

Think of this program as an opportunity for you to reduce customer turnover and potentially increase your revenue; an obvious cost and a revenue loss accompany excessive customer turnover. Also, when you perform a value assessment and find that a customer is not receiving the estimated value, evaluate the situation and make the necessary adjustments. This process is not always a free one for your customers. If you sell maintenance programs, we suggest you tier them (for example, Silver, Bronze, Gold) and add the ROI Value Assessment to the highest level of support for an additional fee. The details regarding such a program can be worked out during the pending sale stage.

Properly executed, the 360 Degree ROI Value Assessment drives greater customer satisfaction through better measurement of the value you are capable of delivering. The 360 Degree ROI Value Assessment can drive other sales opportunities too. It is not unusual to identify up-sale and cross-sale—as well as add-on—revenue opportunities as a result of conducting an ROI Value Assessment. We find that a proactive approach by a vendor shows a commitment to customer success and drives additional revenue from the trust factor.

Summary

Regardless of the ROI model and sales methodology you employ, the integration of ROI into your sales process is a critical success factor. The following chapter summary helps you remember the most important issues you may face when integrating your ROI model into your current sales process:

- ROI Selling can be integrated into any selling methodology.
- Use ROI data and selling techniques to drive customer loyalty, document decisions, and create partnerships with your prospects.
- When a stakeholder gives you time, be prepared with the right questions for the appropriate individual in the organization.
- Don't introduce your ROI model until the meet-and-greet stage—or at least until you have identified the key pain indicators during the qualify stage.
- The presentation stage offers a learning experience for both parties, at which time you want to confirm the data you have gathered to date and determine the impact statement.
- Regardless of the number of steps in your sales process, ROI Selling tools and techniques play a role in each of these steps.
- Your goal is always to shorten the time to revenue! Use the cost of waiting to prove there is a cost to not buying from you now.
- The development of a selling proposal is critical for presenting your ROI model.
- You are the one who holds the statistical analysis data your prospects want, so use it effectively.
- Use 360 Degree ROI Value Assessments and follow-up as an opportunity to increase revenue.

17

INTEGRATING ROI AND SALES FORCE AUTOMATION

Many companies use Sales Force Automation (SFA) programs to help track and manage the activities of their sales personnel. Typically, SFA programs are used to collect customer information, monitor trends, develop sales forecasts, and provide other sales data for sales staff, managers, and investors. If your sales team is using SFA, you have a great opportunity to make using it more effective and valuable by integrating your ROI Selling tools into the SFA application. When you integrate ROI into your SFA application, you reduce the level of effort required to keep SFA data up-to-date by feeding information from the Needs Analysis Questionnaire. This integration also ensures that your sales team is pursuing the best opportunities by enforcing objective qualification criteria at each stage of the sales cycle. Finally, you simplify the forecasting process and improve the accuracy of forecasts by using ROI Selling data to drive projections.

This chapter discusses the use and effect of ROI Selling on Sales Force Automation programs. As we discussed with sales methodologies in Chapter 16, it shouldn't matter which SFA program you are using. The concepts described in this chapter can also be used at any stage of your SFA implementation.

Key Benefits of Incorporating ROI into Your SFA Program

The ROI model offers significant benefits to organizations using SFA programs by making the programs more useful, more flexible, and more effective in their implementation. SFA projects to date have typically focused on collecting customer information, tracking trends, and reporting forecasts and other data back to management and investors. What is missing in many SFA implementations is a tool that goes beyond merely tracking the progress of the sale to help *drive* the sale, keep the sales force focused on moving the opportunity through the sales process, and increase the accuracy of forecasts. The ROI model offers such a tool.

As of this writing, many of the popular sales methodologies have been integrated with SFA systems. Few of these integrated tools, however, have the ability to accept structured data, such as answers from the Needs Analysis Questionnaire, use the data to drive sales status and forecasts, and feed value estimation information back to customers and prospects. But when you incorporate ROI into your SFA system, you overcome these integration challenges.

Incorporating the ROI model into your SFA system can make the system implementation more effective as well. Everyone who has put in the effort to implement SFA knows the challenges that can limit the chances of a successful outcome. You face many issues during each phase of the implementation process for SFA, including sales force resistance. Sales personnel may balk at using tracking systems for a variety of reasons, such as these:

- **Big Brother syndrome.** Who is looking over my shoulder?
- **Lack of perceived value.** If salespeople perceive no value for themselves in the SFA, they are not likely to invest time and energy in using it properly.
- **Fear of extra work.** Related to the above, the sales team may see time spent maintaining SFA data as time away from what the team perceives as more productive sales activities.

Additional challenges that can interfere with SFA implementation include the following:

- **Incomplete or inaccurate data.** Sales force resistance and other factors can lead to incomplete, inaccurate, and/or out-of-date information in your SFA.
- **Information access.** Even if your SFA data is timely, complete, and accurate, but it doesn't produce meaningful reports, or the information is difficult to access, it won't be a useful tool and will lead to management frustration.
- **Budget overruns.** Like other software implementation projects, SFA implementations are notoriously subject to cost and schedule overruns.
- **Difficulty building accurate forecasts.** If the entered data is not accurate, neither is the forecast likely to be accurate.

We have found that using ROI as your road map to SFA implementation reduces the time and cost required to "go live," increases acceptance of the new system, and improves the completeness, timeliness, and accuracy of data input—all resulting in much better management information and forecasts. Other benefits of incorporating ROI into your SFA system include the following:

- **Reducing GIGO syndrome.** "Garbage in, garbage out" (GIGO) is an old software adage referring to the fact that the information you get out of a computer system is only as good as the information you put into it. GIGO certainly holds true when it comes to SFA applications, as it is often costly to rely on the data from these systems. Many sales management personnel have bet their jobs on their SFA data only to quickly find it can be a career-ending move. ROI integration reduces the amount of "garbage," or bad data, entered into your SFA system and improves both the relevance and the accuracy of the management information it produces.
- **Driving your forecast.** Effectively integrating ROI into your SFA system enables you to automate on-demand production of forecasts. At any point, you ought to be able to tell the status of any opportunity, the next steps in the process, and work completed to date. By requiring your sales personnel to complete the Needs Analy-sis Questionnaire online in your SFA system, you are capturing a complete profile for each opportunity and capturing the objective data you need to drive a forecast that is accurate at any

particular point, not just at month-end when reps rush to produce their reports.

- **Improving performance of both new and experienced sales personnel.** It is sometimes difficult for new salespeople to understand the resources available to them. They are trying to figure out what they need to know each time they visit a new or existing account—an awkward time in their career. Building their company's ROI Needs Analysis Questionnaire into the SFA system gives new salespeople a road map to the people they need to contact, the information they need to gather, a place to record the information, and an output mechanism to return to the prospect. An experienced salesperson is able to drive deals more effectively with a better understanding of how to access resources and drive opportunities to a close.

Implementing the Integration

To build ROI into your SFA system, you have to break your sales process down into stages similar to the sales process stages we described in Chapter 16; in that chapter, we discussed a sample sales process consisting of the following seven stages:

1. Target
2. Qualify
3. Meet and greet
4. Presentation
5. Propose
6. Due diligence
7. Pending Sale

As you break your own sales process into stages, assign a value to each stage based on its importance to the overall opportunity and a series of ROI-based questions from the Needs Analysis Questionnaire. As you record the answers in your SFA system, a very simple algorithm uses the values assigned to the

T *i p*

Many steps are required to integrate ROI Selling into your SFA system. We strongly recommend that you enlist the assistance of your SFA software vendor to help with the software development work that may be required. The vendor is likely to be more familiar with the inner workings of the software and may also be in a position to support the changes once you have them in production.

stages to calculate the progress of the opportunity and recommend actions going forward. The steps to accomplish this are described more
completely in the following sections.

We also described in Chapter 16 how each step of the sales process
uses return on investment to help drive the sale to the next stage. Figure
17.1 illustrates this process and the bell curve of prospect interest over
time. In this chapter, we continue to draw on the same example of sales
process stages used in previous chapters.

Identifying Sales Process Stakeholders inside Your Company and Defining Automatic Notification Procedures

Once you have defined your sales process stages and the requirements for each, define which stakeholders within your own organization
need to be updated with sales status information at each stage as the sale
progresses. For instance, when a target moves to qualify, Marketing may
have to be notified so it can update its database; and when a sale moves
from qualify to meet and greet, presales people may need to be notified
so they can assign a resource for the next step in the process.

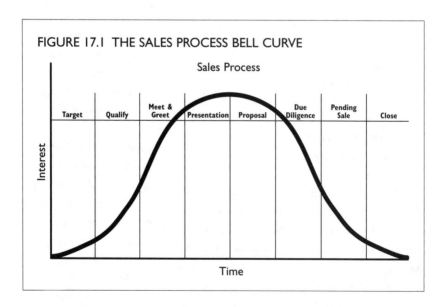

FIGURE 17.1 THE SALES PROCESS BELL CURVE

Automatic notification is a very effective tool for getting buy-in and funding to support sales activity from multiple departments within your organization. When other departments feel they are part of the sales process, you'll find they are more inclined to step up and support a better communication vehicle—especially if it's automated. Automatic notification also keeps everyone in the company abreast of the status of unclosed, pending, and closed opportunities; see Figure 17.2 for a graphical depiction of this concept. We suggest you enter your own notification map in a similar chart.

Building Your Needs Analysis Questionnaire into Your SFA System

Each time a salesperson "touches" a customer or prospect, he or she typically updates the SFA database. The entries include conversations, dates and times, and document management and control leading up to status updates and changes. To automate this process, it is necessary to build your needs analysis questions into the SFA data entry screens so that salespeople are able to complete them before recording their status

FIGURE 17.2 INTERNAL NOTIFICATION SCHEDULE

Sales Process

	Target	Qualify	Meet & Greet	Presentation	Proposal	Due Diligence	Pending Sale	Close
Interest	• Marketing	• Marketing • Regional	• Regional Management • Presales support	• Regional Management • Presales support • Proposal Department	• Regional Management • Legal • Marketing	• Regional Management • Marketing reference management group	• Regional Management • Corporate VP	• Company-wide e-mail

Time

changes. The answers to these needs analysis questions drive the SFA status updates and, ultimately, the forecast, automatically moving the prospect from gate to gate or stage to stage in the process.

For example, for an account to progress from target to qualify, a salesperson asks a series of qualifying questions. These questions become "gates" through which an account must move to progress to the next stage in the process. With this in mind, each series of questions must control the status change or passage to the next stage in the sales process.

Begin with your qualifying questions and build them into your SFA system to control the account's passage from one stage to the next. For example, before a target can be moved to the qualify stage, the salesperson must document the answers to your qualifying questions by entering them directly into the SFA system. Your SFA software can be programmed to capture the answer and compare it with the minimums you have established for an account to move from one stage to the next.

For example, several of our customers specialize in CRM software. The qualifying questions they might use are as follows:

- Do you have a call center?
- How many call takers do you have?
- Are you happy with your hold times?
- Do you perform problem resolution on the phone?

Each of these questions requires a specific answer for the account to move from target to qualify.

Each stage of your sales process requires a different set of questions to move the sale to the next stage. The specific actions (e.g., e-mail notifications, status changes to the account, forecast updates, etc.) that different companies might want to take at various stages in their sales processes are endless. This is where thinking through the alignment of ROI Selling with your sales process as described in Chapter 16 becomes a prerequisite to integrating ROI with your SFA application.

Defining Your "Sweet Spot"

The objective of this phase of the integration process is to define the "perfect" prospect for your product or service. To define this "sweet spot," assign a maximum point value to the perfect prospect and work backward to the minimum and maximum point requirements you defined in Chapter 16 when you defined the qualifying questions for each stage in the sales process. Next, assign point values to the possible responses. These point values provide a basis for your SFA application to calculate an objective "score" for each prospect at each stage in the cycle, and they allow you to use that score to determine when a prospect moves from one stage of the process to the next.

You read about using these questions in a nonautomated sales process in the "Posing Qualifying Questions" section of Chapter 16. At ROI4Sales, for example, we use six questions to help us decide if a company should be moved from the target stage to the qualify stage:

1. How many quota-carrying sales personnel are on your sales team?
2. How many sales managers manage the sales team?
3. What is your annual revenue?
4. What percentage of your sales team achieves quota?
5. What is your established quota for your sales team?
6. Do you utilize a sales methodology such as Solution Selling®, TAS, or VITO?

Lay out your questions in a table like the one shown in Figure 17.3. Determine your sweet spot and assign it the maximum number of points. There is no science to assigning the points, but we like to keep it to a maximum of 15 points between four to six possible response ranges for each question. Next, enter four to six columns for answers to your questions and assign a weighted value based on the combined importance of the range and the question. For example, if you have six sets of questions, as we do, you might assign the most important question a maximum value of 15 and the least important question a maximum value of 6. By assigning different maximums, we build a model of weighted values based on level of importance.

FIGURE 17.3 QUALIFYING QUESTION COMPARISON TABLE

Sales staff?	1–20	21–50	51–250	251–1000+
Points>>	3	7	10	16

Figure 17.3 displays a series of ranges for the number of sales team members and a point value that reflects the ranking of that range in our qualification criteria. Figure 17.4 compares revenue figures to rank our prospects.

FIGURE 17.4 COMPARISON TABLE RANKING REVENUES

Revenue	$1M–$10M	$11M–$50M	$51M–$99M	$100M–
Points>>	2	7	10	16

Figure 17.5 compares sales management head count. Because this qualifier is not so important to us, the point values are lower than are those in the previous two comparison tables.

FIGURE 17.5 COMPARISON TABLE OF MANAGEMENT HEAD COUNT

Sales mgmt.	0–1	2–5	6–10	11–+
Points>>	1	3	5	7

Figure 17.6 compares the percentage of sales personnel who are achieving quota. Notice that the point values get lower as the percentages rise. This is the opposite of the other comparison tables and reflects the fact that the lower our prospects' quota achievement, the better qualified they are for our products and services. The more they are struggling with meeting quotas, the more they need our help.

FIGURE 17.6 COMPARISON TABLE RANKING SALES QUOTAS

Quota achieved	0–10%	11%–25%	26%–50%	51%–+
Points>>	16	10	7	2

Figure 17.7 illustrates the importance of the quota levels the sales team carries. Because some sales team members may carry higher quotas than others, we rank the lowest quota below the sales representatives who carry higher quotas.

FIGURE 17.7 COMPARISON TABLE

Quota amount	$1–$300,000	$301,000–$999,999	$1M–$9.9M	$10M–+
Points>>	2	7	10	16

The table shown in Figure 17.8 compares selling methodologies. Though ROI selling works with all methodologies, in this example we create a comparison suggesting that our products and services may work better with one methodology than with another. Therefore we assign a point value to each sales training methodology in this example.

FIGURE 17.8 COMPARISON TABLE

Sales program	Solution Selling	SPIN	TAS	Other	None
Points>>	16	10	7	5	1

The math involved in ranking our prospects based on all of these data is fairly straightforward. The maximum number of points available in this example is 82, and the least a prospect can score is 11. Somewhere between these numbers you have to establish a minimum point value to move the prospect from one stage to the next. For example, if a prospect answered all six questions and the point value added up to 25, this prospect probably isn't a good candidate with whom to move forward. If, however, a prospect scores 50 points, we would be very likely to move that opportunity to the next stage.

Here are a couple of actual examples to help you better understand the concept:

Response	Point Value
5 salespeople	3
No sales manager	1
Produces a minimum of $2 million in revenue	2
80% of the sales team achieves quota	2
Quotas are $300,000 annually	2
Does *not* use a sales methodology	2
Total	11

At only 11 points out of a possible 82, this prospect is not a very attractive opportunity for us to pursue. The second example tells a different story:

Response	Point Value
Has 100 salespeople on staff	10
6 sales managers	5
Produced $100 million in revenue	16
40% of the team achieves quota	7
Quotas are $2,000,000 per salesperson	10
Uses Solution Selling as sales methodology	16
Total	62

At 62 points out of a possible 82, this opportunity is obviously more attractive for our sales staff to pursue. How do we know this? Not only because the opportunity is larger than the one in the previous example, but because we have a formula we use for the mix of salespeople, management, quota results, revenue, and sales methodology. With this formula, we can establish minimum requirements for an opportunity to move from one stage to the next. The great value of this approach is that it is based on hard, objective data, eliminating subjective or emotional judgments and providing solid criteria for keeping your sales force focused on prospects with the highest likelihood of success.

Building the Evaluation Tables

In Chapter 8, you learned about writing value statements to meet or exceed stakeholders' desired outcomes, resolve stakeholders' business

The Cost of Calls

One of our clients has a sales force of over 100. One afternoon I was talking with Rick, the VP of Sales, who relayed this story to me: "We figure that each time a salesman goes on-site to make a sales call, it costs us on average about $350. We multiplied that out one day and here are the results. We have 120 salespeople on staff. Each salesperson makes one on-site call per week. That comes out to 6,240 calls per year. We then multiplied 6,240 calls times $350 per call, and our annual cost for on-site sales calls is $2,184,000. That is huge if you are not getting it right."

issues, and give your customer or prospect a reason to buy from you. As you learned in Chapters 8 through 10, each of those value statements has specific needs analysis questions assigned to it. The questions we developed for these value statements can be broken down into tables like the ones shown in Figures 17.3 to 17.8. Every time an entry is made into one of the tables, the value is accumulated and the decision to move to the next stage is decided objectively, just as we did in the examples shown above. Don't forget that you must assign a minimum number of points to the set of questions to clear the gate and move to the next stage for this program to work.

Figure 17.9 displays an example of a point system like the one we've just described; here, each stage of the sales process is labeled with the number of points required for an opportunity to enter that stage. Building this into your SFA system is simply a matter of creating the values based on your needs analysis questions.

Remember that each gate you pass prompts a series of actions. The actions move the sale through the process and identify the status and next steps. For example, if your prospect scores above the minimum point value as established in Figure 17.9, then the status changes—for example, from target to qualify. At the same time, the SFA system automatically sends an e-mail to Marketing, notifying it that a lead moved forward. If you assign percentages representing the likelihood that the opportunity will close to each of the stages, work with your SFA vendor to ensure that those percentages are also updated in the SFA system automatically. Using the same example as before, when the prospect scores

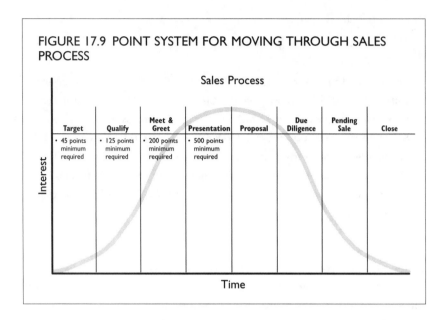

FIGURE 17.9 POINT SYSTEM FOR MOVING THROUGH SALES PROCESS

above the minimum points required to move from qualify to meet and greet, the percentage chance of closing the deal might change from 25 to 50 percent.

When progress from stage to stage is controlled by statistical data and the percentage likelihood is automatically calculated, your forecasting will be far more accurate than the gut feelings of the salesperson or sales manager. Finally, when a prospect has completed all of the gates, the data can be used to publish an Executive Summary Report that you may include in your proposal and that can also be automated as it is based on data in your SFA system.

Automatically Assigning ROI Resources to Stages of the Sales Process

Another way to benefit from the integration of ROI and SFA is by using the pair to automatically assign ROI resources to specific stages of the sales process. These resources can be part of an automatic integration into your SFA system that takes the guesswork out of which resources are best used at every stage. The SFA system recommends and tracks which materials were used during the sales life cycle. Early in the sales process, we recommend using the usual marketing materials, such as brochures, case studies, or demo CDs. As you move the sale along, we strongly recommend the use of management visits or calls, customer site visits or references, and, of course, use of the 360 Degree ROI results.

Figure 17.10 illustrates some of the resources that could be made available to a sales force as a sale moves through the sales process. Notice how each available resource is assigned to a stage in the sales process. For example, a "pitch deck" (materials used in a sales presentation) is available prior to meet and greet to be used during the presentation. Don't be afraid to duplicate resources over multiple stages—for example, suggesting a pitch deck at both the meet-and-greet and the presentation stages.

We hope you've noticed as you worked your way through *ROI Selling* that we are arming your team with tools to help them learn and sell. The resources listed in Figure 17.10 are tremendous sales tools for new and existing personnel. Below is a summary list of just some of the value you'll receive if you take the time to create these documents and procedures for your sales team:

- A salesperson has a road map complete with information on how to move the sale through the process.

FIGURE 17.10 SALES PROCESS AND RESOURCES ROAD MAP

Sales Process

	Target	Qualify	Meet & Greet	Presentation	Proposal	Due Diligence	Pending Sale	Close
	Gate 1 Require	Gate 2 Require	Gate 3 Require	Gate 4 Require				
Interest	• Brochures • Datasheets • Web site	• ROI Needs Analysis Questionnaire • White paper • Case studies • Impact studies	• ROI Needs Analysis Questionnaire • Pitch deck • Partner profiles • Competitive analysis	• ROI Needs Analysis Questionnaire • Presales engineers • Pitch deck • Manager visit	• ROI Needs Analysis Questionnaire • ROI Financial Dashboard • Proposal department	• Impact study • Marketing reference checklist • 360 Degree ROI statistics	• Legal department	• 360 Degree ROI Assessment • Follow-up documentation • Completed sale form

Time

- Salespeople are aware of the resources available at each stage in the process.
- There are several automatic checks and balances with automatic notification at every stage.
- The tool does not threaten salespeople's existence or lead them to think they are going to lose their jobs.
- A properly built tool helps make the sales team more productive.
- Automated resource assignments clearly define what is expected of the salesperson.

Assigning Close Percentages

When you integrate your ROI model into your SFA system, you eliminate manual forecasting on the part of the salesperson and sales management. If implemented properly, the system produces the forecast based on the gates achieved by the prospects in the pipeline. (Note: You need good historical data to assign accurate close percentages.) In Figure 17.11 we added a few sample close percentages. Yours may well be different, so keep in mind these are just a guideline for you to review.

FIGURE 17.11 SALES PROCESS—RESOURCES AND CLOSE PERCENTAGES

Sales Process

	Target 0%	Qualify 16%	Meet & Greet 25%	Presentation 50%	Proposal 60%	Due Diligence 80%	Pending Sale 95%	Close
	Gate 1 Require	Gate 2 Require	Gate 3 Require	Gate 4 Require				
Interest	• Brochures • Datasheets • Web site • Hoovers • Internet	• ROI Needs Analysis Questionnaire • White paper • Case studies • Impact studies	• ROI Needs Analysis Questionnaire • Pitch deck • Partner profiles • Competitive analysis	• ROI Needs Analysis Questionnaire • Presales engineers • Pitch deck • Manager visit	• ROI Needs Analysis Questionnaire • ROI Financial Dashboard • Proposal department	• Impact study • Marketing reference checklist • 360 Degree ROI statistics	• Legal department	

Time

Figure 17.11 illustrates how the chance of closing the opportunity improves as you complete each gate with additional information and move from stage to stage in the sales process. Because each gate has a point value and you are required to complete the needs analysis questions with data related to the prospect's current situation to move from stage to stage, the SFA system has the information it needs to constantly evaluate the opportunity and provide feedback in the form of continually updated forecasts. Using this system, your forecast should not only produce itself but should also be more accurate, because the data that is driving it is validated and objective, not the salesperson's opinion or best guess.

Summary

Keep in mind that ROI Selling is about creating, assessing, and measuring the value your products and services deliver. When you build these ROI Selling tools into your sales process and SFA implementation, you are taking your sales team to a whole new level. In Chapter 18 we give you ideas of how you can use your ROI information in your marketing campaigns. One of our objectives is to get sales and marketing on the same page . . . one voice!

Keep the following summary points in mind as you move forward with integrating ROI with your SFA system:

- Integrating ROI with SFA helps to drive a sale, not merely track it.
- Use ROI and SFA to qualify a prospect automatically.
- ROI with SFA can help to automatically build a reliable sales forecast.
- Don't rely on SFA data without using an ROI model.
- Define and weight your ROI questions to perform automatic qualification and forecasting using ROI in your SFA application.

18

ROI MARKETING

In previous chapters, we have discussed in detail the use of ROI Selling in the sales process and the integration of ROI Selling into your Sales Force Automation program. In this chapter, we talk about integrating ROI Selling into your marketing program. During the course of building your ROI model and conducting 360 Degree ROI Value Assessments with your existing customers, you have assembled a library of extremely valuable data that describe:

- Why people buy your products and services
- The issues, pains, and goals that drive their purchases
- The individuals in your prospects' organization who feel these issues, pains, and goals and who make purchase decisions
- The outcomes those individuals seek
- The features and solutions you offer to meet or exceed those individuals' expectations
- The specific, quantifiable value you deliver
- Actual data about value your existing customers have received as a result of buying and using your products and services

This information is an absolute gold mine for your marketing department! Any marketing manager would pay dearly to have this data at his or her fingertips when creating marketing communications, developing product strategy, and searching for a solid basis on which to establish pricing. And using the ROI information you have gathered to drive your marketing programs and communications results in complete consistency in the messages your prospects receive from your marketing activities and sales representatives.

In most companies, the marketing department is responsible for, among other things, the tangible and measurable objective of generating leads for the sales team to pursue and the potentially less measurable objective of maintaining and enhancing the image and awareness of company brand(s) and products in the marketplace. Some marketing departments are also responsible for product enhancements and pricing. To promote these objectives, marketing personnel conduct a number of activities, including but not limited to the following:

- Creation and maintenance of marketing materials for the company Web site
- Preparation and distribution of sales literature and collateral materials
- Trade show preparation and deployment
- Advertising
- Customer conferences
- Public relations, including speaking, press releases, article placement, and so on
- Case studies
- Telemarketing
- Product management
- Potential investor marketing documentation

The cumulative effect of these activities is to bring prospects into a company's sales process and to provide them with favorable impressions about how they can use the company's products and services to address their most pressing business pains and issues. Does this sound familiar? Clearly, your company's chances of success in the sales process will be improved by consistency between the enticing messages your prospects have heard through your marketing campaigns and the tailored message your sales team delivers to them as individual prospects.

Many companies struggle with a disconnect (and occasional animosity) between the sales, product development, and marketing teams as a result of the disparity in compensation, misaligned objectives, and poor communication between the teams. To be successful, it is critical to combine these separate teams into a single, cohesive machine—one that completely shares the same objectives, agendas, and understanding of what is required to get the job done. Marketing must be aligned with your sales methodology and ROI process. Conversely, Sales needs to buy into the media or communication vehicles the marketing department is pursuing. Sales also needs to understand the value of feedback to Marketing to enable a continual refinement of product development and marketing processes.

Building this type of cohesive team is a daunting task, best accomplished through clear, consistent, and continual communication. The participation of members of the sales force in critical marketing events and program design provides the marketing team with valuable information about what is actually occurring in the trenches—and what needs to be accomplished at home in the corporate boardroom. Leveraging the power of shared ROI materials and information is another important factor in forging a cohesive team of the sales and marketing groups in your company.

In this chapter, we discuss how our customers have achieved tighter integration between their sales, marketing, and product development groups and activities as a result of making their ROI Selling tools the focal point of each discipline. We also provide specific suggestions for how you can use your ROI Selling materials to enhance the effectiveness of your company's marketing activities.

Key Concepts and Guidelines

Your goal is to develop one unified message that will be consistently echoed by sales, marketing, and product development. As you consider the most efficient and best ways to create and make use of your company's ROI Selling materials in your marketing programs, keep in mind these fundamental concepts and principles:

- **Powerful value statements are critical for both sales and marketing.** Remember that value statements sum up the entire value proposition about your products and services. The very qualities that make value statements an important part of your ROI model also make them vital components of a strong, effective marketing message and program.

- **Leverage the Needs Analysis Questionnaire.** The content of the questionnaire drives the sales process. That same content must come through loud and clear in your marketing messages. Use ROI questions as part of your lead-generation programs, trade-show kiosks, and telesales programs.

- **Use 360 Degree ROI data in marketing campaigns and messages.** You'll find that 360 Degree ROI Value Assessments are your vehicle to track, measure, and prove the value you have delivered to your customers; this data includes valuable success stories for use in marketing efforts. When Marketing is challenged on the validity of your impact statements, the 360 Degree ROI analysis provides the answers it needs to address those challenges.

- **Integrate marketing campaigns and ROI.** Every marketing campaign your company currently runs can benefit from using ROI Selling tools and techniques.

- **ROI and value-based pricing.** Use your 360 Degree ROI to assess the value you are delivering compared to the price you are charging. Several of our customers have evaluated and changed their pricing models based on the value they have measured and delivered using ROI Selling.

- **Use ROI Selling for more than selling.** A well-documented ROI Value Matrix is one of the most impressive documents you can provide to potential investors. It explains all the reasons people buy, their business issues and desires, and the solutions and value your products offer. The value matrix tells a complete success story of your products and services. It's also an excellent summary that you can use to educate new staff members and thus help move your entire organization to the same message and same voice.

- **Make the best use of the value matrix workshop.** If you conduct a value matrix workshop, the resulting materials reflect the best knowledge and ideas from your sales and marketing organization. Use this information to drive your sales efforts and sharpen the message you are presenting to the market and to potential investors.

Leveraging Strong Value Statements in Marketing

Although you may not be aware of it, you are probably already using value statements throughout your marketing plan and materials. A value statement definitively expresses the value your products and services can deliver. ROI Value Statements provide the foundation for a value-based marketing campaign, including making the sometimes challenging transition of your marketing program from feature/benefit messaging to value-based messaging targeted to a particular vertical market, industry, or industry segment.

The value statement helps ensure that you are sending the right message to the right stakeholders through both your marketing messages and your sales activities. As part of creating your value statements, you associated stakeholders with the pains, issues, or goals your customers and prospects experience. The first step in creating any communication, especially in marketing, is to consider who the audience is for the message and then build the message around that person's point of view. A well-crafted value statement spells out this information explicitly: "This person feels this pain, and expects this outcome, which our products and services address with these features, resulting in this value to the customer."

Most sales methodologies stress that your message must meet or exceed the stakeholders' expectation. Marketing is tasked with developing campaigns to carry a message to these same stakeholders. Therefore, doing a good job building your value statements is a very important step in defining the messages for both Sales and Marketing. When developing corporate ROI Selling programs, most companies have Marketing create the value statements, aided by sales department input provided during the ROI workshop.

Using the Needs Analysis Questionnaire as Both a Sales and a Marketing Tool

There is no substitute for direct contact with prospects, and the Needs Analysis Questionnaire presents a great opportunity to demonstrate your knowledge of the issues and concerns that your prospects face (see Figure 18.1).

FIGURE 18.1 NEEDS ANALYSIS QUESTIONNAIRE—ROI SELLING

Increase revenue from less customer turnover

Use 360 Degree ROI Selling to ensure your customers stay with you long after the sale. Periodic reminders of the value you are delivering help your customers understand the value you bring to their business.

Enter the number of customers currently on maintenance agreements:	1,800
Enter total maintenance agreement revenue:	$25,000,000
Calculated revenue per customer for maintenance agreement:	$13,889
Enter the percentage of existing customers lost annually:	10%
Calculated number of existing customers lost annually:	180
Calculated maintenance revenue lost annually because of customer turnover:	$2,500,000
Enter the total amount of revenue annually from existing customer base for add-on, upgrade, services, etc. (Do not include revenue from maintenance.)	$0
Calculated additional annual revenue per existing customer:	$0
Calculated "additional annual revenue" lost from customer turnover:	$0
Calculated summary of total revenue lost from annual customer turnover:	$2,500,000
Calculated annual revenue loss per lost customer:	$13,889

A typical ROI4Sales customer reduces his or her customer turnover ratio by 5%–25%

Enter the percentage of lost customers retained annually using 360 Degree ROI:	5%
Calculated number of customers retained from utilizing 360 Degree ROI:	9
Total revenue gained from reducing annual customer turnover rates:	$125,000

You can use your needs analysis questions in many marketing activities:

- **In your lead-generation programs.** Presenting a portion of the Needs Analysis Questionnaire as a tease followed up by offering an ROI analysis has proven to be an effective lead-generation mechanism for many of our customers.
- **At trade shows.** One of our clients used a portion of the Needs Analysis Questionnaire at a trade show event. He put up kiosks around the booth and collected information from attendees, who were attracted by the client advertising a drawing. At the end of the trade show, the client drew one name and gave away $1,000 in cash. This brought in quite a crowd. The program far exceeded the expectation for the number of qualified leads generated.
- **As a guide for your telesales and telemarketing groups.** The general information or qualification questions can be used as part of your standard telemarketing program. By including selected portions of the Needs Analysis Questionnaire in your telemarketing scripts, you have an opportunity to populate a portion of the data required by the sales team directly into the questionnaire based on the work of your telemarketing group.

N *o t e*

Many companies now include Needs Analysis Questionnaires on their Web site in an attempt to "self-qualify" prospects as they come to the site. In our experience, this technique has limited success, although your competitors may be enjoying it. We suggest that you put up a small piece of the questionnaire on the Web site as a tease and offer a complete version via e-mail or, best of all, in person. See "Integrating ROI Selling into Your Marketing Programs" later in the chapter for more information on this topic.

Using 360 Degree ROI Value Assessments and Other ROI Tools in Marketing Campaigns

In Chapter 15, "360 Degree ROI Selling," you learned how 360 Degree Value Assessments provide critical validation data, which you can use to support the synergy between sales and marketing activities. When your team returns to a client to measure the value delivered by your company's products and services, your marketing department gets a new success story.

Impact statements offer critical measures for tracking and verifying the returns delivered by your products or services. As such, these statements are another important source of product success stories for use in marketing materials and campaigns (see Chapter 13, "Designing the ROI Needs Analysis Questionnaire Interface," to learn more about impact statements). The validity of your impact statements are questioned consistently by prospects, and Marketing must be the touch point for all sales personnel when your impact statements are challenged. By consistently tracking and measuring the value delivered using 360 Degree ROI, you can respond to those challenges with factual data and stay one more step ahead of your competition.

But the marketing value of ROI information and materials isn't limited to the 360 Degree ROI Value Assessment data. As you can see in Figure 18.2, each ROI tool you have created throughout this book is associated with a marketing or lead-generation program. As an additional exercise, you may want to create your own table for reference.

N *o t e*

Remember that company size doesn't play a role in determining whether ROI will benefit sales and marketing campaigns. Regardless of the size of your organization, ROI Selling integrated into your marketing programs and plans helps increase the effectiveness with which you communicate your value to the market. Small to medium-sized businesses gain a competitive edge, and large companies learn to focus their message for greater impact. In both cases, investors better understand to whom you are marketing and what message you are presenting.

Using ROI Data as a Foundation for Value-Based Pricing

One of the biggest challenges all of us face in selling is the question, How much does it cost? ROI Selling is about changing this paradigm. When using ROI Selling in your sales process, you are leading with value; you are measuring potential value; and, after the sale, you are assessing the actual value you delivered. The discussion of price becomes something of an after-the-fact consideration in the sales process that can be handled in part by your proposal. The "how-much-is-it" discussion needs to take place when price and value come together after the pre-

FIGURE 18.2 MARKETING ROI TABLE

Marketing Campaign	ROI Selling Integration
Web site	• Value statements • Needs Analysis Questionnaire
Literature and collateral	• Value statements • Success stories • ROI Financial Dashboard (inset)
Trade shows	• Value statements • Kiosk with KPI input form and Needs Analysis Questionnaire
Advertising	• Value statements • Needs Analysis Questionnaire offer
Customer conference	• ROI Value Matrix workshop exercise • Value statements • 360 Degree ROI—Gather data for comparison and analysis
Public relations	• Value statements • 360 Degree ROI results/impact statements • Case studies for press releases and article placement
Case studies	• 360 Degree ROI results
Telemarketing/Telesales	• Value statements • Needs Analysis Questionnaire • Value matrix
Product marketing	• 360 Degree ROI analysis • ROI Value Matrix

sentation stage. In companies with corporate ROI Selling programs, the marketing department typically maintains the ROI model, collects the value assessment data in one location, participates in determining pricing structures, and drives the product development process that leads to the value ultimately delivered to your customers.

Making the Best Use of the Value Matrix Workshop

Companies implementing ROI Selling as a corporate program often choose to conduct the information-gathering activities described in Part

One in a workshop format. The value your company receives from conducting an ROI workshop extends far beyond a data-gathering exercise to build the ROI Value Matrix. For virtually all of our customers, an ROI workshop has been a rare opportunity to bring sales and marketing personnel together. The exchange of ideas and transfer of knowledge present an opportunity to gather information about case studies, success stories, and advertising testimonials. The workshop helps your marketing team learn about the "value" your products and services deliver directly from the personnel who deliver it—the sales team. Marketing can also use the data gathered during the interactive workshop for building literature and trade show collateral.

If you are considering an ROI workshop for your organization, please review Appendix B, "Conducting an ROI Workshop," for more information about this process and about the workshops we facilitate for our ROI4Sales customers.

Integrating ROI Selling into Your Marketing Programs

Integrating ROI Selling into your marketing programs is a natural progression in the shift from feature/benefit selling to value-based selling. The same concept applies to your marketing methodology. Shifting from feature/benefit marketing to value-based marketing is a natural progression when developing ROI Selling tools.

We suggest a phased approach to the integration process. Begin with your marketing message. Ask yourself what the overall value message you are trying to send to the market is. Review the ROI Value Matrix to answer this question and compare the marketing message to your value statements; the messages should be very well aligned. If you detect any inconsistencies, review both the marketing message and the value statements to determine where adjustments are needed. This is an opportunity to either update your value matrix with new information from a marketing perspective or sharpen the marketing message to reflect the information in your value matrix. Either way, this exercise tells you the most important messages your marketing programs and sales team need to promote and also ensures that your marketing department and sales team are sending a consistent message.

Once you have confirmed alignment between your marketing message and value statements, use your value statements as the basis for new literature development, case studies, and white papers. This is not a static, one-time activity. Your value statements are powerful tools that must be updated frequently to conform to changes in your markets and products.

Also, update your Web site to reflect both your value statements and Needs Analysis Questionnaire. As mentioned earlier, you don't want to give away the entire model on your Web site, but pieces of the ROI model can make an excellent teaser that entices prospects to request additional information and ROI analysis. Many of our clients have built their ROI model in HTML or other Internet-based tools to facilitate Web deployment.

In the next phase—360 Degree ROI Value Assessment—postsales support and marketing come together to drive a successful program. At the same time the postsales group is performing assessments and following up with the customer base, Marketing needs to be gathering data for case studies, impact statement updates, and success stories.

Finally, you can use the ROI Value Matrix in conjunction with training new marketing personnel, both in telemarketing and product mar-

Making Best Use of Web Questionnaires

One of our clients put a subset of its ROI questions on its company Web site so prospects could sample an ROI analysis. The client also added a "barometer" that graphically measures and displays the value its product is expected to deliver based on a prospect's answers to the ROI questions.

This company conducts very successful "Webinars" (online seminars) on return on investment. After the Webinar, participants are directed to the corporate Web site, where they are asked several questions that identify the site's visitors and obtain their thoughts on the Webinar's content. These questions are followed by a sample set of ROI value-based questions. On completion, visitors are offered a free needs analysis assessment. This campaign has netted many new prospects for our client.

keting. This document holds many of your organization's secrets and treasures as they relate to the value you are capable of delivering, so make sure you manage the value matrix distribution and use. As new products become available, Marketing should spearhead the effort to add a new value matrix to your portfolio of marketing materials.

Summary

Marketing departments in most organizations can take ownership of the ROI modeling process. They are truly the stakeholder for a successful implementation.

- Use the ROI Selling tools developed through reading *ROI Selling* in your marketing programs, campaigns, and plans.
- Remember that company size doesn't matter when integrating ROI into your marketing program.
- Use your ROI Value Matrix to improve your relationship with:
  - Investors
  - Prospects
  - Telemarketing personnel
  - New hire training groups
- Marketing management is a great candidate to take ownership of the ROI marketing program integration, which involves the following:
  - Keeping the model up-to-date and spearheading new development
  - Managing the distribution of the value matrix
  - Developing, modifying, and enhancing the value statements

N *o t e*

We have emphasized the importance of using your customer base whenever possible to gather baseline data for your impact statements. We have also suggested the use of industry benchmarks for comparisons. Both of these activities normally fall under Marketing's responsibility. If you find that the data is not readily available within your customer base, take additional time to perform a customer impact study using the Needs Analysis Questionnaire. When performing this study, ask your customers to estimate the value you have delivered to them. The results of your customer impact study increases the validity, credibility, and objectivity of your entire ROI model.

- Use the 360 Degree ROI Value Assessment to capture data for up-dating your:
  - Impact statements
  - Marketing programs and campaigns
  - Case studies/literature
- Integrate ROI materials and tools throughout your marketing campaigns.

A

EXAMPLES AND TEMPLATES

Throughout *ROI Selling,* you've seen numerous examples of the forms, tables, and templates used to compile and present ROI materials. This appendix presents you with additional examples to further demonstrate these important tools.

Examples in this appendix include the following:

1. Value Matrix Template
2. Sample Needs Analysis Questionnaire 1
3. Sample Needs Analysis Questionnaire 2
4. KPI Input Sample
5. Financial Dashboard Example 1
6. Financial Dashboard Example 2
7. Financial Dashboard Example 3
8. 360 Degree Data Entry 1
9. 360 Degree ROI Sample
10. Start Screen Example

VALUE MATRIX TEMPLATE

No.	Why Buy?	Business Issue	Stakeholder	Desired Outcome	Feature/Solution	Category	Value Metric	Group
1								
2								
3								
4								
5								
6								
7								
8								
9								
10								

SAMPLE NEEDS ANALYSIS QUESTIONNAIRE 1

Powerful programming software tools to reduce programming costs and increase revenue from faster operation start-up

Tag-based programming: Use of tag-based addressing means that your memory mirrors your application. It allows you to create and maintain separate documentation for data table layout, eliminate the need to select a logical address (just create the actual name like "tank rate" and "flow rate"), eliminate the need to create documentation for many objects, and reduce the need to look up details of a device.

Enter the average amount of time (hours) spent per person monthly programming your PLCs: 30

Enter the number of personnel involved in the programming process: 3

Enter the average hourly burdened cost of personnel involved in the programming process: $34.00
Calculated annual rate: $70,720

Calculated estimated annual cost of programming PLCs: $36,720

Rockwell Automation customers have saved up to 40% in programming time.

Enter your estimated savings from using tag-based programming: 40%

Potential cost reduction in programming time: $14,688

Programming reduction cost summary

SAMPLE NEEDS ANALYSIS QUESTIONNAIRE 2

Increase revenue from indirect channel

Using ROI Selling; questionnaire; Financial Dashboard; workshop; and 360 Degree Value Assessment, for your indirect sales channel increases their accuracy and effectiveness. Our questionnaire helps your partners become more knowledgeable about your products, drives a consistent data-gathering method, and ensures they are selling your products and services the way you want them marketed and sold.

Do you currently have an indirect sales channel? Yes

Enter the total number of indirect channel participants: 80

Enter the annual revenue for the indirect channel: $11,300,000

Calculated average revenue per channel partner: $141,250

A typical ROI4Sales customer increases the yield for indirect channel by 5% - 10%

Enter the increase in yield per channel partner from utilizing ROI Selling sales tools: 5%

Calculated revenue per channel partner increased: $7,063

Total revenue increased for indirect sales channel using ROI4Sales in your sales process: $565,000

KPI INPUT SAMPLE

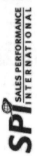

SALES PERFORMANCE INTERNATIONAL

Return on Investment Analysis - KPI Questions	
Prepared for: Zachary Corporation	01/21/04

The answers to these questions **measure the cost of existing annual customer turnover.**

Does your customer turnover exceed 5% annually?

Enter the number of customers currently on maintenance agreements:

3,500

Enter total maintenance agreement revenue:

$10,000,000

Enter the percentage of existing customers lost annually:

10%

Enter the total amount of revenue annually from existing customer base for add-ons, upgrades, services, etc.: (Do not include revenue from maintenance)

$1,200,000

Notes:

Our customer base is made up of many very small companies and some very large ones. Not all customers take the maintenance program from us. Therefore we spend most of our time focusing on the large companies.

FINANCIAL DASHBOARD EXAMPLE I

Customer Name: ABC Company

Netliant ROI Financial Analysis Dashboard

Investment vs. Return

Summary Potential Return on Investment		
Netliant Investment:		$2,000,000
Payback period:		0.25
Annual Return on Investment:		370%
Net Present Value:	Enter Rate: 10%	$4,909,517
Internal Rate of Return: (Annualized)		307%
Cost Reductions:		$1,448,286
Cost Avoidances:		$768,316
Revenue Increases:		$5,923,913
Total Potential ROI >>>		$8,140,515

KPI Summary	
Reduce time to create designs and quotes	$344,280
Reduce cost of supporting indirect sales channels	$4,750,582
Increase revenue and decrease cost of sale	$2,090,220
Reduce inventory and logistics costs	$720,308
Reduce cost of deployment	$235,125

Summary Return Values

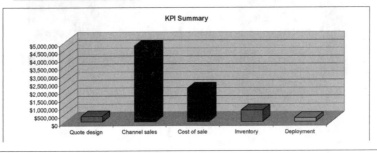

KPI Summary

Copyright VMC 2002

FINANCIAL DASHBOARD EXAMPLE 2

Rockwell Automation

Value Estimation Tool - Financial Dashboard

Date	January 1, 2003	Prepared for:	Enter Company Name

Summary Potential Return on Investment

Rockwell Automation Investment:	$145,000
Payback period:	5.5
Return on investment:	218%
Net present value: Enter rate: 8%	$136,684
Internal rate of return: (One-year basis)	118%
Cost reductions summary:	$189,597
Revenue increases summary:	$126,432
Estimated value delivered:	**$316,029**

Key Pain Indicators

Cost reductions from unscheduled downtime:	$144,518
Increased revenue from increased throughput:	$21,600
Reduction in planned maintenance costs:	$10,135
Reduction in inventory costs:	$0
Reduction in scrap rate:	$34,944
Increased revenue from reduced scrap rate:	$104,832
Summary >>	**$316,029**

Investment vs. Return

(bar chart: $400,000 / $300,000 / $200,000 / $100,000 / $0 — Investment, Payback)

Value Estimation Category Breakdown

(pie chart: Revenue increases 40%, Cost reductions 60%)

KPI Value Justification Summary

(bar chart: $150,000 / $100,000 / $50,000 / $0 — Unscheduled downtime, Throughput, Planned maintenance, Spare parts, Scrap)

FINANCIAL DASHBOARD EXAMPLE 3

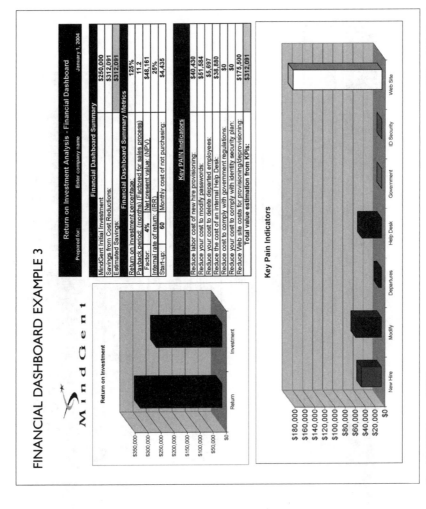

Return on Investment Analysis - Financial Dashboard

Prepared for:	Enter company name	January 1, 2004

Financial Dashboard Summary

MindGent Initial Investment	$250,000
Savings from Cost Reductions:	$312,091
Estimated Savings:	$312,091

Financial Dashboard Summary Metrics

Return on investment percentage:		125%
Payback period: (months) (Factored for sales process)		11.2
Factor:	4%	Net present value: (NPV)	$48,161
Internal rate of return: (IRR)		25%
Start-up:	60	Monthly cost of not purchasing:	$4,435

Key PAIN Indicators

Reduce labor cost of new hire provisioning:	$40,430
Reduce your cost to modify passwords:	$51,584
Reduce your cost to delete departed employees:	$5,697
Reduce the cost of an internal Help Desk:	$38,880
Reduce cost to comply with government regulations:	$0
Reduce your cost to comply with identity security plan:	$0
Reduce Web site costs for provisioning/deprovisioning:	$175,500
Total value estimation from KPIs:	$312,091

Return on Investment

Key Pain Indicators

ROI Financial Dashboard

360 DEGREE DATA ENTRY I

Reduce your cost of sale by reducing the sales cycle

Our goal is to reduce our cost of sale. The goal is achieved through reducing the sales cycle. Each day you do not close a sale there is a cost. That cost will continue to accumulate until the point when the opportunity is signed or abandoned. If your cost of sale increases over time, the savings will increase too based upon the average cost per day of not closing the sale.

	Current	Baseline Goal	
Annual revenue for product only:	$62,000,000	$60,000,000	
Number of deals that produced annual revenue:	650	625	
Calculated average sale size:	$95,385	$96,000	
Cost of sale: (Percentage)	37%	40%	
Calculated cost of sale: (per sale)	$35,292	$38,400	
Length of sales cycle:	142	150	WARNING
Calculated cost per day if original sales cycle continued:	$235	$256	
Calculation of actual cost per day with reduced sales cycle:	$249		
Calculated reduction in sales cycle: (days reduced)	8.0	10.5	
Calculated percentage reduction in sales cycle:	6%	7%	
Actual cost reduction in cost of sale:	$1,292,394	$1,680,000	WARNING

Goal Achieved?	Warning, Goal not reached

Baseline goal vs. achieved

Actual reduction in days — 8

Sales cycle day reduction goal — 11

360 DEGREE ROI SAMPLE

ROI4Sales
Strategic ROI Sales Tools

Value Assessment Follow-up Analysis - Measurement Analysis
Prepared for: ABC Company

This follow-up Value Assessment was created for the purpose of measuring the actual value delivered by ROI4Sales. The column labeled "Original" contains the data your team entered when we first performed this ROI analysis. The column labeled "Current" is where you will need to enter your current data. The analysis tool will take your original responses and compare them to the current entry and feed back to you valuable information on the value delivered by ROI4Sales. Take note in areas where you did not achieve the goal you set out to achieve; there are actions that can be taken to ensure success. ROI4Sales will cover these potential actions during a follow-up debrief.

Statistics Center

Date of original ROI:	January 1, 2004
Current Date:	October 1, 2004
Days between	273
Initial Investment:	$450,000
Expected Return:	$1,105,481
Return to Date:	$457,476
ROI Percentage:	246% Warning: Goal not achieved
ROI to Date:	102% Over PbP

Warning

Percentage KPIs Achieved
60% / 49%
■ Goal achieved
■ Goal not achieved

Goal vs. Return to Date
■ Goal ■ Return to date

ROI Achieved

Key PAIN Indicators	Original Baseline Goal	Current	Percent of baseline achieved	Goal Status
Reduction in cost of sale:				
Reduce cost of getting new sales reps productive:	$20,769	$35,769	172%	Goal Achieved
Revenue increase factored for quota achievers:	$138,462	$190,769	138%	Goal Achieved
Reduce annual lead generation cost:	$0	$0		
Revenue increase from increased close ratio:	$0	$0		
Reduce the amount of time spent on account debriefs:	$256,250	$14,938	6%	WARNING
Increase revenue by selling more services:	$0	$0		
Increase revenue moving reps above quota:	$0	$0		
Increase revenue from less customer turnover:	$125,000	$216,000	173%	Goal Achieved
Increase revenue from indirect channel:	$565,000	$0	0%	WARNING
Key PAIN Indicators Summary:	$1,105,481	$457,476	41%	WARNING

(Continued)

360 DEGREE ROI SAMPLE *continued*

Original Goal vs. Current Achieved

The above chart compares the original revenue goal for return (cost reduction, revenue increase, cost avoidance) to our current revenue amount achieved.

START SCREEN EXAMPLE

T N C
The Navigator Company

Return on Investment Analysis - Start here

This Value Estimation tool was created by VMC, Inc. a company specializing in return on investment modeling since 1998. To use this tool press the "Clear" button. The sheets will be cleared and the cursor will arrive in the first data entry field. Enter company information first, followed by General Information and then press the "Needs Analysis Questionnaire" button below.

Date: January 21, 2004

Company Name:	Zachary Corporation		
Contact Name:	Zachary Reich		
Address:	23432 N. Peako Road		
City:	Scottsdale	**State:** AZ	**Post:** 85254
Country:	USA	**Phone:** 602-555-1234	

Clear all input
Needs Analysis Questions
Financial Dashboard

	Name	Title	Phone
Contact 2:	Joe James	VP Sales	602-555-1235
Contact 3:			
Contact 4:			

General Information Questions

Enter the number of units produced annually:					2,000,000
Enter the number of units produced per hour:					200
Enter the value of each unit produced:					$4.000
Enter your estimated cost per hour of unscheduled downtime:					$20,000
Hours of production per day:	12	Days per week:	5	Weeks per year:	52

B

CONDUCTING AN
ROI WORKSHOP

We created this book to make the exceptionally powerful ROI Selling concepts and tools that we have developed with and for our major corporate clients over the past six years available to individual salespeople and to companies of all sizes. ROI Selling is a very flexible sales tool. In Chapters 15 and 16, we describe how you can use ROI Selling to increase the effectiveness of any sales methodology and Sales Force Automation software. Another hallmark of ROI Selling is its ability to be used by any size organization, and even by individual salespeople, to shorten the sales cycle, increase sales revenues, and reinforce customer relationships.

When we work with corporate clients to develop ROI Selling programs for their products and services, we conduct the initial information-gathering activities for the program in a workshop format. We adapted that approach for this book to allow anyone, from a Lone Ranger out to enhance his or her sales skills and resources to a large company or product division, to collect the necessary information and build a compelling ROI Selling model. The directions in Part One reflect a retooling of the ground we cover in our ROI workshops, restated to allow the process to be completed by a group or an individual.

Conducting an ROI workshop provides a number of benefits to your company and team. First and foremost, the brainstorming approach to information gathering increases the likelihood that you really will identify every possible reason people buy products and services like yours. You are also certain to gain additional insights from the group into the stakeholders—the individuals who are affected by those business issues, the outcomes those individuals are seeking, and the ability of your products and services to address those concerns.

An ROI workshop is also a valuable team-building and knowledge-sharing exercise. It is not unusual for us to facilitate workshops for our customers in which many of the participants have never spent significant time together and certainly haven't engaged in serious discussion about their customers, their customers' issues, and their company's products. This is especially true in groups "cross-pollinated" with both sales and marketing personnel.

If you are part of a larger team and want to make use of the workshop format in the information-gathering phase of your ROI model development, this chapter is for you. The following is a brief overview of the ROI development process as it is conducted with our corporate customers. The phases and individual steps are the same as those presented in this book—the following sections describe the participants and their roles in each phase in a corporate deployment as well as the steps involved in preparing for and conducting an ROI workshop.

Phase 1—Information Gathering

During the information-gathering phase, we want to fill the value matrix with as much data as possible about your customers, their issues, and the ways your products and services help. Therefore, whenever possible, we conduct an ROI workshop for the Phase 1 activities, bringing together the best minds we can find from our clients' sales and marketing departments to collect this information. The objective for this phase is to:

- Identify every possible reason people buy products and services like yours
- Document the business issues, pains, and goals that drive those why buy statements from the customer's point of view
- Associate stakeholders within a prospect's organization with each why buy and business issue statement

- Define the desired outcomes those stakeholders are looking for to address their issues, pains, and goals
- Attach features and solutions that your products and services offer to meet or exceed stakeholders' expectations for desired outcomes
- Assign ROI categories and value metrics to measure the tangible benefits your features and solutions deliver to your customers
- Document all of this information in a table called a value matrix that has one row for each why buy and each business issue statement and one column for each piece of information listed above

We know from experience that knowledgeable individuals can do a pretty good job of pulling this information together on their own, but there is something about the brainstorming dynamic of an ROI workshop that gets the ideas flowing and results in a more complete product. This section of *ROI Selling* tells you how to conduct an ROI workshop for your company.

Phase 2—Building the Model

During this part of the process, we distill all of the information collected during Phase 1 into the components of an ROI model:

- Value statements, which reduce each row of the value matrix into a single statement
- Key pain indicators (KPIs), which are questions you ask your customers during the early stages of the sales cycle to find out which of your value statements represent areas of pain for a prospect
- Needs analysis questions, detailed follow-up questions that you use to drill down into the KPIs for obtaining data you can use to document the cost of a customer's current situation and the potential ROI you can deliver
- ROI calculations, or formulas, that turn the data you collected with your needs analysis questions into projected ROI for your customers
- Needs Analysis Questionnaire, which is a document containing the KPIs, needs analysis questions, and ROI calculations that you use as the vehicle to collect prospect information and develop your initial ROI results

- ROI Financial Dashboard, which is a single-page document that summarizes the projected ROI for your prospect and forms a vital part of your sales presentation and proposal to a customer
- 360 Degree Value Analysis Tool, which is an extension of your ROI model that lets you return to your customer after a sale and prove the actual value you have delivered

Again, the objective of Phase 2 is to distill the information gathered during Phase 1 into an ROI model. This represents a significant shift from brainstorming mode to analytical mode. For example, one of the first steps in Phase 2 is analyzing the value matrix to group-related items, eliminating duplicates, and focusing on the items where your products and services can deliver the greatest value. In Phase 2, we also venture into some of the more "technical" areas of ROI development in terms of developing the actual model, calculations, and presentation tools.

At this point, therefore, responsibility shifts from the group to an individual. When you are developing the ROI model as part of a company-wide workshop, Phase 2 tasks should be performed by someone designated as your company's ROI specialist. The ROI specialist facilitates the workshop and then distills the data collected into an ROI model for your products and services. If the specialist is an internal resource, he or she generally comes from the marketing department, although some companies bring in outside expertise for this role. These are the services that we perform for our customers.

Phase 3—Deployment

At this point you are ready to roll your new ROI tools out to the troops. We discuss three aspects of deploying ROI tools in Phase 3 of ROI Selling:

1. **Integrating ROI into your sales process.** This involves analyzing the stages in your sales cycle and identifying which specific ROI activities and tools are most appropriate to each stage.
2. **Integrating ROI into your Sales Force Automation (SFA) software.** Linking specific ROI activities and milestones into your SFA software helps guide new and experienced reps through the sales

cycle, improves lead qualification, and automates the production of forecasts and sales reports.

3. **ROI marketing.** The information in your value matrix is a gold mine for the marketing department. Implementing ROI Selling represents a great opportunity to consolidate and unify the message you are presenting to your market across the spectrum from marketing to sales and customer service.

Executing the deployment actions in Phase 3 is typically a joint effort involving your ROI specialist and a dedicated team of sales managers and marketing personnel.

Planning the Workshop

To achieve the best results, workshop participants should include a cross section of individuals involved in selling and supporting your products. Cast a wide net to pull in as much expertise and as many perspectives as possible. Again, the workshop is a brainstorming exercise, and the objective is to capture every possible reason to buy, business issue, stakeholder, and so on. At this point there are no "bad" suggestions.

The following are four important steps in preparation for your workshop:

1. **Identify participants.** As noted earlier, try to choose workshop participants who represent a cross section of individuals involved in marketing, selling, and supporting your products. We have had mixed experiences with product developers, who sometimes bring strong emotional feelings about the product that may get in the way of the objective perspective that is needed at this point in the process. With that caveat in mind, cast a wide net to pull in as much expertise and as many perspectives as possible. Balance this with keeping the group to a manageable size. We find that between 10 and 20 participants is ideal.

2. **Identify facilitator.** We have found that marketing management personnel make good facilitators for an ROI workshop. They are typically not directly involved in the sales process, but they have a good understanding of the products and services your company

sells. The person who facilitates the ROI workshop needs to be im-partial, unbiased, and open to new thoughts and ideas. Marketing is usually a pretty good source for the facilitator of the value ma-trix building process. We generally use a two-person team, one to actually run the workshop and another to build the value matrix by recording the group's ideas and suggestions in a worksheet.

3. **Set up facility.** The ideal venue for an ROI workshop is a large room (big enough to be comfortable for the planned number of participants) with tables set up in a U-shaped configuration to encourage interaction among the group. The facilitators should be at the front and center of the group and should set up a PC and projector to display the developing value matrix as they work.

4. **Prepare the group.** Encourage the group to review your market-ing literature and any information that is available about your primary competitors (Web sites, etc.) to get the juices flowing be-fore the meeting. Then, a few days before the meeting, distribute a "Why Buy" worksheet to the participants and ask them to write down as many ideas as they can about why people purchase prod-ucts and services like yours. The facilitator should also prepare some thoughts in advance to "prime the pump" and ensure the meeting starts off at a brisk pace.

Conducting the Workshop

Most ROI workshops extend through almost two full working days. Beginning around 9 AM and ending at 3 or 4 PM allows participants time to attend to urgent messages and calls before and after the meeting. It's essential that the facilitators have the undivided attention of the group, so set some ground rules: We recommend that you don't permit any PCs other than the facilitator's in the room during the meeting, and that you discourage cell phones. Also, try to enforce a "no interruptions" rule, encouraging participants to take care of calls and e-mails before and after the meeting and during breaks.

The workshop itself follows the sequence outlined in Chapters 2 through 7. Capture why buy statements until the group has exhausted every possibility. Remember to keep the exercise wide open—you want to encourage as many ideas as possible at this point. The ROI specialist will be able to filter the list to the most compelling items during Phase 2. Then have the "scribe" add a column for business issues and repeat the process, continuing until you have completed all of the columns in the value matrix.

The facilitator's role is to maintain order, keep the meeting focused on the task at hand, and stimulate discussion if things slow down. As you move through the columns, the facilitator also helps the group's thought processes by introducing the prompter and connector words described in Chapters 2 through 7 to help pull together the concepts across the rows of the value matrix.

At the end of the ROI workshop, you should have a value matrix with 45 to 60 rows representing why buy and business issue statements. If you end up with a lot more, the filtering process at the start of Phase 2 will be more complicated. If you have many fewer, you may find it worthwhile to engage the services of a third-party ROI expert to review your situation and help build up the list.

After the Workshop

The ROI specialist will clean up the value matrix and proceed to the steps outlined for Phase 2. Depending on the level of product expertise the specialist possesses, it may be necessary to provide access to one or more product experts for a month or two after the workshop to help the specialist with detailed questions and follow-ups.

Summary

The ROI workshop is an important first step in the deployment of a corporate ROI selling program. The information you gather during the workshop forms the foundation for your ROI model and for its deployment throughout your sales process, SFA software, and marketing programs. The quality of that information is the biggest single determining factor in the quality of your model and your results. The following summary recommendations should help you ensure the success of your ROI workshop:

- **Assemble the right group.** You want a team that really knows your customers and products.
- **Use a good facilitator.** Make sure the person running the meeting is thoroughly versed in the concepts of this book, especially Chapters 2 through 7, and that this facilitator is experienced in running meetings and keeping groups focused and on task.
- **Prepare.** Require both the facilitator and the participants to prepare ideas before the meeting so the workshop gets off to a rolling start.
- **Record results.** Assign a scribe to record the group's input in a value matrix during the meeting. Trying to re-create the results later from cryptic notes and memory results in your losing valuable data. For the same reason, don't put the facilitator in the awkward position of running the meeting and recording the results.
- **Maintain discipline.** Assembling the best group of product experts won't do you any good if they are distracted by e-mails, phone calls, and pages from the receptionist. Make sure a member of senior management communicates the importance of dedicated attendance and attention during the short duration of the workshop.
- **Be objective and honest.** As we have emphasized throughout the book, your ROI model must be credible; and to be credible it must be based on honest, objective data about your customers and your products. Don't let wish list features and services creep into your ROI workshop—focus on solid deliverables.

The descriptions in this glossary don't always echo classic dictionary definitions. We have tried to describe the words in the context of ROI Selling tools and techniques. In most cases, we have provided examples of these terms in use at some point within the book.

360 Degree ROI Value Assessment An ROI model that includes the tools and processes used at specific periods after a sale to assess the value delivered by the product or service. The 360 Degree ROI Value Assessment is used as an ongoing program, not an event.

baseline goals The goal for your cost reduction, cost avoidance, or revenue increase that is defined on the Needs Analysis Questionnaire and summarized on the ROI Financial Dashboard. Baseline goals are used as a comparison point in the 360 Degree Value Assessment.

benchmark goal A goal based on an industry standard. Sometimes the benchmark goal is used for comparison purposes in the 360 Degree ROI Value Assessment.

benefit statement A statement that defines which features or functions of your product or service are used to deliver the estimated value calculated on the Needs Analysis Questionnaire. Typically, the benefit statement is printed after the value statement on the Needs Analysis Questionnaire. Also referred to as *product benefit statement.*

burdened rate The annual cost of an employee including all associated expenses such as benefits and overhead. See also *full-time equivalent.*

business issue The quantifiable logical explanation for the pain, issue, or goal referenced in the why buy statement of the ROI Value Matrix; typical components of business issues are time, wages, costs, or other numerical attributes that can be used in a calculation. Writing business issues is Step 2 in the process of building an ROI Value Matrix.

comparison table A table used to assign point values to qualifying question responses in order to determine how well a prospect qualifies as a potential customer for your product or service. Comparison tables contain a range of levels of a given criteria, such as sales quota amounts, management head count, and so on; and point values are assigned the varying levels within that range.

cost avoidance An ROI revenue category that represents savings achieved by eliminating an expense.

cost justification Explaining the value of a product or service based on its cost rather than its benefits. Cost justification is a reactive approach to selling rather than the proactive approach of *value justification.*

cost of waiting In ROI Selling, the calculated cost of not purchasing the proposed solution or feature. This calculation includes the start-up factor, initial investment, expected return, and payback period. The calculation is as follows: ((expected return − initial investment) ÷ (payback period + start-up period)) = variable X. Next, initial investment ÷ variable X = new payback period.

cost reduction A category of ROI revenue resulting from the diminishment of an expense; an act that results in a reduction in costs regardless of its source.

CRM - customer resource management A software application that supports your customer base and typically includes Sales Force Automation, Call Center, Dispatch, and contract management functions.

desired outcome A section within the ROI Value Matrix that lists the results stakeholders seek to resolve their why buy and business issue statements.

discount rate The interest rate at which companies are able to borrow money. The higher the discount rate, the lower the present value of future cash flows. For a typical investment, with costs concentrated in early periods and benefits following in later periods, raising the discount rate tends to reduce the *net present value (NPV).* In our ROI Financial Dashboard, we call the discount rate the "factor."

double-dipping Counting the same value two or more times.

due diligence stage Step 6 in our sample sales process where your customer or prospect confirms you are capable of delivering the value you estimated in the proposal and ROI model.

estimated value delivered This figure is the anticipated amount of value (cost reduction, cost avoidance, or revenue increase) your product or service will deliver on a particular KPI or value statement.

feature/solution The specific component of your product or service that resolves your prospect's business issue, meets or exceeds the prospect's desired outcome, and gives the prospect a reason to buy from you.

financial summary The culmination of the KPIs summarized on the ROI Financial Dashboard.

full-time equivalent (FTE) The annual cost of an employee, including all associated expenses such as benefits and overhead. Also known as *burdened rate.*

garbage in garbage out (GIGO) A term used to refer to the process of feeding flawed data into, and receiving faulty results from, a computer system.

gate A concept used when forecasting sales opportunities. A gate contains a series of Needs Analysis Questionnaire questions. Each question has an arbitrary value assigned it. When the question is answered, a related number of points accumulate; the total point value of all questions is summarized and compared with a minimum requirement chart that determines whether the opportunity status can change. If the minimum number of points is not achieved, the sales opportunity will not be forecast.

general information The section of your ROI model where you collect data that is to be used in calculations in more than one location on your Needs Analysis Questionnaire.

impact statement Impact statements answer your prospect's basic question: "What impact will your product have on our business?" There are two components to the impact statements on the Needs Analysis Questionnaire: The first is a statement of fact based on research and includes the value your company has typically delivered to customers or prospects; the second is a question asking for an input of the expected cost reduction or revenue increase (impact) your product or service will have on the value statement.

intangible An intangible return is a savings benefit that is quantifiably indefinable. An example might be levels of customer satisfaction or employee satisfaction.

internal rate of return (IRR) The rate of return you are receiving from your investment.

investment The cost for a solution that may include hardware, software, services, maintenance fees, set-up fees, dealer prep, and the like. In ROI Selling, the investment is displayed on the ROI Financial Dashboard.

key pain indicator (KPI) Describes a primary issue, pain, or goal your customer or prospect experiences.

key pain indicator question A restatement of a business issue in the form of a question; KPI questions are designed to force prospects to describe the pain they feel as a result of business issues.

KPI summary The list of KPIs from a Needs Analysis Questionnaire summarized in a table on the ROI Financial Dashboard and the 360 ROI Value Assessment.

marketing criteria Minimum quantifiable standards that "targets" must meet in order to move to the qualify stage of the sales process.

meet and greet The third step in the sales process where you meet directly (face-to-face or through a teleconference) with the prospect to, among other things, identify the key pain indicators.

Needs Analysis Questionnaire The document within an ROI model that includes questions used to define the status quo, or current cost or pain, and estimate the benefits and impacts of a proposed product or service on a prospect's business.

Needs Analysis Questionnaire development template A table used to assist in creating the questions for a Needs Analysis Questionnaire.

Business Issue	Component of Issue	Questions
Feature/Solution	Value Statement	

net present value (NPV) The dollar value of an expected future return expressed in today's dollars (for comparison to the investment).

payback period The time it takes to recoup an investment.

pending sale Step 7 in the sales process, in which your prospect works on the agreement and financing and completes the necessary due diligence.

presentation stage The stage in the sales process in which you present a demonstration or presentation of your products' capabilities as they relate to the key pain indicators you defined earlier in the sales process. Also, the stage in which you confirm the KPIs and update the impact statement percentages.

product benefit statement See *benefit statement.*

proposal stage An important step in the sales process, in which you present the investment, cost, and value you expect to deliver.

qualify The second step in the sales process, in which you identify the KPIs and confirm that this prospect is worthy of pursuing. The decision to move forward is typically determined by your qualifying questions.

qualifying questions A set of questions that will help determine whether a prospect is worthy of continuing the sales process. Examples might include: Does this prospect produce enough revenue? Have enough sales people? Each question must return a yes answer to continue through the sales process.

return on investment (ROI) Accumulated net benefits over a fixed period divided by your initial cost. Typically, the ROI is presented as a percentage.

revenue increase An act that leads to an increase in top-line revenue that may or may not lead to an increase in profit.

ROI category One of three types of benefits to be received through purchase of a product or solution: either cost reductions, cost avoidances, or revenue increases.

ROI deliverable The tools that make up your ROI model. They include Needs Analysis Questionnaire, ROI Financial Dashboard, and the 360° Value Assessment.

ROI Financial Dashboard A summary of calculations taken from the Needs Analysis Questionnaire graphically displayed and summarized on one sheet. Examples are available in Appendix A.

ROI goals The impacts your prospect is expecting based on estimated cost reductions, cost avoidances, or revenue increases defined on the Needs Analysis Questionnaire.

ROI marketing The process of integrating ROI Selling into your marketing programs, process, and plans.

ROI model The final collection of ROI tools.

ROI questionnaire Needs Analysis Questionnaire made up of quantifiable questions to be used throughout the sales process.

ROI Value Matrix A table used to collect data to build an ROI model. The ROI Value Matrix includes: Why Buy?, Business Issue, Desired Outcome, Stakeholder, Feature/Solution, ROI Category, Value Metric, Group, and Value Statement.

ROI value table A table used to isolate Business Issue, Feature/Solution, and Value Statement to assist in creating the questions for the Needs Analysis Questionnaire.

Sales Force Automation (SFA) A software tool used to automatically track, document, and drive the sales process.

sales input form A version of the Needs Analysis Questionnaire with the mathematics, benefit statements, and impact statements removed. Also,

Does your cost of sale exceed your budget?	
Enter your annual revenue. (Exclude service revenue)	
Enter the number of sales closed to produce the annual revenue listed above:	
Enter your current cost of sale percentage:	
Enter the length of your average sales cycle in days: (e.g., 3 months = 90 days)	
Notes:	

there are no calculations of value. This form is strictly used to gather ROI data and reinput it into the ROI model.

sales process A series of steps used to identify the progression of a sale over time. Examples include meet-and-greet stage, presentation stage, or due diligence stage.

soft dollar savings Savings achieved by shifting costs to a more attractive activity.

stakeholder The decision maker or person of influence within your prospect's organization who has the most to gain or to lose if the organization doesn't purchase your product or service.

start-up factor The period required for clients to become capable of using a newly purchased product or service to its full functionality and value.

status quo The current cost of the pain, issue, or goal defined by the KPI question.

tangible ROI modeling Modeling with the ability to *quantifiably* measure the financial impact on your customer or prospect of the implementation of your product or service.

target One of a list of companies that your sales personnel will pursue for qualification into their pipeline. The identification of this group is the first step in a sales process.

value assessment summary dashboard See *360 Degree ROI Value Assessment.*

value justification Using ROI in the sales process to prove you are delivering more value than you are charging in costs for a product or service.

value matrix Typically, a spreadsheet or table that contains the following information: Why Buy?, Business Issue, Desired Outcome, Stakeholder, Feature/Solution, ROI Category, Value Metric, and Value Statement; used as a research tool to gather information to create a Needs Analysis Questionnaire.

value matrix participant worksheet A printout of a spreadsheet used in preparation for and during the course of an ROI workshop that contains columns for Why Buy?, Business Issue, Desired Outcome, Stakeholder, and Feature/Solution.

Workshop Participant Worksheet				
Product>>>				
Why Buy?	Business Issue	Desired Outcome	Stakeholder	Feature/Solution

value metric The unit of measure delivered by the Feature/Solution. It must fall into one of the ROI categories of cost reduction, cost avoidance, or revenue increase.

value statement A phrase that summarizes one line of an ROI Value Matrix, which you write in order to better understand and explain exactly the value your products are capable of delivering to your customers or prospects.

value statement table A table used to break down the value matrix and create value statements.

Desired Outcome	Feature/Solution	Category	Value Metric
I want to reduce the time to revenue and shorten the sales cycle.	Solution Selling Sales Process and Job Aids	Reduce cost	Reduce the cost of sale
Value Statement	**Reduce your cost of sale by shortening the sales cycle using Solution Selling Sales Process and Job Aids**		

why buy statement A phrase used to describe the emotional reason a prospect or customer would buy a product or service like yours. Writing why buy statements is the first step in building an ROI Value Matrix.

why buy value matrix table A table used to illustrate reasons people or companies purchase products or services.

Product	Why Buy?
Why buy a sales training program?	I want to reduce our cost of sale.
	I want to increase revenue per closed lead.
	I want to reduce the amount of time we spend performing account debriefs.

wishware A term sometimes used in software development to refer to features that are wished for but don't currently exist. In ROI selling, this term refers to any feature or service you might be able to sell a prospect but one your company doesn't currently offer. Also known as "vaporware."

Share the message!

Bulk discounts
Discounts start at only 10 copies and range from 30% to 55% off retail price based on quantity.

Custom publishing
Private label a cover with your organization's name and logo. Or, tailor information to your needs with a custom pamphlet that highlights specific chapters.

Ancillaries
Workshop outlines, videos, and other products are available on select titles.

Dynamic speakers
Engaging authors are available to share their expertise and insight at your event.

Call Kaplan Publishing Corporate Sales at 1-800-621-9621, ext. 4444, or e-mail kaplanpubsales@kaplan.com

PUBLISHING